D0710660

On Consciousness

On Consciousness

Ted Honderich

University of Pittsburgh Press

© Ted Honderich, 2004

Published in the United States by the
University of Pittsburgh Press, Pittsburgh, Pa., 15260

First published in the UK by
Edinburgh University Press

ISBN 0-8229-4245-3

A CIP record for this book is available from the
Library of Congress.

Contents

To Ingrid at Fountain House

Introduction

Philosophy of the analytic kind, some say, goes back to the ancient Greeks and in particular Aristotle. Certainly it was already flourishing with Hobbes, Locke, Berkeley, Hume and Kant in the seventeenth and eighteenth centuries. Science as we know it was also under way. Newton published his *Principia* in 1687. Philosophy of the analytic kind and physical science in particular are endeavours and traditions of accredited intelligence, with great leaders and strong supporters. They have both changed the world. They have for centuries remained independent, often sceptical of one another, often given to vain ideas of superiority.

One thing that follows from all this is that they must have different virtues. As it seems to me, the virtue of philosophy, if it can be got into a sentence, is that it is logically more hard-headed than science. The virtue of science is that it knows a lot more about how the physical world works and certainly about its empirical nitty-gritty. Connected with the latter fact of empiricism, and despite the existence of grand theories, science is less general.

That philosophy is logically more hard-headed than science has little or nothing to do with the formal logic that officially is part of philosophy. Philosophy is somewhat better than science at seeing the whole wood despite the attraction of the trees – and seeing what a pile of theory comes to despite the way it is put together and the sign put on it by the owner.

When it is good, it struggles really to be clear, does not lose sight of the subject, say consciousness, or confuse questions, or operate with circular or elusive notions. It separates a thing from the relations it is in, and doesn't run things together. It doesn't mistake other connections between two things for the things actually being identical – one and the same thing. It is intolerant of nonsense, even when it is adventurous theory, and sceptical of standing and repute, including the standings and reputes of other disciplines. It attends closely to making all of its propositions consistent, to giving a complete picture, and so on. What all this amounts to, of course, is a reliance on the logic of intelligence – reliance on rather than sole ownership.

The most prominent part of the current philosophy of mind has been a little invaded by science, some say infected.[1] Notably cognitive science, but also physics. So long as it remains philosophy at all, it is not greatly more empirical than it was, but somewhat more empirical. It has also been computerised – subjected to the conviction that the mind is no more than events of computation, or not much more – and also made curiously speculative. Perhaps speculation is the nature of scientists when they are on holiday, or retired.

Could your lingering thought at this moment about that last sentence *be* nothing other than microtubules? Microtubular activity? Could your hopeful feeling about this book, or your early resistance to it, be microtubules? Those are indeed little tubes in your head and elsewhere in you, making up the cytoskeletons that give cells their shape.[2] Could your conscious thought or feeling instead be magnetic forces, the pulls and pushes we know about? Or that funny stuff in Quantum Theory, or rather interpreted into the theory – the stuff taken as having the consequence that Schrodinger's cat is neither definitely alive or definitely dead in the box until and *because* someone has a look to see which.[3]

Well, it could be. Maybe your conscious thought or feeling could conceivably be those things. Certainly, if I myself have to choose between consciousness as a mystery, as it is in traditional and true dualism, the etherealism of Descartes, I will be ruefully inclined to the inner tubes. With them, you at least have a starting point, at worst something false. There has been reason why philosophers of mind have invited friends from neuroscience and the rest of science into their subject.

In fact, however, there is hardly anything about the microtubules and the cat in what follows. That, of course, is because of the customary generality of philosophy, connected with its logic. Certainly sorts of physicalism or materialism in connection with consciousness get a great deal of attention. It is near to being the subject of at least half of the book. There is not much attention to what can also be called the spiritualism of Descartes, who has not been so fortunate in his successors as Hobbes. They are pretty well limited to defenders of free will, who require something grand to do the willing, and the remaining defenders of the soul of traditional religious belief.

The book was made from papers that appeared in journals of philosophy and collections of papers after being read out to departments of philosophy and consciousness conferences. They have been much revised, purged of an error or two, much shortened, and conceptually defragged. So as to try to sustain a line of thought clearly, I have kept back from expositions of books of importance that come to mind – first those of Block, Brewer, Chalmers, Dennett, Fodor, Heil, Kim, Lycan and Galen Strawson. The papers are easier to read than they were. They do come together into a sequence of argument too. They are also a narrative of a struggle with the subject. It goes somewhere, maybe gets somewhere.

Do they make up a book that has the virtue of philosophy as against science? Do they instead put in question the proposition that there is such a virtue? Well, I don't have to write a review. See for yourself.

Even if they have the distinctive virtue of philosophy, they do not make consciousness into other than a subject for science, or, of course, make out philosophy to be somehow superior to science. They are not philosophically standard or safe. They do not preserve a certain doctrinal trinity with respect to episodes of consciousness. A perception or thought or whatever does not in the end remain a matter of the trinity made up of the subject or self, the content of the perception or whatever, and the world.

They move towards and into a theory of consciousness that is not more of the same. Some will say a dream from which we must awaken to reality. The difficulty with that conventionality may be that reality as we have it is unbearable – which is to say that what philosophers have made of the reality of consciousness fails to do what an adequate theory needs to do. We have a grip on consciousness. In a sense, we know what is needed in an analysis or account of it.

For more of an overview of what follows, you can look through the little introductions to the papers. You will indeed see that first thoughts give way to second thoughts. Will you see that second thoughts are best?

Notes

1. For good introductions to the recent philosophy of mind, see Tim Crane, *Elements of Mind* (Oxford University Press, 2001), Jaegwon Kim,

Philosophy of Mind (Westview, 1998), E. J. Lowe, *An Introduction to the Philosophy of Mind* (Cambridge, 2000), Peter Morton, *A Historical Introduction to the Philosophy of Mind* (Broadview, 1997), Stephen Priest, *Theories of Mind* (Penguin, 1991).

2. Roger Penrose, *The Emperor's New Mind* (Oxford University Press, 1989), *Shadows of the Mind* (Oxford University Press, 1994).

3. For one example of such lines of thought, see Johnjoe McFadden, 'The Conscious Electromagnetic Information (Cemi) Field Theory: The Hard Problem Made Easy?', *Journal of Consciousness Studies*, 2002.

Chapter One

Anomalous Monism, and the Champion of Mauve

In the philosophy of mind, on the main subject of the mind and the brain, there are philosophers known by themselves or others as physicalists, mind-brain identity theorists, materialists, eliminative materialists, reductionists, monists, naturalists, and, we might add, neuralists. Some also present themselves as functionalists or philosophical cognitive scientists. These various personnel differ among themselves, greatly. They certainly differ in what they mean by saying or seeming to say that mind and brain are *one* thing, maybe that mental or conscious events in some sense or other *are* neural events. They also differ in how they arrive at whatever they mean – their arguments or evidence for their conclusions. They do stand together, or anyway say they do, against the philosophers who say mind and brain are *two* things, however they may be connected. Certainly the physicalists, identity theorists and so on make common cause against traditional dualists who say your mind, unlike your brain, is not anywhere in space or anyway takes up no space.

Donald Davidson's Anomalous Monism, as he names it, has rightly got much attention, for at least three reasons.

The first reason has to do with lawlike, law-governed, necessary, nomic or nomological connections. Two things or events are in such connection as a matter of causal or other natural necessity. They may be at the high level of generality of a natural or scientific law, or they may be a long way below, and readily perceived as lawlike without the aid of a scientific education – as in the case of the event of the egg on the marble floor being hit with a heavy hammer and the event of the egg breaking.

It is Davidson's idea that a mental and a neural event are only 'anomalously' one thing. That is, they are not one thing as a matter of lawlike connection. This is a lawless monism, whatever other sort of monism it may be. Putting the matter in a way that some may suppose is contentious, it is the idea that it is a kind of accident that the two things are one thing. Did anyone else before Davidson think that whether two things are one thing, whether one and the same thing falls under two different descriptions, is not a matter of natural or scientific law? Did anyone really think that whether two things are one *is* a fact that is a matter of natural or scientific law?[1]

A second reason that Anomalous Monism has got attention, although not so prominent a reason, is the particular sense it makes of the very idea that a mental event and a neural event are one thing. As you will be hearing, the idea does not make it at all natural to call our monist Davidson a materialist. Maybe, if there is any difference, not a physicalist either.

The third attraction of Anomalous Monism is the ingenious argument he supplies for its conclusion. It begins with an inconsistent triad, three propositions that cannot all be true. Making them consistent in his way also makes for a surprise.

The anomalousness or lawlessness or disconnection with mind and brain, the particular sense given to talk of identity, and the ingenious argument – all of these help to raise a question. It is the question of whether Anomalous Monism falls into the disaster of epiphenomenalism. That is the nineteenth-century doctrine of neurophysiologists that denies the efficacy or worth of the mental. It is what first raised a persistent scepticism about science's contribution to understanding minds as against brains. It supposes that our minds – our thoughts and feelings as ordinarily conceived, say our memories and desires as ordinarily conceived – are no part at all of the explanations of our actions, or indeed of such later mental events as other thoughts and feelings. Thinking changes nothing. It is now believed, perhaps, only in Australia.

My piece below looks mainly at the matter of the charge of epiphenomenalism against Anomalous Monism, concentrating on the ingenious argument. But there is a wider relevance – to other accounts of mind and brain that, so to speak, take mind and brain out of the ordinary connection that seems to be the main fact of the natural world. What we are looking at is a good example, but an example.

My remarks below bring together one earlier piece with part of another one. They were the beginning and the end of a

philosophical set-to in the journal *Analysis* between me and
Peter Smith, a good but Davidsonian fellow. (For details, as
with each chapter in the book, see the acknowledgements note
at the back of the book.) The pieces helped, as did pieces by
one or two others, to make the inventor of Anomalous Monism
think again,[2] if not to give it all up.

---

1   From an Inconsistent Triad to a Mind-Brain Identity Theory

Davidson's monism, his engrossing identity theory of the mind,[3]
emerges from reflection on what seems to be a contradiction. The
seeming contradiction is a matter of three fundamental claims, the
first of which is that there are causal connections between mental
events and physical events. Who could doubt it? The second is the
principle of the nomological character of causality: wherever there
are causal connections between events, the events are connected by
law. Can you doubt it?[4] The third fundamental claim is that there are
no lawlike or necessary connections between mental and physical
events, no psychophysical lawlike connections. It's supposed to be
another undeniable fact. Well, we can all grant it *is* undeniable, if
a little vague, that the mental and the physical can be said to be
different realms.

We escape the seeming contradiction in the three fundamental
claims, the inconsistent triad, and we get to Anomalous Monism,
by way of a certain understanding of the second claim. While causal
connection holds between events however we describe them,

> laws are linguistic; and so events can instantiate laws, and
> hence be explained or predicted in the light of laws, only
> as those events are described in one way or another...the
> principle of the nomological character of causality must be
> read carefully: it says that when events are related as cause
> and effect, they have descriptions that instantiate a law. It
> does not say that every true singular statement of causality
> instantiates a law.[5]

So when events E1 and E2 are cause and effect, it does not follow that
they are in lawlike connection *as* E1 and E2, or *under the descriptions*
'E1' and 'E2'. The two events may be connected in that way, but need
not be.

If a mental event causes a physical event, they can therefore be in
lawlike connection under *other* descriptions than 'a physical event'

and 'a mental event'. Given the third fundamental claim, that there are no psychophysical lawlike connections, any such mental event *must* be in lawlike connection under some other description. What? Well, there seems to be one alternative. They must be in lawlike connection as a *physical* event. We therefore have an identity. The mental event *is* a physical event.

However, the third fundamental claim comes into operation a second time at this point, and so what we have is a lawless identity. It is not a matter of law that the mental event is what it is, identical with a physical event. As the idea of Anomalous Monism is also expressed, on the assumption that laws, which are general, are a matter of *types* of things, not instances or tokens of types. What we have is token-identity but not type-identity.[6]

2   Causally-Relevant Properties and Lawlike Connection

Davidson is also known for his conception of an event as an irreducible entity, not something to be removed from or played down in our ontology. Events, it seems, are in a category somehow as basic as the category of physical things, say pears or apples. An event, further, has an indefinite number of properties, features or aspects. When I speak of Dora's fall, I do not in those words fully describe all of that event. It was a fall from the top of the table, during her birthday speech, and so on.[7] This conception of events is not necessary to the proposition that causal connection as ordinarily conceived need not entail a lawlike connection in the same terms. But it will be simplest to talk in terms of the given ontology, to use it in thinking a little more of what we have.

Certainly it is true that when I put some pears on the scale in the kitchen this morning, something green and French did cause the pointer to move to the two-pound mark, but there in fact is no entailed law connecting greenness and Frenchness with the pointer's so moving. There is in fact no law at all connecting the event in virtue of its being of something green and French with the pointer's moving to the two-pound mark. Other green and French things do something else when they are put on the scale. There is no lawlike connection connecting the first event in virtue of greenness and Frenchness with the second event in virtue of its being the pointer's moving to the two-pound mark.

It is to be noticed that we have given clear sense to talk of something's being such and such *as* something or *other*, or under a *description*. To talk this way is just to speak of certain properties of a thing rather than others. To say two things are not in lawlike connection *under certain descriptions* is to say that certain of their properties are not in lawlike connection. Or, perhaps, that the things are not in lawlike connection in virtue of certain of their properties. It could be that everyone has always understood 'under a description', and 'as' when it is so used, in this way. So far as I can see, Davidson does not disagree.[8]

Certainly the proposition that lawlike connection holds in virtue of certain properties is not in conflict with that remark you heard a minute or two ago, that 'laws are linguistic', understood as it must be. Davidson's doctrine of the nature of laws – not at all an easy matter – is not fully developed.[9] But presumably it takes lawlike connection to be no more a matter of language than causal connection is made a matter of language by the remark that 'causal statements are linguistic', which of course they are.

To return to the event of the pears, there is no denying that it is only certain properties of the event that are relevant to its being the cause it is. Does Davidson disagree? As already noted, he rightly allows that causal connection holds between events, or doesn't, whatever descriptions or names we put on them. To express this another way, the substitution of coextensive descriptions in causal statements does not affect truth value.[10] Or you can say we must distinguish between a cause and the feature we hit upon for describing it.[11] All of that, however, is consistent with the truth that neither the greenness nor the Frenchness of the pears was relevant to the event of the pears being put on the scale in so far as that event caused the pointer to move to the two-pound mark. So with effect-events. That the scale's pointer is steel made in Sheffield rather than Birmingham is irrelevant to the event of the pointer's moving to the two-pound mark being the effect in question.[12]

Is there a difficulty in the idea that it is in virtue of certain of its properties rather than others that an event is the cause it is? Well, you can say the event of the pears being put on the scale would not have been the event it was if the pears were not green and French. Thus there would be a barrier to saying that *that* event would have caused the pointer's moving to the two-pound mark if the pears had not been green or French. *That* event would not have occurred. Does this upset the apple-cart – make the pears being green and French causally-relevant to the given effect?

It seems clear that it does not. Certain conditional connections in the world – the very sinews of causation – hold between the weight of the pears and the pointer's movement. They do not hold between the greenness or Frenchness of the pears and the pointer's movement.[13] The greenness and Frenchness were necessary to the event's being the event it was, but they were not necessary to the event's being the cause it was. The greenness and Frenchness were not necessary to the pointer's movement and they were not part of the causal circumstance that made it move. It was only true of the *weight* of the pears that if it had been different the pointer's movement would have been different, and that since it and other things were as they were, the pointer's movement was what it was.

Certainly it may even be said that *the cause* that there was would not have existed if the pears had not been green and French. That is consistent with the greenness and Frenchness being causally irrelevant to the effect. That we say, as we do, that the cause that there was would not have existed if the pears had not been green and French – this is owed to a fact of language, roughly the fact that we take the whole for the part, and not to any fact of causal necessity about *all* properties of the pears. There is no such fact.

So much for the truth that if event E1 caused event E2, that is a matter of only a certain property or certain properties of E1 and E2. Now to press on, to something that needs to be added, it seems clear that lawlike connection is a matter of only these properties.

It seems clear, that is, that it *does* follow, from the fact that event E1 caused event E2 in virtue of a property F of E1 and property G of E2, that E1 and E2 are in lawlike connection partly or wholly in virtue of properties F and G. If the ground for saying that two events are in some lawlike connection is that they are cause and effect, and it is the case that all of their properties save one or two are irrelevant to their being cause and effect, then they are in the given lawlike connection solely in virtue of those one or two properties.

It can be granted not merely that not every true singular statement of causality entails that the events are in lawlike connection under the same descriptions, but also that none does. 'Something weighing two pounds being put on the scale caused the pointer to move to the two-pound mark' does not entail that the events are in lawlike connection under the same descriptions. However, it *does* follow from any statement that the event of the pears being put on the scale caused the pointer to move to the two-pound mark, and the statement that it did so in virtue of only certain properties, that the events were in lawlike connection *by way of those properties*.

This is a pretty fundamental proposition too. We can call it the principle of the nomological character of causally-relevant properties. It is consistent with and indeed required by any tolerable account of causation, and is integral to any account which takes causal relations precisely specified to *be* a species of lawlike relations.

3   A Dilemma with Epiphenomenalism in It

What follows from all this about Anomalous Monism? A question does, for a start, and then a dilemma.

According to Anomalous Monism, if a mental event causes a physical event, what is the causally-relevant property, or what are the causally-relevant properties, of the mental event? In the case of a physical event that is an action, the mental event for Davidson is, very roughly, a belief and an attitude. More generally, mental events are formally indicated, despite serious problems, in a logico-linguistic way related to what Franz Brentano called intentionality and others have called aboutness.[14] Any mental event, however, is identical with a physical event. To speak of a mental event is to speak of an event which also has physical properties. To repeat, then, what is causally-relevant with respect to the mental event?

As we noted at the beginning, and since then, Davidson remarks truly that causality is a relation between individual events no matter how described. He goes on to remark that his first fundamental claim, the principle of causal interaction between the mental and physical, 'deals with events in extension and is therefore blind to the mental-physical dichotomy'.[15] With respect to the first remark, we now also know we can do better – specify causal relations as holding between the relevant properties of the events. Is the second remark to be taken as denying the proposition that the mental event is a cause in virtue of *certain* of its properties? If taken in that way, it is surely false. It is not in general mistaken to distinguish causally-relevant properties. There is no reason to think that mental events are any exception.

Davidson's account of an action as being caused by a reason, roughly a belief and an attitude, suggests that he takes the mental events in question to be causal *as mental*. Elsewhere he accepts what can be called the conviction of the efficacy of the mental, 'the efficacy of thought and purpose in the material world'.[16] Again, we have it that Anomalous Monism is not to be confused with 'nothing-but' materialism: for example the idea that 'conceiving the *Art of the Fugue* was nothing but a complex neural event.'[17] This suggests an ordinary idea or understanding of the mental, whatever that comes to.

1. One possible answer to our question, then, is that it is *as* a mental event that a mental event causes a physical event. It is not a mental event as physical that does the work. Such implicit denials of epiphenomenalism are of course common. But if it *is* a mental event as mental that causes a physical event, we have a very unhappy upshot as soon as we add the truism, about a typical physical event said to be caused by a mental event, that the physical event is an effect *as* a physical event. This is easy enough to spell out.

If we accept the first two of the fundamental claims that issue in Anomalous Monism, along with the present idea that the mental as mental causes the physical, and the equally fundamental principle of the nomological character of causally-relevant properties, the upshot is plainly the denial of the third claim, that there are no psychophysical lawlike connections. On the contrary, there are. Hence we get to nothing other than a denial of Anomalous Monism. If, on the other hand, we wish to retain the third claim, and accept the idea and the principle just mentioned, we must give up the first claim as we are now understanding it, that there is causal interaction between the mental as mental and the physical. We still have self-contradiction in the theory. So much for the first horn of the dilemma.

2. The question of what is causally-relevant with respect to a mental event can be given another answer. It is the answer that it is not the mental event as mental that causes the action, but the mental event as physical. To give this answer is of course to cast a new light on the first claim, that the mental interacts causally with the physical. It becomes merely the claim that the mental *as physical* interacts causally with the purely physical.

What is really important, however, is that the resulting picture seems not to account for a conviction that lies behind acceptance of his first claim when it is naturally understood, as the claim that the mental as mental causes the physical. This is the conviction of the efficacy of the mental, already mentioned. It is the conviction that an event as mental is an ineliminable part of any full explanation of an action. It is the very root of the conviction of the absurdity of epiphenomenalism in its several versions. Here we have the second horn of the dilemma.

Can this horn and therefore this picture of the mind somehow be made tolerable? It cannot be done by a means already noticed – we cannot just say that an event would not be the cause it is if it were not a mental as well as a physical event. That will not make the mental character of the event causally relevant with respect to the action, and hence safeguard the conviction of mental efficacy. Nor, evidently, can we gain the end by way of the simple fact that an event can be said to be a cause even when it is picked out by way of a description of its causally irrelevant properties.

A doctrine of what is called *supervenience*,[18] so far unmentioned, will come to the minds of some philosophers at this point. Is it any help? The picture we get if we add in the doctrine is as follows. It is a mental event as physical that causes an action; lawlike connection holds between the mental event as physical and the action, but not between the mental event as mental and that same event as physical; however, since the event as mental *supervenes on* the event as physical, the event as mental is efficacious with respect to the action.

The final claim turns on what supervenience comes to. What it comes to cannot be lawlike connection between the mental and the physical, of course. It is indeed to be understood as no more than the holding of certain universal material conditionals – statements of the form 'If P, then Q' understood in a formal logician's peculiar way.[19] That is to say that the connection between the mental and the physical is accidental. There is no nomic necessity about the event as physical being the mental event it is. Here, it seems, we do not get the efficacy of the mental.

4   The Worth of Being Mauve

We have not looked too closely at Anomalous Monism itself, this identity theory in itself, as distinct from the ingenious argument for it. Does it make good sense?[20] As for the argument for it, we have not looked into the question of the truth of the third of the fundamental claims on which it rests, the denial of lawlike connection between mental and neural events.[21] All I have tried to establish is that the three claims, together with the fact of causally-relevant properties, the principle about their nomological character, and the conviction of the efficacy of the mental, are bad news for Anomalous Monism. They result not in a proof, but a fatal dilemma.

Have I gone badly wrong in thinking so? Peter Smith said so in a number of articles.[22] They led me to imagine, finally, the Champion of Mauve. If he does not advance the argument you have heard, he maybe fortifies it.

As we go through his household, we notice many things painted mauve. Here a light-switch, there a bottle of gin, here his bedroom slippers. Take the slippers. The Champion of Mauve notes that they are splendid slippers – they have the effect of keeping his feet really warm. This is the effect, he more particularly allows, of just the Hibernian fleece with which they are lined. He also allows that their being painted mauve isn't nomically necessary to their Hibernian fleece, their causal property whose effect is the keeping of his feet really warm.

But, he adds, it would be a wonderful confusion to move on from that truth to any *underrating* of mauve in connection with his warm feet. The slippers with Hibernian fleece *are identical with* the mauve slippers. So too the light-switch with its effective circuit-breaker *is* the mauve light-switch. The bottle with the gin in it *is* the mauve bottle of gin. Let us, he adds, have no confusion about efficacy in these matters either.

Enter Smith, speaking of mind and brain, under the influence of Davidson. More particularly, he speaks of a man's noticing of a kipper, his wondering if it is too old, and his intending to eat it anyway. Consider the intending, says Smith. In this connection, there was a neural event that was a cause of the man's then eating the kipper. More particularly, there was an event with a neural property, which property was a cause of the action. Of properties of the event, only the neural property was a cause of the action.[23] The event did also have a mental property, that of being our man's intention to eat the kipper. That property, Smith says, was not nomically necessary to the event having the neural property.

But, says Smith, do not fall into the wonderful confusion of underrating the man's intention to eat the kipper. That intention was a property of an event that *was identical with* the event that had the neural property. Noticing and wondering about the kipper involve like facts. Do not confusedly suppose, says Smith, that what I have said offends against any conviction that we actually have about the efficacy of the mental, any conviction we actually have of the falsehood of epiphenomenalism.

My dispute with Smith, at bottom, is over whether he can distinguish himself in a relevant way from the Champion of Mauve. He does not persuade me that he can.[24] He is committed, for all he says, to an epiphenomenalism or denial of the efficacy of the mental that is quite as impossible to accept as the mauvism of the Champion of Mauve. His policy, in which he persists, is to go on saying that an event that has a mental property *is* an event that also has a physical property – a physical property that *is* causal with respect to an action. It won't do, and no amount of repetition and emphasis will help. It ignores or tries to fly in the face of the fact of causally relevant properties of events as against causally irrelevant properties, the example of the pears. It still leaves the mental out of the explanation of the action. Your desires and beliefs, ordinarily speaking, are not why you do things, ever.

There are many more problems and possibilities in this neighbourhood than have actually surfaced in the controversy. But it is plain that the so-called identity proposition is of no more use to Smith than is the like proposition to the Champion of Mauve. The Anomalous Monist can be as wedded as he wants to the proposition that *of course* a mental event in his sense causes a physical event. By way of that truth he is no nearer getting mental efficacy than the Champion of Mauve is to getting mauvish efficacy by going on saying that it *is* the mauve slippers that keep him really warm.

So much for all of that, except for a footnote.

To go back to the beginning, there are the philosophers known to themselves or others as physicalists, mind-brain identity theorists, materialists, eliminative materialists, reductionists, monists, naturalists and neuralists, some of them functionalists or philosophical cognitive scientists – functionalism being a matter of the functions or effect-and-cause roles of things. They say or seem to say mind and brain are somehow or other one thing. In what sense is Davidson among them?

Well, as you may well have gathered already, when he speaks of his monism but denies nothing-but materialism, and when we take into account his doctrine of events and their various properties, and a good deal else, there seems to be a simple and clear sense in which he takes mind and brain to be one thing, a mental and a neural event to be one thing.

A mental event is identical with a neural event in that there
is one event that has both a neural and a mental property.

Do you say that is surely not a real identity theory but a *dualism* – a dualism of properties? So indeed it seems. It must seem so, certainly if mental properties are understood as having a distinctive nature, as they ordinarily are, as against merely indicated by something mentioned earlier, a certain logico-linguistic means having to do with the language used to describe them and other things.[25] That mental properties are really understood in an ordinary way in Anomalous Monism is indicated, first of all, by the warning that the theory is not nothing-but materialism.

Do you say, too, that no light is shed on these properties, on the distinctive nature of consciousness, no analysis given of our ordinary conception of it as a somehow *subjective* thing or fact? That no plain sense is made of my consciousness being a fact pertaining to me that is not like my weight or location or my producing good sounds in answer to at least some questions? So indeed it seems – Anomalous Monism, you can say, is about the relation between mind and brain rather than about the mind.[26]

One last thought. It's a good idea, generally speaking, not to be confident about who and what is in which of the two classes of philosophers and philosophies with which we began, the physicalists and so on and the dualists. Also a good idea not to suppose that a philosophy, although it has been put into one class, does have the supposed general virtues of that class – or the vices. For a start, what are called physicalisms or monisms may be mysterious. What are called dualisms may turn out to be more naturalistic. Get beyond the labels.

Notes

1. Davidson names some candidates in his main paper on Anomalous Monism, to which we are coming, but you may well wonder. The subject comes up again in the next paper of this book.
2. Donald Davidson, 'Thinking Causes', in *Mental Causation* (eds) John Heil and Aflred Mele (Clarendon Press, 1993). Reprinted, like the papers from which the one you are reading derives, and several by Smith, in *Mental Causation and the Metaphysics of Mind*, ed. Neil Campbell (Broadview Press, 2003).
3. 'Mental Events', in Donald Davidson, *Actions and Events* (Clarendon, 1980). See also 'Psychology as Philosophy' and 'The Material Mind' in the same book.
4. For one account, not Davidson's, of the nature of nomic or lawlike connections between things, and thus the nature of laws, and the relation of both to causation, see Chapter 1 of Ted Honderich, *A Theory of Determinism: The Mind, Neuroscience and Life-Hopes* (Oxford University Press, 1988) or *Mind and Brain* (Oxford University Press, 1990), the latter book being the first half of the former.
5. 'Mental Events', *Actions and Events*, p. 213.
6. The names can be misleading. In an ordinary sense of 'type', types of mental properties might go with types of neural properties without nomic connection. To assert mental properties are in nomic connection with neural properties is indeed to assert that types go with types, but to assert that types go with types is not necessarily to assert nomic connection.
7. 'The Logical Form of Action Sentences', in Nicholas Rescher (ed.), *The Logic of Decision and Action* (Pittsburgh University Press, 1967); 'Events as Particulars', *Nous*, 1971.

8. 'Eternal vs. Ephemeral Events', *Nous*, 1981; *Actions and Events*, pp. 194–5.
9. 'Emeroses by Other Names', *Journal of Philosophy*, 1966.
10. 'Causal Relations', *Journal of Philosophy*, 1967; *Actions and Events*, p. 152.
11. 'Causal Relations', ibid., pp. 155–6; 'Mental Events', *Actions and Events* p. 215.
12. John Mackie sets out the fact of causally-relevant properties clearly. See *The Cement of the Universe* (Clarendon Press, 1974), p. 260 and Chapter 3 of the book. See also my *A Theory of Determinism* and *Mind and Brain*, Chapter 1 in both cases.
13. There are several analyses of causation in terms of conditional statements, one being mine in *A Theory of Determinism* and *Mind and Brain*. The present point does not depend on my account.
14. 'Mental Events', pp. 210–12.
15. 'Mental Events', p. 215.
16. 'Mental Events', pp. 224–5.
17. 'Mental Events', p. 214.
18. 'Mental Events', p. 253. See also 'The Material Mind', p. 253.
19. Clarified by Davidson in discussion.
20. The question is given some attention in Chapters 2 and 3 below.
21. For evidence and arguments against the third claim in particular, see *A Theory of Determinism*, Chapters 2, 3 and 5 in particular.
22. See the acknowledgements note at the back of the book.
23. Smith thus embraces the second of the two possibilities in the culmination of the objection to Anomalous Monism. See p. 12.
24. Do have a look at his vigorous attempts, and at my replies, particularly my replies in paper (5) mentioned in the acknowledgements note, 'Smith and the Champion of Mauve', of which only part is reprinted here.
25. See above, p. 11. See also 'Mental Events', pp. 210–12, and *A Theory of Determinism*, pp. 71–3. One main point of the formal means, which faces fatal counter-examples, is that a mental event may fall under a sentence that is true, for example 'He wants a smart fast car for £4,000', even if there is nothing that falls under the contained description. Another main point is that a mental event may fall under a sentence, for example 'He thought of Penelope', that is supposed to become false when it is turned into another sentence containing an equally true designation of Penelope – for example 'the woman who would poison him'.
26. It is possible to run together the question of the nature of the mind with the question of its relation to the brain. Many do. *Introducing Consciousness* (Icon, Totem, 2000), the engaging book of the admirable philosopher of science David Papineau, is a clear example. It is on the question of the nature of consciousness, as it most often says, in accordance with its title, but you are also told that this is the question about consciousness of 'how it relates to scientific goings-on in the brain' (p. 15) and the question of 'where the feelings come from' (p. 21). There is the cover of the book, too, which says it is about 'the relation between mind and matter'. This conflation can lead you in the direction

of 'nothing-but' materialism – there is *some* question in front of you that does not need an answer in terms of subjectivity itself. I had the feeling once, too, on a radio programme with Sir Roger Penrose of the microtubules, that he wasn't at home with the difference between the proposition that consciousness just is the microtubules and the proposition that consciousness depends on the microtubules. That can help you past a problem, the problem of the nature of consciousness.

Chapter Two

The Thinking of Some Neuroscientific Friends

Anomalous Monism is properly called a philosopher's theory of mind and brain, and it is none the worse for that. It is a theory, that is, that has in it a lot of that mainstay of philosophy, ordinary logic – nothing much to do with and not relying on formal logic. The world is a better place on account of such theories. It is also a better place on account of theories of another character. They have in them more of the nature of science. They may be less reflective, and less complete. One of these theories of mind and brain, probably still the main one, is the subject of this second paper. There are flurries of philosophy in neuroscience from time to time, but this view persists and underlies them. It is what most or many working neuroscientists would say if they could be got into a corner and drawn into general discussion of a philosophical kind.

As you have heard, there are physicalists, mind-brain identity theorists, materialists, reductionists, monists, naturalists and neuralists, some of them also professing functionalism. That list of categories, we know, is deceptive. For a start, it seems that a monist so-called can be a kind of dualist, as in the case of the Anomalous Monist. What is also true, plainly, is that the mentioned schools of thought, if that is what they are, are not all on a level but rather are complexly related. If physicalism is the view that that mental events are only physical events, then neuralism, being the view that mental events are only neural events as neuroscience now knows them, is a species of physicalism.

Does the theory that will first concern us in what follows, that of Mind-Brain Correlation with Non-Mental Causation, fall into one of the mentioned six categories? Well, it is certainly not traditional dualism of the Cartesian kind. But that is

actually about as much as can usefully be said. Until actual definitions are supplied of the categories, as they rarely are, you
can pretty well say what you want, in terms of the categories,
about the theory first to concern us. The one that follows it, an
identity theory different from Anomalous Monism, is, as we
now say, *something else*.

Mind-Brain Causation with Non-Mental Causation, at bottom, gives a fundamental place to the brain, but not by actually denying the mind. It seems to fare well when faced with
some rather elevated Wittgensteinian objections, and also with
some rather technical objections of the American-speculative-
philosophical kind. Is it adequate in terms of expressing one
of our convictions about the mind? I mean the conviction that
the mind itself *does something*, the conviction of mental efficacy.
If you feel that the theory isn't satisfactory here, you may be
tempted by a tough-minded rather than a tender-minded alternative – the mentioned identity theory. But happily tempted?
There may be a general objection to identity theories, an embarrassing one. And it may be that anyway you do not have to
risk the embarrassment.

The paper below, although revised, is pretty much the one
that seemed to me to survive the doubts and animadversions of
four other philosophers in an issue of the same worthy journal,
Inquiry – Mackie, Stich, Sprigge and Wilson. But no doubt you
would be wise to have a look at their words. Maybe even my
rejoinder to them. See the acknowledgements note.

---

1   The Correlation Hypothesis, and Alternatives

We have an ordinary, settled and obscure idea of consciousness or
mentality, of our conscious or mental events in their streams. A
stream or event or fact of consciousness, we say, is in a special
relation to some particular thing. A stream, event or fact of consciousness is *of*, *to*, or *for* some one thing, in unusual senses of those
prepositions. It is also somehow a personal or individual matter in
another way. There is some uniqueness of consciousness and what
makes it up – some difference between mine and yours and between
either of those and anybody else's.

We can fairly confidently go further and say our idea of consciousness is the idea of a subject or self, or maybe just awareness, and of

certain somehow subjective contents of consciousness in relation to it, somehow different from the world itself, and also the interdependency of the subject or whatever and the contents. It seems contents do not merely occur on their own, despite Lichtenberg's thought to the contrary against Descartes' famous premise '*I* think'. The contents seem to occur for or to a subject.[1] Nor do we suppose there are bare subjects – subjects without contents, awareness of *nothing*. This idea of consciousness was perhaps not much improved by Brentano in talk of the subject's 'activity' with respect to and its 'direction onto' what he called contents or objects, let alone the 'inexistence' of the contents or objects.[2] Certainly the ordinary idea calls out for explaining or analysing.

We can also have the idea of whatever can be distinguished by a person as occurring within his or her consciousness and very likely of a type different from all other types. Each such distinguished thing, say my wondering a moment ago if it is 7 o'clock and therefore time for a glass of wine with Ingrid, is itself a matter of subject and content. Such a thing, which we shall call a *mental event*, and can as well call a conscious event or an event of consciousness,[3] is almost certainly of a type that almost certainly distinguishes it from all others. The type is a matter of its character. This is to be understood at least in terms of content, as with thinkings, believings, desires, conscious intentions and the like, or quality, as with sensations, or a kind of datum in the case of perception, or . . . There is no need here for a taxonomy of consciousness.

We need not really try now to explain or analyse the nature of a mental event, go beyond saying that it is a matter of interdependent subject and content, or try to say much more about how this generalization fits in with the different facts of belief, sensation and so on. Nor do we need to look further into distinguishing mental events from other things. Evidently they do not include dispositional beliefs, or those mental episodes, if they can be called such, that fall under epistemic or causal definitions. So they include neither all of what is contained in my knowing that I am in Bath, nor my seeing the abbey, where the latter episode is taken to bring in a causal reference to the abbey. Neither of these is precisely a mental event.

On two occasions when I describe two of my mental events by saying, truly, 'I was thinking of the Royal Crescent's fanlights', it is unlikely that the events will be of the same type – indistinguishable in content, quality or whatever. Whether two mental events are of the same type is not a matter of whether they are included under the same natural-language description. We can leave unsettled the question, among others, of to what extent the discerning difference or sameness in mental events requires conceptualization. What *is* required is that we have powers of self-awareness after the fact, which we have, and that we be able to fix identity-conditions, which we can. With respect to the latter, and hence countability, the idea of a mental event is of course wide, say like that of *a thing in this room*.

Despite what was said of our ordinary idea of consciousness, it is a conceptual possibility that two mental events, in the conscious lives of two different individuals, be of the same type. There are overwhelming difficulties in the way of confirming directly that such a thing has happened, which is not all that important. What needs to be true of Brown's mental event and Green's is that if either man had also had the other's experience, he could not discern any difference in character.

Finally, by way of introduction to one view of mind and brain – Mind-Brain Correlation with Non-Mental Causation – we have ideas of neural events. They go with mental events, somehow. A neural event is something's having a property of a central nervous system. Indeed such an event is a neuron or a collection of such cells having a property. The property is an electrochemical one, maybe of the axons of cells or transmitter-substances, a property of more or less the kinds that are the subject of existing and anticipated neuroscience. Neural events are of course a species of physical events. Physical events, very roughly speaking, are those that involve a thing being in space, actually taking up some space, and either being perceived by us or being in lawlike connection with perceived things – events of things like sofas and things like atoms.[4] Neural events, like mental events, are particular events rather than types of events.

You should and may well ask at this point whether mental events as just spoken of are also taken to be physical. Did the account of them in terms of subject and subjective content suggest something else? It is reasonable to say so. But in fact we shall leave this question open. By doing so, as already remarked, we have in front of us what has perhaps been the commonest scientific view of mind and brain.

It is far from true that working neuroscientists – as evidenced, say, by their ruling textbooks – embrace or even spend much time on theories of the nature of consciousness itself. But it is a safe generalization that despite their science most of them are not 'nothing-but' materialists, and that they do think that the mind is necessarily tied up with the brain, and that there are non-mental explanations of both brain and mind. That the view is incomplete with respect to the general nature of mental events is a shortcoming but in fact no bar to our considering it. Incomplete views can be better than other views.

Much science in addition to neuroscience, and much reflective belief and disbelief, including disbelief in disembodied consciousness, support the idea that there is some intimate connection, some close and non-accidental connection between simultaneous neural events and mental events. What it comes to is that mental events are either in some satisfactory sense identical with neural events or they are in a lawlike connection with them. We are no longer confident, however, that any particular mental event occurs as a matter of lawlike or necessary connection just in case a very simple or local neural event occurs simultaneously. It has turned out to be the case in neuroscience that one part of a brain can do what was previously thought to be done only by another. Could it be that different species have different neural correlates for mental events of a single type? Some philosophers have thought so.[5]

Well, to go along with all this, we can think of a type of mental event, as defined, as being in lawlike or necessary correlation with *one or another* type of neural event – a disjunction of types of neural events. What we get is the Hypothesis of Lawlike Correlation or just the *Correlation Hypothesis*, which is as follows.

> Any mental event of a given type occurs in any person just in case as a matter of lawlike connection a neural event of one or another of a set of types occurs simultaneously in that individual.

On my understanding of lawlike correlation, the hypothesis states what can be called a *whatever-else* connection. Given a mental event, and whatever events also occur that are logically consistent with it, there occurs in the individual a neural event of one or another of a set of types – and given the neural event, and whatever else logically consistent with it, there occurs the mental event of the given type.[6] To use some familiar and general terms, the occurrence of a neural event is sufficient for the occurrence of a mental event, and the mental event is in a special way necessary to the occurrence of the neural event. There is a *many-one* relation between the neural and the mental – given a neural fact, the mental fact is fixed, but not the other way on. The hypothesis is about necessity in the world, of course, the way the world works, not definitions or conceptual connection. It is not reductionist in the particular sense of asserting the existence of bridge laws whose terms are one-one rather than one-many. It is certainly different from certain hypotheses of supervenience or correspondence, but it may be like or even the same as others.[7]

Does the Correlation Hypothesis assert more uniformity in us as a species than you think there is? Does it go against an instinct or intuition having to do with the individuality of each of us? Does it go beyond our science? Should we, in this neighbourhood, be considering other things than the Correlation Hypothesis? Well, we can think of a related pair of generalizations. The *Individual Correlation Hypothesis* is as follows.

> Any given mental event occurs in a given individual – say *you* – just in case as a matter of lawlike connection one or another of a specific set of neural events occurs simultaneously in the given individual.

The *General Correlation Hypothesis* is this.

> Similar mental events occur in individuals generally just in case as a matter of lawlike connection one or another of a specific set of neural events occurs simultaneously in an individual.

The Individual Correlation Hypothesis says nothing at all of all humans in general, and hence by itself would be unpersuasive for a clear reason. Take the fantasy of two persons such that *all* the neural events occurring in one for a time are identical with the neural events occurring in the other. The individual hypothesis would allow that their conscious experience was *wholly* different. Anyone who takes up the individual hypothesis, and is familiar with even a small report of neuroscience, is likely to want the general one as well, or a variant, in order to give recognition to what seems undeniable – that there is *more* uniformity in connections between central nervous systems and conscious lives than is required by the individual hypothesis.

How well the uniformity is recognized by the general hypothesis is wholly uncertain, however, since as it stands it is indeterminate. How *similar* must the mental events be? There would be a related problem with asserting a probability relation between a given mental event and one or another of a set of neural events.

To forget the general hypothesis for a moment, what might be said for the individual one? An attempt can be made to explain in a general way how it comes to be true, as it was taken to be by several philosophers.[8] Consider the following story. At a certain time the young Green is aware of something, and, as it happens, neural event N occurs. The type of awareness, say of a wheel, comes into correlation with events of the same type as N. Thereafter there is a lawlike connection in his case. We say, perhaps, that N was blank in Green's case until a certain time, and then was wheel-imprinted. The young Brown, on the other hand, if a neural event of the same type as N occurs in him at a certain time when he is aware of his thumb, comes to have *that* awareness correlated by law with neural events of the same type as N. In him, N-type events are thumb-imprinted.

The individual hypothesis as it stands is not merely unpersuasive but inconsistent, and this is not avoided by the metaphorical imprinting story. Take Green grown older. We are to suppose that N-type events in his case are correlated in a lawlike way with wheel-type mental events. That is, a neural event of the type of N is nomically sufficient for or necessitates a wheel-type mental event. How can we suppose so? There is the flatly contradicting proposition that the neural event itself is not in this lawlike connection with the mental event, since if this were so, the neural event *would* be accompanied by the wheel-type mental event when it turns up in Brown. Any tolerable account of lawlike correlation gives this conclusion.

What may now come to a hopeful mind is a certain kind of thought. Neural events of the same type as N plus something else, events of type X, constitute the lawlike correlate of the wheel-type mental event, and N-type neural events plus something different, Y, constitute the lawlike correlate of the thumb-type mental events. This does not conform to a plausible reading of the individual hypothesis as given, but we might try to rewrite it into something better.

Before trying, let us ask what X and Y are. It would be pointless (1) to take X and Y as neural events themselves. The result would be tantamount to accepting the ordinary Correlation Hypothesis. Wheel-type mental event occurs if neural events N+X occur, and thumb-type mental event occurs if neural events N+Y occur. So, as some seem to suppose, can X be taken to be just (2) Green's history, or, more precisely, the original fact of awareness, or (3) the 'storing' in him of the original wheel-awareness or something related to it?

With respect to (2), it cannot be that later wheel-type mental events of the older Green are owed in part to the direct or unmediated influence across time of an event in his past. The past awareness must work through a causal sequence, somehow reaching the later wheel-type mental event. As for (3), there is no avoiding the question of the nature of the storing. If it is somehow a matter of consciousness in some other sense than the one we have, which is difficult or impossible to conceive, lawlike correlation as we have it is wholly abandoned. If the storing is neural, we are back in sight of the Correlation Hypothesis. If it is anything else than somehow conscious or else neural, we have abandoned lawlike correlation as we have it. We have also embraced mystery.

Let us then abandon the Individual Correlation Hypothesis, and, partly in consequence and partly for independent reasons, the General Correlation Hypothesis. Objections of an analogous kind, by the way, also apply to a species correlation hypothesis, to the effect that any given mental event occurs in individuals of a given species just in case as a matter of lawlike connection a neural event or one of a set of types occurs. What we carry forward in our reflections is only the Correlation Hypothesis.

2   Non-Mental Causation of Neural Events, and of Actions

A second and overlapping hypothesis on mind and brain is about the neural events that enter into the Correlation Hypothesis. It requires the idea of a causal sequence, one of the things called a causal chain. A causal sequence consists in certain lawlike connections, each holding between a causal circumstance or actually sufficient condition and its effect – one of the conditions in the circumstance typically called the cause of the effect. A causal sequence has no gaps. Save for initial events, very likely arbitrarily selected, each event in a causal circumstance is by definition also something else: the effect of a prior circumstance. Initial events, which may occur at various times rather than just at the beginning in time of a sequence, are those whose own causal ancestries are not within the sequence. The end-effect of the sequence is the effect of the initial events that compose a causal circumstance for it. It may also be said, of course, to be the effect of mediating circumstances.

Neural events are effects of causal sequences that are wholly physical and which do not include mental events, even if these latter things in their obscurity are somehow contemplated as physical. Some of the events in the sequences are neural events, others muscular or other bodily events, and the rest are external to our bodies but impinging on them. The initial events of the sequences also divide into bodily and external.

One gets very different pictures of mind, and very different philosophical problems, depending on what initial events one specifies. Let us not consider, say, sequences which begin with or just after certain mental events, perhaps acts of will just prior to actions. Let us have in mind sequences whose initial events occurred (1) when a conscious individual came into existence, and (2) also thereafter. If we do not pause for closer definitions, we come to a certain proposition.

> The neural events specified by the Correlation Hypothesis are such that each is the effect of a causal sequence, all the events in the sequence being physical and non-mental – they are environmental, bodily or neural events. The initial elements of the sequence are events in the individual at the beginning of consciousness and environmental events thereafter.

This *Hypothesis on the Non-Mental Causation of Neural Events* is evidently related to familiar beliefs about a person or an aspect of a person being a product of heredity and environment. It itself is to the effect that there are certain non-mental rather than mind-brain or psychophysical lawlike connections. Each neural event, being the effect of initial events which constitute a causal circumstance for it, is in lawlike connection with that circumstance, and of course other mediating circumstances.

However, these lawlike connections also enter into the longer lawlike connections produced by conjoining them with the particular brain-mind connections specified by the Correlation Hypothesis. Above all there is the longer such connection between initial events and each mental event, mediated by very many non-mental events. The first and second hypotheses taken together, for good reason, are often understood as being in conflict with doctrines of free will and responsibility, but these are not our present business.[9]

The third hypothesis in the view of mind and brain we are considering has to do with the causation of actions. It has to do, that is, with certain of our physical movements and stillnesses, instances rather than types. These are those that derive from an intention, a mental event involving desire and belief in a certain way. The deriving in question comes roughly to this: the action falls under a description that also occurs in description of the intention. It is not to be taken that an action's deriving from intention is its being *caused* by the intention. This is not part of the idea. The *Hypothesis on the Non-Mental Causation of Actions* is as follows.

> Each of our actions is the effect of a physical causal sequence, either neural or bodily, the initial events in it including the neural correlate of the intention from which the action derives.

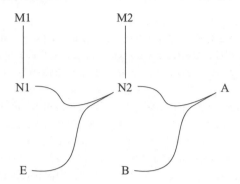

Figure 1: Mind-Brain Correlation with Non-Mental Causation.

This, which might be complicated in several ways, evidently over-laps with the Correlation Hypothesis. It presupposes propositions asserted by the Correlation Hypothesis. In this third hypothesis, we have the assertion or presupposition of both non-mental and psy-chophysical lawlike connection. Psychophysical connection, medi-ated by a neural correlate of the intention, holds between the inten-tion and the action. The hypothesis can be differently expressed, so as to accommodate other conceptions of action. It has fewer rivals than its predecessors. It does conflict with the view that a causal cir-cumstance for an action consists not only in neural or bodily events but also in mental events, both being causally necessary to it.[10]

A very simple model pertaining to the three hypotheses will be of use for illustration and of more use for the conduct of the argument to come. It is a model of a bit of a little historical episode. The event M1 was a mental event simultaneous with the neural event N1 and in lawlike connection with it. E was a simultaneous environmental event, physical, that impinged on the person in question. N1 and E made up a causal circumstance for the later neural event N2. That neural event was in lawlike connection with mental event M2. Event B at the same time was a bodily event. N2 and B made up a causal circumstance for the later action A, also physical. We can think of mental event M1 as someone's noticing a dish of olives on the table, M2 as intending to have one, and action A as reaching for one.

The Correlation Hypothesis is modelled by M1 and N1 and by M2 and N2. The Hypothesis on the Non-Mental Causation of Neural Events is modelled by the connection of N1 and E with N2. The Hypothesis on the Non-Mental Causation of Actions is modelled by the connection of N2 and B with A.

So there we have it – the theory of the Mind-Brain Correlation with Non-Mental Causation, a view of many neuroscientific friends.

You may well say it does not include an explanation or analysis of consciousness or mentality itself, an explanation of our somehow distinguishing it from, so to speak, the world of objective fact. Yes, there is that lack, but it is a shortcoming shared with most of the philosophy of mind. Putting that aside, are there problems with correlation?

3   Wittgensteinian Objections to Correlation

Are there objections to the Correlation Hypothesis? Are there in fact no such psychophysical lawlike connections as the hypothesis asserts? Let us first consider objections of a Wittgensteinian kind.[11]

If the Correlation Hypothesis is true, then, in virtue of part of it, if a certain neural event occurs in an individual, there also occurs in the individual a mental event that was also instantiated in me this morning when I had the thought that I expressed by saying that the art galleries in Paris close at 7 p.m. It may forever remain beyond the capability of neuroscience to bring about a neural event by techniques of electro-stimulation of a brain and the like. Nonetheless, it is said, there is no barrier to scientifically fictional speculation, and from it, together with the Correlation Hypothesis, a certain conclusion follows.

It is that if a certain neural event *were* brought about artificially, an individual would experience the given conscious or mental event – even if the individual were an African lad who had never heard of art galleries, Paris, or clock-time. It follows that he would experience the mental event even if his life-experience had been such that he had had no conception whatever of these things.

This, we are told, is an absurd conclusion, one that destroys the Correlation Hypothesis. To state the objection generally, it is not enough, for an individual to think or feel certain things, that a certain neural description be true of him. He must be an individual with a certain history, a certain learning-history. The Correlation Hypothesis, seen clearly, is unacceptable. It leaves out of account something essential to thinking and feeling, which is the experience that precedes it.

Does the Correlation Hypothesis issue in absurdity? Well, it does not force us to give up our conviction that in the world as it is, and very likely will be, an individual has a certain thought only if he has a certain history. Neuroscience is not remotely in sight of bringing about what has just been imagined. The Correlation Hypothesis asserts no such absurdity. The absurdity to which the

Correlation Hypothesis is supposed to be committed must be some contradiction or some related incoherence. Is there such an absurdity in concluding that an individual might conceivably have a certain thought without having had the experience that always, in the world as it is, goes with it? What is it that may move us in the direction of supposing that the conclusion is somehow incoherent?

One thing, despite what has just been said, may be the confusing of factual or practical incredibility with conceptual defect. Another, worth more attention, is the truth that for the individual to have the given thought, he would have to have the possibility of many more. It is necessary for having the thought, as we can say, that he has an awareness of *forms of life*. It is incoherent to suppose that the African lad could have a thought about 7 p.m. without having the possibility of thoughts about other clock-times. It is incoherent to suppose he could have a thought about art galleries without having some grasp of the existence of a good deal else.

But then what moves one towards supposing that our conclusion is incoherent is an accidental aspect of it: the suggestion that a thought might be had, so to speak, *in isolation*. This has nothing to do with the lad's lack of a certain learning-history. This can be brought out by an alteration of the science-fiction. The neuroscientists in a long campaign produce many neural events which go with an appreciation of the relevant facts of life. They begin with certain fundamentals and go forward to the final moment when there occurs a neural event correlated with the thought that the art galleries in Paris close at 7 p.m. Here, whatever else needs to be said, there is no 'isolated thought' incoherence.

This will not satisfy all comers. They will say that whatever is true of the African lad at the final moment in terms of some ramified neural counterpart of my neural states when I had my thought this morning, he will not be *having a thought*. The declaration may have a good ring, but why? The inexplicit supposition of incoherence may be this: to have a thought of something is by definition to have something of a certain ordinary ancestry, perhaps causal. This ordinary ancestry takes spelling out, but it excludes an ancestry of neurophysiological construction. The proper response to this supposition will be anticipated. There can be no doubt that if *having a thought* is so defined, then it is self-contradictory to conclude that the African lad could have the thought that the art galleries in Paris close at 7 p.m. Mental events were not so defined.

But does our own conception of a mental event fail to catch hold of an, or the, essential subject-matter? Does it fail to cover having thoughts? Again the answers can be anticipated. The conception of a mental event is the conception of whatever can be distinguished by an individual from other things in consciousness. Certainly some such things are properly described as havings of thoughts. They are havings of thoughts where these are not defined as requiring a certain ancestry. They seem to be havings of thoughts, indeed, as these are ordinarily understood, since surely a certain ancestry is not logically necessary for having a thought as ordinarily understood.

One further supposition of incoherence may be contemplated briefly. Having a thought, it may be said, is something that has a *semantic* character. Would it not be absurd to say that the African lad's mental event was *of* something? The question, of course, raises many issues, and presupposes that reference is not itself a matter of causal ancestry. I shall not attempt what has not been done, which is to articulate the given supposition of incoherence. There is no apparent reason to conclude that the African lad's thought could not be of something in the way that mine was of something. There seems no reason to think that he could not have a mental event of the relevant character. In terms of the constitutive subject and object of the mental event, the object could be for him what can be called *designative*. This would be a fact about him, not the world.

A contrary view might be derived from a semantic theory that required of each and every thought of a certain class that its owner had perceptual experience of precisely its referent, but there are no such theories. Perhaps it is to be granted that thoughts of the given class, which includes the one in our example, require some perceptual experience on the part of the individual. That requirement, however, seems to be of a factual kind. It appears to be a factual rather than a conceptual impossibility that an individual of no perceptual experience should have certain thoughts. A factual impossibility, a constraint on neuroscientific construction, is not to the point.

4   The Objections from Holism, Indeterminacy, and Rationality

Has something been missed which is to the point but not given explicitly in these objections? Perhaps, if so, it will turn up in others to be considered, indeed the next one. It derives from writings by Quine, Davidson, and others,[12] and rests on the fact just noticed, that to ascribe a single mental event to someone requires that we also do much more. Despite our use of the fact against the African lad objection, this in fact may be held to be more enemy than friend to lawlike correlation.

If I suppose that at some moment a man thought or believed that a half-bottle of wine is a decent amount at dinner, I must also attribute to him a large number of dispositions, most importantly dispositional beliefs. He must have the idea of a whole of a thing, and so on. Consciousness is holistic, which is to say, here, that the ascription of a mental or conscious event, a passing thought, requires the ascription of many dispositional beliefs and attitudes. These are necessary conditions of the given occurrent belief.

It may now be thought to follow that any neural correlate of the belief in this situation must be a correlate of the whole indefinite corpus of dispositions. If I cannot ascribe a believing of something to him, a certain mental event, without also ascribing to him many dispositional beliefs, then what we must contemplate, it may be thought, is a neural correlate for the lot. We cannot suppose there is a neural correlate for just the passing belief. But the Correlation Hypothesis depends on precisely such suppositions. Must we not give it up and try to conceive of something else by way of correlates of beliefs? This, however, would be something obscure, a large and indefinite physical structure correlated with the large and indefinite body of dispositional beliefs and what-not. If we were to try to pin down this thing by labelling it in some way as a general neural correlate, that would take us nowhere. We would not know what we were talking about.

Something like this objection from holism, although it seems that nothing so explicit has been specified, may have persuaded some philosophers to abandon hope of anything like the Correlation Hypothesis. Let us reflect on the crux. Why is it supposed that if we cannot have the passing belief without the corpus of dispositional beliefs, we cannot suppose that there is a neural correlate for the passing belief by itself?

The only reason for the supposition is surely the confusing of dispositions with mental or conscious events. In setting out the objection, as you can look back and see, this was done. But dispositions are neither mental events nor of course types of mental events. Dispositions in general, and not only those that have to do with the mind, are not puzzling, although some philosophers have made heavy weather of them. Any disposition is a set of standing conditions such that when it is conjoined with a further condition or conditions, the resulting whole constitutes a causal circumstance for something.

In consonance with the three hypotheses, and indeed many other pictures of mind, dispositional beliefs and other such things are best regarded as persistent neural structures. There is surely is no possibility other than that our dispositional beliefs are neural if they are not within consciousness. Certainly no other possibility has been made clear. The idea of subconscious or unconscious dispositions, where these are not themselves either mental events or neural structures, has some currency. But surely this idea, which perhaps need not be fastened on the already battered Freud, is without essential content.

If dispositions are taken as neural, however, we have no problem. They do not complicate the mental or conscious side of things. We regard them as somehow contributing to the neural correlates of mental events, and in particular as contributing to the neural correlate for the man's thinking that a half-bottle of wine is a decent amount at dinner. That is no reason for thinking that the correlate cannot be determinate. We may also suppose, for what it is worth, that many of the same dispositions contribute to other neural events, again without making those events indeterminate. Certainly it is unclear how the dispositions relate to the particular neural events. Whatever premises neuroscience can provide for the three hypotheses, it has barely begun any progress towards answering such particular questions. The important point for us is that there is no obstacle to identifying dispositions with neural facts functioning in a certain way and hence no objection of the kind we have been considering.

Another point may be necessary. Many dispositions are naturally taken as having extended histories. Each of us has *known* things, in the relevant sense, for a long time. It can therefore be argued that in ascribing a mental event we must also accept that there occurred a succession of neural events prior to the correlate of the mental event. There is no embarrassment here. That certain things were prior necessary conditions of a neural event in no way prevents that event from being a lawful correlate of a mental event. By way of distant analogy, having a car-door key, and so on, may in a situation be necessary conditions of turning the ignition key, and so on, which does not stand in the way of turning the ignition key, and so on, being a correlate of the car's starting. It is an oversight to suppose that an actually sufficient condition of an event, which condition comprises

necessary conditions of the event, comprises all the necessary conditions of the event.

The objection from holism can be connected with others having
to do with an indeterminacy. They derive from Quine's doctrine,
but are not given by him.[13] Some bare bones of the doctrine are
as follows. In attributing beliefs to a man, what we have to go on
mainly is what he says. Given that, however, does he mean A, with
the consequence that he believes X, or does he mean B, with the
consequence that he believes Y? It is like decision theory. Just as a
man's choices do not tell us what he believes unless we also have a
view of his desires, so we cannot have a view of what a man believes
when he says something unless we have a view of what he means.

With respect to these issues, furthermore, we can only try to deal
with them by considering the whole corpus of a man's beliefs, attitudes, and so on. We cannot decide these issues one by one. We
cannot do one thing at a time, but must take on many together. For
these reasons, and others of a related kind, there is the conclusion
that we can come to no exact or final answers. There necessarily is
indeterminacy in our understanding.

An objection based on this doctrine of indeterminacy, I take it, is
that there are insuperable difficulties in the way of even beginning
to try to confirm the Correlation Hypothesis, since there must be
indeterminacy in the ascription of beliefs and other mental events.
There are three brief replies.

1. We can be too ready to be overwhelmed by difficulties raised up
in the way of grasping the experience of others. Not all our attribu-
tions are as uncertain as some are. To take an entirely rudimentary
but relevant example, we can have a fully-warranted belief, about
a man reporting his experience at two moments as he sits facing a
red wall, that his perceptual experience was indeed identical. It is
also possible to have too grand a view of what would be needed to
confirm the Correlation Hypothesis, which is a matter of inductive
extrapolation from several kinds of evidence,

2. The fact that often we cannot do one thing at a time, when
judging someone's experience, seems to have no fatal consequence.
One might think, with not much weaker reason, that the interdependence of judgements about categories of fossils, sediments, variations in traits and a great deal else puts into question the theory of
evolution. Complexity does not inevitably produce impossibility of
judgement,

3. *If* we need a certain grip on a man's experience in order to answer a question about certain mental events and neural events, and

we have not got that grip, then we are unable to answer the question. To be in trouble is to be unable to see which of two answers is correct, one for and one against lawlike correlation. It is not to be able to see that one answer is mistaken. If exact and final judgements about some mental events are impossible, then this contributes precisely as much to uncertainty about the non-existence of psychophysical lawlike connection.

Another objection deriving from the doctrine of indeterminacy consists in the conclusion, drawn from the premise that there is indeterminacy in our view of a man's experience, that his experience is actually not determinate. Large issues are raised here, but they cannot stand in the way of the observation that the conclusion, which undercuts virtually all reflection and theory about the mind, does not follow from the premise. Or, to take up a position that may be excessively cautious, the conclusion has not been shown to follow from the premise. It has not been shown that our uncertainty entails 'that there is not even . . . an objective matter to be right or wrong about'.[14] Furthermore, any demonstration would surely depend on philosophical and other theory that could not be of greater persuasiveness than a proposition that a man is at a time thinking or feeling *something*, of whatever elusive character, rather than thinking or feeling something else.

The objection from holism can also be connected with the objection from rationality, explicitly advanced by Davidson.[15] A man with one belief, as we know, necessarily has a system or network of beliefs. These must be regarded as having a certain rationality. It is impossible to describe it closely, but it consists in part in consistency. We cannot think that the man who really has the idea of a half-bottle of wine supposes that two wholes make a half. If his utterances showed no consistency from moment to moment, and we took them to reflect his actual on-going consciousness, it would follow that he had no beliefs. Indeed, an absolute inconsistency would stand in the way of his producing for us what counted as utterances, since sense itself is importantly a matter of consistency.

To describe a man's beliefs, then, and indeed to ascribe a single belief to him, we must ascribe criteria or standards of consistency to him. However, there is no such constraint on us in our descriptions or theories of the physical. We have no use for ideas of rationality in the description of synapses, potentials, and impulses. Here there is no echo of imputations of rationality.[16] There are, however, very different ruling ideas in our description of the physical. To describe it we depend, for example, in the measurement of temperature and time and a great deal else, on the postulate of transitivity.[17] There are then two descriptive domains or systems, depending upon disparate assumptions or principles. Therefore there cannot be lawlike connections between the systems. There is the conclusion that there can be no psychophysical lawlike connections.

There is no denying the difference between the two domains, and the account given of the mental is in a way striking. It is apparent too that what is said must constrain in certain ways the further confirmation of the Correlation Hypothesis. Still, we are not actually given a reason for thinking that the given conclusion follows from the description of the two domains. As others have asked, what reason is there for thinking an item which falls in one domain, and whose description then depends on X, cannot be in lawlike connection with an item in the other domain, whose description then depends on Y?

There is no clear general truth to the effect that there cannot be lawlike connection between items whose descriptions have different necessary conditions. There appears to be no relevant sense in which two domains can be said to be 'closed' and which precludes lawlike connection without begging the question.[18] What then is the relevant feature of this admittedly unique pair of domains? Davidson remarks that his argument is no proof. It must also be said I think that it is at least crucially incomplete as an argument.

The issue calls for more discussion, but I shall leave it with a couple of comments. (1) It is implied or not denied by Davidson, and fairly widely accepted, that there are lawlike connections between the neural and that part of consciousness that seems *not* to fall under the intentional characterization mentioned at the beginning of this paper.[19] Given that all of consciousness is also a possible domain, doubts must arise about the postulated discontinuity – surely overwhelming doubts. In particular, there is perception which seems to saddle the intentionalist and the other. (2) It is allowed that there are in fact lawlike connections between the physical and the mental, but, of the mental as neural or anyway physical. The possibility of this position depends on the strength of an Identity Theory. Here too there are at least serious doubts, of which more in a moment.

5   The Mental Efficacy Problem, and Identity Theories

So much for a consideration of some principal objections to mind-brain lawlike connection in general and the Correlation Hypothesis in particular. Objections are also made to the second and third hypotheses, about the physical causation of correlates and of actions but I pass them by. My own conviction, on which I shall now proceed, is that these three hypotheses are well formed, and survive the philosophical attempts to dismiss them that we have considered. That is not to say they are without problems. They issue in a considerable problem, to which we now turn.

We have the conviction that consciousness is efficacious, that the doctrine of epiphenomenalism is impossible to believe. This conviction has the character of a datum, not a part of theory. It is not identical with the proposition that mental events *cause* other mental events and actions, although that is the most likely rendering of it. Common expressions of it are that thoughts and desires *give rise to* or are the *sources* of other mental events and actions. These are not necessarily causal locutions. Those who use them may suppose that an *acausal* self, familiar in reflections on free will, is part of the connection between two mental events. Nor are the locutions to be taken as conveying, merely, that actions and mental events derive from earlier mental events, where that is just the idea that the later falls under a description that brings in the earlier.

What the locutions do convey, for our purposes, is this: mental events are *ineliminable parts of the explanations* of later mental events and actions. You cannot have a full explanation that leaves them out. They must be mentioned in answer to the general question of why later mental events and actions occurred. That is the fundamental thing about our conviction. We do not contemplate the possibility of overdetermination, of there being two or more explanations, each complete, of a mental event or action. If we did, we would require the inclusion of the relevant earlier mental event in each of the explanations of the later mental event or action.

How does this conviction of the efficacy of the mental stand to the three hypotheses? To return to the model, interpreted as before, the mental event of noticing the olives, M1, is in lawlike correlation with the neural event N1; and the event of intending to have one, M2, is in lawlike correlation with N2; and N1 is in the causal background of N2; and both N1 and N2 are in the causal background of the action A, reaching for an olive. More generally, the three hypotheses offer this account of the relationship between an earlier mental event and a later mental event: the earlier was a lawful correlate of a neural event that occurred within a causal sequence for a later neural event that was a lawful correlate of the later mental event. As for the relationship between mental event and action, it is this: the neural correlate of the event occurred in a causal sequence for the action.

Do the hypotheses give a place to our conviction of the efficacy of the mental? Is the theory far enough from epiphenomenalism? To repeat, earlier mental events are correlates of neural events that cause actions and also neural correlates of mental events – the earlier mental events are not themselves causes of the later actions and mental events. Is their being correlates of causes, in a way necessary to them, good enough?

There seems to be room for different judgements here. Things are not so clear as in the case of Anomalous Monism and epiphenomenalism, where mental events were not lawlike correlates of neural events. Some philosophers and neuroscientists do indeed say or assume that the view we are considering is epiphenomenalist, or does not assign *enough* efficacy to the mental, enough explanatory power. They say or assume that we have to do better. They say or assume that to provide for the efficacy of the mental, we must supplement the three hypotheses by *identifying* neural events and mental events, thereby joining those philosophers who pursue an identity theory of mind.

We must identify M1 with N1, giving ourselves what we can refer to as M1/N1. Then we shall have as much efficacy as can be asked, since that event will be a *cause* of the later mental event M2/N2, and also the action A. This Nomological Monism, such that M1 is N1 as a matter of law, is the answer. This is a picture of mind that Davidson contemplates and takes to be coherent but regards as false. It has, he supposes, been accepted by others.[20] As it seems to me, however, all relevant identity theories are in need of more than friends, and are of no help to us. First, however, some words on Nomological Monism in particular.

What shall we mean when we say that M1 was identical with N1? We must certainly have a relation that gives us what we are trying to acquire, mental efficacy. We must have 'M1' and 'N1' designating one thing, in the sense in which certain 'theoretical reductions', say, do not produce one thing. We must have the intuitively-understood identity of which a number of criteria have been proposed: the Leibnizian, to the effect that each of seemingly two entities has all and only the properties of the other; sameness of spatio-temporal position; same causes and effects;[21] sameness of general property, instantiating individual, and time.[22]

Can we have X and Y identical in the intuitive sense and also in lawlike connection? It seems plain that we cannot. The simple fact here is that for lawlike connection you need two things – as indeed you do for the most familiar kind of lawlike connection, which of course is standard causal connection. If 'X' and 'Y' occur in the relevant places in the statement of a lawlike connection, then X and Y cannot be identical. There is an old proposition, affirmed by Hume among others, that the causal relation can hold only between what he called distinct existences. It is at bottom the truth that cause and effect must be non-identical. It is as clear that all lawlike connections require non-identical terms.

This is independent of conceptions of such connection, at any rate of tolerable conceptions. Whether we say that if X is in lawlike connection with Y then (1) X and Y are a kind of instance of a constant conjunction or (2) X and Y are in a whatever-else connection, mentioned at the outset, or (3) even that the terms 'X' and 'Y' somehow 'fit' one another,[23] if that is a serious contender – whatever we say, we must have X and Y non-identical in the fundamental sense. This remains true, certainly, when X and Y are, as we can say, properties of some one thing. If it were a matter of law that this olive's being green goes together with its being moist, then its moistness would have to be non-identical with its greenness.

Can the conclusion be avoided by concentration not on the intuitive idea of identity but on one of the four proposed criteria? It will be agreed, I think, that only the third offers hope: what seem to be two things can surely be in lawlike connection if the identity-relation between them is that each shares all causes and effects with the other. Indeed so, but this criterion does not in fact produce identity. There is the fact that seemingly one thing by this criterion, can have a property lacked by the other. In terms of the example, suppose M1 and N1 share all causes and effects. For a start, there is the fact that M1 has a lawlike correlate N1, which is lacked by N1. Again, consider two things with different spatio-temporal positions. It is a conceptual possibility that they are joint effects of a single causal circumstance, and that through overdetermination all and only the effects of each are also effects of the other.

I conclude we cannot conjoin an identity of mental event and neural event with the Correlation Hypothesis, thereby doing better to give expression to our conviction of mental efficacy. Do you now propose that we should just abandon the Correlation Hypothesis, give up on it and start again? Secure everything we want of mental efficacy by way of just an identity theory? There may be other recommendations.[24] This lurch, it has to be said, is another thing that turns up among neuroscientists when reluctantly they turn to philosophy.

Well, there is a reason against this, a general argument against identity theories. It is, in sum, that they divide into two categories: real identity theories that amount to what can be called local idealism or true materialism, and are therefore unacceptable, and those which in fact issue in the inefficacy of the mental. This can be shown easily enough.

Let us have in mind ordinary or Leibnizian identity, which is fundamental. To return to M1, noticing the olives, what is its nature? The sense of the question can be caught by way of a natural answer, which is that its nature is a matter of consciousness and only that, consciousness conceived in the way mentioned at the outset – a matter of subject and subjective contents. Let us say, correspondingly, that N1 is neural and only that. Its nature or properties are wholly neural. These two things, if they exist, are respectively wholly mental and wholly neural.

If we now contemplate that M1 = N1, and read from left to right, we begin with M1, any property of which is mental. It follows that any property possessed by N1 is mental. We have local idealism – certain contents of our heads, which we took to be neural, are in fact mental. What we have is not the large and paralysing metaphysical doctrine of past centuries to the effect that everything that exists is mental, but the doctrine that what is located in our heads, neurons and transmitter substances and the two hemispheres and so on, are only mental.

If we read from the right, what we have is a particular materialism – neuralism. That is, reality no longer includes consciousness as ordinarily understood, anyway with respect to us. What we call thoughts and desires have only neural properties. In each case we have efficacy, but at an unacceptable price.[25] The second choice, if not the first, has been attempted by some bold philosophers. Many have elaborated the fact, certainly, that the neural properties in question are causal ones. In this functionalism, which will have our full attention in the next chapter, there is no escape from the true materialism.[26]

Other philosophers of a materialist but compromising persuasion have proceeded somewhat differently. Their endeavours follow the same pattern.[27] We have it that N1 = M1, and there exists only the neural, but there is the further point (1) that there is a kind of special presentation of the thing in question. I as owner have it 'from inside'. The fact of mentality, not to be got rid of, is allowed to persist within the *presentation* of the neural. Or (2) we are given a distinction between the *evidence* and the evidenced, with the mental associated with the former.

Or (3) we are reminded of Frege and hence his distinction between the sense and referent of a term or expression.[28] The expression 'the evening star' has the same referent as 'the morning star', picks out the same heavenly body, but has a different sense. Similarly, the referent of expressions for the mind is neural, but then sense conveys something else. This third proposal is not attractive, since it is absolutely not true that 'feeling sad' standardly has a neural referent. Still, remembering the definition of sense as 'mode of presentation of the referent', and detaching this third proposal from anything about natural language, we can take it that this saving of the mental comes to the same thing as one or both of the previous two.

We have a new dualism of properties or characters in these compromising proposals. Such proposals, while they may escape from a true materialism, are on a certain understanding not identity theories at all. It is indeed right to say they are not real identity theories. More important, there is the fact that we seem as much as with the three hypotheses taken by themselves to run afoul of our conviction of the efficacy of the mental. The introduction of the 'presentation' as against what is presented, or the evidence against what is evidenced, makes self-defeating the line of argument we are considering. It really runs as follows.

We begin with N1 and M1, and N2 and M2, and N1 causing N2. Convinced of the efficacy of M1 with respect to M2, and wanting to do well by the fact in our theory, we identify the mental event and the neural event. However, putting aside the pretty mad idealism option, this issues in a true materialism. In an attempt to avoid the true materialism, we add in the mental presentation MP1 of that which is M1 and N1, and the mental presentation MP2 of that which is M2 and N2.

Sadly, however, we now have the fact of mentality as inefficacious. It is not that MP1 is efficacious with respect to N2 and M2, or with respect to MP2, but, to put the point one way, that it is *somehow* in relation with that which caused N2 and M2, and perhaps MP2. Let us put aside these additions.

Some will say impatiently that something has been left out of this whole line of reflection. Indeed something *has* been left out – another identity theory, also Leibnizian. Not a real or a compromising identity theory but something different. Go back all the way, they will say, to where a question was asked about the natures of M1 and N1, and where M1 = N1 was read in such a way as to produce either local idealism or a true materialism. Read it instead as follows: that which has or in a sense is M1 is that which has or is M2. Thus M1 and N1 are taken to be parts, properties, characters or whatever of some one thing. The idea is that there is one thing which has just these two parts or whatever. That which is M1 has all and only the properties, including some neural ones, that are had by that which is N1.

In this weak sort of identity theory, of which Davidson's seems to be an example, we again have a dualism of properties. More important, we are again left with the inefficacy of the mental. We can grant that that which is N1 is in a certain sense that which is M1, and that which is N2 is that which is M2. But we have it from our hypotheses that there is a full explanation of M1 and M2 that mentions N1 and M1 only as N1. Only the character or property-set N1 enters into the causal sequence.

It appears, then, that an identity theory will be one of certain categories. It will be (1) a real identity theory, and such as to secure efficacy, but at the excessive price of a true materialism or local idealism. Or (2) it will be a compromising identity theory or (3) a weak identity theory, in both cases a dualism of properties that fails to secure efficacy. Anomalous Monism, on the view taken of it in the first paper in this book, is a weak theory.

6   Mental Efficacy, Fly in the Ointment

Let us go back, then, to Non-Mental Causation of Neural Correlates and Actions. What else can be done to deal with the problem of mental efficacy? In terms of the model, the problem comes to this: there is a full explanation of M2 that does not mention M1, and a full explanation of A that does not mention either M1 or M2. This is so, to put the point one way, and to speak only of M1 and M2, because there is a causal circumstance for M2 that is prior to M1 and that does not issue in M2 by way of a sequence that includes M1. That is what gives some affront to the conviction of efficacy.

It is important to see that it is all that affronts it. The three hypotheses do not give any other affront.

It is indeed not part of the hypotheses that N1 *causes* M1. All that is asserted is that these two items are in lawlike correlation. Therefore we are not committed to one particular epiphenomenalism, in fact the original one, which makes mental events precisely into mere side-effects of neural events. It is not asserted that N1 is a cause or a causal circumstance for several effects, one being M1 and another being N1 and so on. That is consistent with but not entailed by the three hypotheses. We are therefore not committed to an epiphenomenalism that reduces the mental to merely a sign, a guaranteed sign, of some of the physical. The mental is not made just an ideal barometer of neural weather.

Nor, very certainly, is it part of the three hypotheses that M2 might have happened, in the situation, even if M1 had not happened. On the contrary, M2 would *not* have happened if M1 had not happened. That is to say that the two are in lawlike connection, by way of N1 and N2. In one sense, M1 is a necessary condition of M2. In a related sense, however, the reverse is also true. We are thus not committed to a certain gross epiphenomenalism which, as might be said metaphorically, would actually *disconnect* an earlier mental event from a later, or *disconnect* relevant mental events from an action.

So – there is a full explanation of M2 that does not mention M1, but M1 is not asserted to be merely a certain side-effect of N1, and we do have it that M2 would not have happened without M1. There are pictures of mind, then, that would give greater affront to our conviction of the efficacy of the mental. That is not to say that ours does not give some.

Can it be shown to give still less than might now be supposed? If I think of the episode of the olives, assuming myself to be the person in question, what thoughts of it would be unacceptable? Let us cast around. Any thought of it is unacceptable which makes *me* inefficacious. One thing that is not on, whatever is said about mental events, is that *I* should be on the sidelines. No picture of the episode is acceptable which has no place for *personal efficacy*. Whatever other proposition in this neighbourhood is true, this one is. How do the three hypotheses stand to personal efficacy?

It seems unnecessary that in answer we provide a full conception of the person, or opt for one of several competing conceptions. Any adequate one will give a place to on-going dispositions of belief, notably memory-belief, and desire. These are, so to speak, grounds of mental events. As already noted in another connection, they are identifiable with what are underdescribed as neural structures. These, to say the least, are consonant with the three hypotheses. With this proposition we evidently have good hope of accommodating our conviction of the efficacy of persons within the framework of the three hypotheses. A person occurs ineliminably in our explanations. This is a matter of the second hypothesis, on the physical causation of neural correlates.

It is arguable, perhaps, that our conviction of the efficacy of persons is more fundamental than our conviction of the efficacy of the mental, or, as we might now call it, the efficacy of mental events. Can enough be said, perhaps, if the three hypotheses save personal efficacy? It was natural to suppose that M1 must be an ineliminable part of any explanation of M2, and that M1 and M2 must be such parts of any explanation of A. But if you stand back a bit, and look again at the episode of the olives, can you suppose that not much is wrong about the report to which we come? It is one that above all makes a person into an ineliminable part of the explanations of M2 and A. It allows, also, that M2 would not have happened without M1, and that A would not have happened without M1 and M2. Furthermore, neither M1 nor M2 is mere side-effect of the physical, and A can be said in a sense to derive from M2. What is not included is only that M1 is ineliminable with respect to the explanation of M2, and that both are ineliminable with respect to the explanation of A.

Implicit in these last reflections is the idea that in this neighbourhood of one's self we may have what is best summed up not as a conflict of seeming truths. We rather have a conflict between seeming truth on the one hand, by which I mean the three hypotheses, and, on the other hand, desire and volition. This is our desire and volition to believe a certain thing about desire, volition and the like. It is at least arguable that there is this desire and volition about desire and volition rather than philosophical perception in the demand for the efficacy of mental events.

Does this bring the theory of Mind-Brain Correlation with Non-Mental Causation to a happy end? Bring calm and confidence to the more philosophical departments and laboratories of neuroscience? Let me avoid unnecessary suspense. More needs to be thought about, because in fact there is a fly in the ointment.

Come back to the model. The mental event M2 and the neural event N2 were in lawlike or necessary connection. M2 was a kind of necessary condition for N2. If M2 hadn't happened, N2 wouldn't have happened. This, of course, is an instance of familiar stuff. As we say, more generally, if one thing is sufficient for a second one, you don't get the second without the first. But if M2 was a kind of necessary condition for N2, then, to come to the crunch, how could other things be a sufficient condition for N2? In particular, how could N1 and the environmental event E be enough to bring about N2?

Something is needed for calm and confidence.

Notes

1. For an acute discussion of Lichtenberg see Bernard Williams, *Descartes: The Project of Pure Inquiry* (Penguin Books, 1978) p. 95 ff.

2. Franz Brentano, *Psychology from an Empirical Standpoint*, eds O. Kraus and L. McAlister (Routledge & Kegan Paul, 1973).
3. There are non-conscious events and things that are in another sense mental, of course. These are things and events subject to rules or programmes that in our case issue in conscious events. The most familiar of these are dispositional beliefs and the like. These non-conscious things and events, more or less the subject of cognitive science and the like, are not our primary subject. Our subject, brain and mind, is better served by using the word 'mental' in the most ordinary way, as more or less synonymous with 'conscious'.
4. For an exposition of something close to this fundamental conception of physicality see Anthony Quinton, *The Nature of Things* (Routledge & Kegan Paul, 1973) pp. 46–53, a wonderfully better book than some others opened more often.
5. Hilary Putnam moves towards his functionalist conclusions by way of the point about species: 'The Nature of Mental States' in his *Mind, Language and Reality: Philosophical Papers* (Cambridge University Press, 1975).
6. As remarked in a note to Chapter 1, see my *A Theory of Determinism* or *Mind and Brain*, in both cases Chapter 1, for a full discussion of causal and lawlike connection. There is also a further discussion of Mind-Brain Correlation with Non-Mental Causation (pp. 154–6) and of related theories, one of them Jaegwon Kim's strong one (pp. 156–63).
7. Here is a fuller version of the Correlation Hypothesis. For each mental event of a given type there exists some simultaneous neural event of one of a certain set of types. The existence of the neural event necessitates the existence of the mental event, the mental event thus being necessary to the neural event. Any other neural event of any of the mentioned set of types will stand in the same relations to another mental event of the given type.
8. e.g. John Thorp, *Freewill: A Defence against Neurophysiological Determinism* (Routledge & Kegan Paul, 1980) ch. 3, sect. 6.
9. They are the business of a companion volume to this one, *On Determinism and Freedom* (Edinburgh University Press, 2004).
10. The Union Theory is such a view. See Chapters 3 and 4.
11. Derived from G. E. M. Anscombe, 'The Causation of Action', an address to the Institut International de Philosophie. There is a revised version in *Knowledge and Mind: Philosophical Essays*, eds Carl Ginet and Sidney Shoemaker (Oxford University Press, 1983).
12. W. V. O. Quine, *Word and Object* (Wiley, 1960) ch. 2; Davidson, 'Mental Events' (see ch. 1 Notes).
13. Quine, ibid.
14. Ibid., p. 73.
15. 'Mental Events'.
16. 'Psychology as Philosophy', p. 43 (see ch. 1 Notes).
17. 'Mental Events', p. 95.
18. Further arguments against Davidson's denial of psychophysical lawlike connection are advanced by Jaegwon Kim, 'Psychophysical Laws', in *Actions and Events: Perspectives on the Philosophy of Donald Davidson*, eds Brian P. McLaughlin and Ernest LePore (Blackwell, 1985).

19. See p. 21. See also p. 11.
20. 'Mental Events'.
21. Davidson, 'The Individuation of Events', in Nicholas Rescher et al. (eds), *Essays in Honour of Carl G. Hempel* (Reidel, 1969).
22. Richard Brandt and Jaegwon Kim, 'The Logic of the Identity Theory', *Journal of Philosophy*, 1967. Kim, 'Events as Property Exemplifications', in Myles Brand and Douglas Walton (eds), *Action Theory* (Reidel, 1976).
23. Davidson's brief account of law, involving 'fitting' predicates, is given in 'Emeroses by Other Names', *Essays on Actions and Events* (Oxford University Press, 1980).
24. See above, p. 23.
25. That the price is unacceptable is clear to everybody, I think, anyway in private, but more will be said of it later (p. 54, p. 206). In the meantime notice that you can be helped in the direction of being willing to pay the price, accept neuralism or the like, by a certain ambiguity. Our subject is one thing, consciousness itself, rather than four things. Our subject is not consciousness + the purely neural or brain facts that go with consciousness + the causes of consciousness + the effects of consciousness. But there is certainly a tendency in much current philosophy of mind to think that this large bundle is the subject of consciousness. It is evident, to take a good example again, in Papineau's *Introducing Consciousness* (Icon/Totem 2000) (p. 10, p. 13). There is a tendency to regard consciousness itself as just an 'ingredient' in the bundle-subject that is consciousness (p. 7). There is 'the conscious pain' and the 'conscious visual experience', so presumably there are also the other ones – the neural pain and the neural visual experience (p. 1). Well, anybody can think of anything they want, but if they are thinking about what we take to be *consciousness itself*, they aren't thinking about the three other things. What happens on my retinas, for a start, or in the world before it gets to my retinas, is not part of my consciousness itself. We don't usually run the four things together, although it's unkindly said without reason that we do, and certainly we don't have to (p. 14). The important point here is not a matter of argument strictly speaking. It is that people can drift into thinking that a pile of materialistic doctrines is pretty good on three-quarters of a subject – and therefore that its not doing well with the last bit, even missing it out, is tolerable. Just *one* 'ingredient' missing. But that is not the situation at all. If the subject is supposed to be and is said to be consciousness, and the pile leaves all of *that* out, every last scintilla, the pile is a disaster, isn't it? Even if it's the cat's pyjamas with respect to the three other quarters of a bundle? For more along these lines, see my piece 'Consciousness and Inner Tubes', *Journal of Consciousness Studies*, 2000.
26. The proposition is a main subject of the next chapter.
27. For an account and defence, see Edgar Wilson, *The Mental as Physical* (Routledge & Kegan Paul, 1980).
28. Gottlob Frege, *Translations from the Philosophical Writings of Gottlob Frege*, ed. P. Geach & M. Black (Blackwell, 1960).

Cognitive Science's Philosophy, and the Union Theory

This paper in its first part is about a view of consciousness that has been deferred to in philosophy and is in or underlies a good deal of the thriving inquiry into consciousness known as cognitive science.[1] That is the science of consciousness that is inspired by the computer, or at any rate has the computer looking over its shoulder. The philosophical view in question, functionalism, does certainly make consciousness into a subject for science. Consciousness so conceived raises problems, of course, but problems no different in kind from those elsewhere in science – and only problems that call for the same assumptions, methods and indeed kinds, strengths and uses of intelligence.

The view does greatly more to make consciousness a subject for science than the theory of Mind-Brain Correlation with Non-Mental Causation. The latter, after all, does something like leave consciousness on one side. Consciousness in that theory has a distinctive nature about which we are not clear, may or may not be physical, correlates with neural activity, and has a secondary explanatory role. The science in which this most immediately and naturally issues is the main endeavour of neuroscience – the discovery of particular brain-mind correlations and the explaining of neural correlates in terms of previous neural causes. As against this, functionalism conceives of consciousness in such a way that it itself simply is and must be an *immediate* concern of science – neuroscience as much as cognitive science. Consciousness itself is as much the concern of science as atoms, hydrogen, trees, electricity, bridges, planets, and the origin of the universe.

Functionalism has its name because it finds the nature of consciousness in how certain things function – which is to say what place or role they have. Such a role or place has usually been conceived of causally. The view, then, very roughly, is that mental or conscious events are to be understood in terms of their causes and effects. It is therefore related to the truism that things are often conceived partly in terms of their effects. No doubt functionalism is an improvement on behaviourism, which in its strong form somehow conceived of mental events in terms of their effects in behaviour. It has had proponents, made converts, and attracted fellow-travellers. It has been taken as crucially different from materialism somehow understood in that it does not eliminate consciousness but rather preserves and explains it.

But this paper is not only about functionalism. In its second part, maybe for two good reasons, it sets out something different, the rudiments of the Union Theory, a contribution of my own that has fewer supporters, more discriminating. It is an entirely different theory of consciousness, but one of which you know a good deal already. It has in it the Correlation Hypothesis as one basis, and the ordinary idea of consciousness in terms of subjectivity. It comes out of what seems to me to be the wreck of functionalism but also that fly in the ointment of the theory of Mind-Brain Correlation with Non-Mental Causation and of course the problems of some identity theories, the real ones and some others.

---

1   What Functionalism Is Not, and Is

A person's mind includes a sequence of mental or conscious events – sensations, perceptions, thoughts, beliefs, emotions, desires, intentions, and the like. A person's mind may also be taken to include, not so naturally and more as a matter of stipulation, a set of dispositions to mental events – no doubt to all those mentioned kinds of them. We can also add in the unconscious operations, procedures, computations, calculations, programme-followings and what-not by which the dispositions come to issue in mental or conscious events. This sort of thing includes my knowing my two middle names when I am not thinking of them, and how, as we naturally say, they come into my mind. It also includes not only dispositional beliefs but also dispositional desires, intentions and what-not, if not at all necessarily the supposed sexy desires so pleasing to Freud and his followers.

All of these unconscious dispositions are neural, since there is not anything else they can be. That a neural structure (or anything else) is a disposition is merely the fact that it is persistent and the fact that it together with something else will or would make up a causal circumstance (p. 26) for a later event, say my conscious hope at this moment that this paper will persuade you of something. So too, of course, are the unconscious operations and so on neural.

Hume has the fame of first seeing that there seems no reason to take a person's mind to be any more than the sequence of mental events and maybe the set of dispositions and so on.[2] (Of course there is the implicit fact that the sequence is internally related in several ways, most notably in that some of the events are memories of others – that is what makes it a single sequence.) Hume has the fame, more particularly, of noting that when we look into our mental lives themselves, or better, when we recollect the moment just past of our mental lives, we never recollect anything but mental events.

That is, we never recollect anything that is in any sense mental or conscious that is *external* to the mental events, which thing possesses, underlies or organizes them. We find no such *self*. A person is not such a mental entity, but, in so far as mental facts are concerned, just a single sequence of mental events, and maybe the dispositions. Hume's truth should neither be overlooked or taken for anything else. It is definitely not a denial of the subjectivity of mental events in all senses, of which more in due course, much more.

The mind-body problem is the problem of the relation of mental to simultaneous neural events. It is not the problem of the relation of mental events to their explanatory antecedents, including neural dispositions. To deal with the mind-body problem we evidently need conceptions of both mental and neural events. What in general are mental or conscious events? What is their nature? This, really, is the fundamental problem in the philosophy of mind. This is the *hard problem* or the *hardest problem* in the philosophy of mind – however those terms are used elsewhere.[3] Can we replace our ordinary, settled and obscure idea of them in terms of a subject or subjective parts or awareness and somehow subjective contents? (pp. 20–1)

Functionalism, which at least underlies cognitive science, and in fact shades into cognitive science of a philosophical kind, or cognitive science with philosophical ambition, has in the past couple of decades offered an answer to this question at the bottom of the philosophy of mind. Does functionalism really provide an answer, an adequate analysis or characterization of mental events in general?

There is a lot of loose talk in this neighbourhood, and much argument by slogan, and rich complication that obscures main propositions. There is also a lot of scientized reflection of uncertain philosophical virtue – by, as you might say, those with the policy of Penelope's wooers.[4] Also, if you are looking for something that has multiple realizations, of which fact a bit more will be said, you could do worse than by starting with functionalism itself. So it will be as well to be definite about what I have in mind in speaking of functionalism. Let me first exclude quite a few things.

Functionalism is not the banal assertion that

> all mental events, conceived in whatever way, at least typi-
> cally have certain causes and effects.

Everybody believes and knows something of that sort, save perhaps some remaining defenders of free will and a couple of epiphenom-enalists. Nor is functionalism the assertion we should distinguish, that

> all mental events, conceived independently of their causes
> and effects, at least typically do have certain causes and ef-
> fects.

Perhaps most non-functionalist philosophers of mind accept some-thing like this, while strict functionalists, as I shall come to call them, do not, since they deny the possibility of a conception of mental events independent of the causes and effects. Nor is functionalism to be taken as the somewhat stronger proposition of determinism that

> all mental events, conceived independently of their causes
> and effects, do always and without exception have certain
> causes – and effects.

At least very many non-functionalists accept this, while strict func-tionalists do not, again because of the contained assumption of an independent conception.

Nor, to turn away from mental events in general, the genus, is functionalism to be understood as the proposition that

> kinds or species of mental events, say beliefs or intentions,
> do have typical kinds or species of causes and effects.

That is very true, but not relevant. Nor is functionalism the propo-sition, which I and many other accept, that

> each of beliefs, intentions and other kinds of mental events
> are to be understood or defined partly in terms of kinds of
> causes and effects.

Whoever set out to understand desires wholly independently of action or behaviour? Another thing to be put aside is the belief that

types or kinds of mental events, as well as particular mental
events, can be successfully discriminated, individuated or
identified just by their causes and effects.

– where that is not a claim about their nature, or the whole of their
nature. The belief is very likely true. With respect to events of any
kind, what is more common than successful individuation by cause
or effect or both? But, for present purposes, who cares?

Functionalism as I am understanding it is also not just the programme, obviously a fruitful one, of investigating, theorizing about,
giving formal accounts of, and finding analogies to the causal sequences in which human mental events occur – the genus of them
or its species. That programme of research into dispositions and operations, computations, programme-followings and so on will contribute to any full account of mental events, but is not to be confused
with something else.

Let me add, finally, that there are various theories and doctrines
that fall under names got by adding a prefix to 'functionalism'. The
prefixes have included 'classical', 'metaphysical', 'methodological',
'machine ', 'homuncular', 'wide', 'narrow', 'teleological', 'sober',
'weak', and so on. I am concerned only with any of these that is
functionalism as I am going to understand it, or anyway approxi-
mates to this.

Functionalism as I and others understand it, to get there at last,
purports to be a complete answer to the question of what mental
or conscious events in general are. That is, it purports to give all of
the common nature of mental events. It is to replace our ordinary,
settled and unfortunately obscure and elusive idea of consciousness
or mentality. That is what makes it interesting. Does it? If so it will
of course distinguish mental events from all else. Keep that in mind.

Functionalism so understood, comes in two kinds. In strict functionalism, the first and most important of the two kinds, probably
the only important kind, mental events at bottom are said to consist in no more than events that stand in certain causal relations.[5]
That is,

an event in so far as it is mental is at bottom no more than
an event that stands in certain causal relations.

We are to understand, of course, that there is no other or further
true and very different characterization of mental events, events in
so far as they are mental. They have no further and very different
mental character. In particular, our ordinary conception of them in
terms of subjectivity is an illusion. To speak frankly, as functionalists
explicitly or at least implicitly do, it is an illusion of no use to us.

Mental events, to say a word more of functionalism's central idea, are in causal relations with input, what are called other 'inner' events, and output. That is the basic answer to the fundamental question of the philosophy of mind. Hence my wanting that glass of wine over there consists fundamentally in an event that was (1) an effect of such things as the glass of wine, (2a) also an effect of such things as an inner event having to do with my seeing the glass, (2b) a cause of other inner events, maybe having to do with my intending something, and (3) also the cause of such things as an arm-movement in the direction of the glass.

This account of my wanting the glass of wine, already far from simple because of the occurrences of 'such things as', can be enlarged by saying of the causal relata of the wanting that they stand in causal relations to other things than the wanting. We thus get a 'holistic' account of the event, something in accord with 'the holism of the psychological'. But what we have in description of the mental event or the event as mental remains no more than causal relations.

All that is pretty vague, but there is no need to be more precise. It is to be understood, though, in such a way as to leave one question open. This needs a little attention.

Shall we take it that strict functionalism asserts of the mental events of which we know most, our human mental events, that they have *no* other properties than the causal ones? Shall we take it, that is, whatever we say about how the events are 'realized' in our brains, that they themselves do *not* have neural properties? Philosophers who do this puzzling thing evidently make their account of our minds, of our mental events, even less than ethereal. They make them abstract, as some of them say – of the order of the number 5 itself, or the proposition $5 + 5 = 10$, these items not to be confused with marks, sounds or anything at all in space and time.

Those functionalist philosophers who are fleeing traditional mystery about the mind, fleeing dualistic talk of ethereal stuff, ghostly stuff, succeed in making our mental events into yet less than ethereal and ghostly stuff. These philosophers at least aspire to make our mental events into no more than *relations*, as distinct from things in relations, and, what is more, relations of an abstract kind, like the one between $5 + 5$ and 10, as distinct from *being heavier than* or *being two feet to the right*. In defining strict functionalism, let us not take this disastrous path.

Let us rather follow other philosophers to be found in this neighbourhood and take it that in strict functionalism the mental events of which we know most, human mental events, *are* also neural events. This identity theory, which I shall take as contained in the functionalism in question, evidently reduces to just the proposition that certain of our neural events have certain causes and effects. The proposition both completes this functionalism's account of our mental events and serves as its solution to the mind-body problem in so far as we humans are concerned.

It is also noted, certainly, as a part of the doctrine, that it is a possibility of some sort that events of other kinds than neural, say silicon events in computers for a start, could stand in the same causal relations. Indeed, silicon events could have replaced our neural events without any repercussion for the given facts of mentality. The silicon events could have stood in the same causal connections. Theoretically, you could get rid of a batch of my important neurons, put in silicon, and I would on occasion still be thinking of Aunt Sarah. This is the proposition of multiple realizations or variable realization, of which a great deal is made.

2   Functionalism as Unswallowable

So much for how functionalism is properly understood and in particular strict functionalism. We will get to the other kind, which is lenient, in a while. Supporters of strict functionalism typically pass by a basic and general objection to their conception of our mental events – often pass it by in the course of considering what seem to me lesser objections that are by-products of the basic and general one. Let us not follow them, but hesitate.

What we have at bottom is that human mental events in so far as they are mental consist in no more than events that are certain effects and causes – effects of input and other inner events, causes of other inner events and output. Add more talk of causal relations if you like. And, whatever might have replaced them, our human mental events are also neural. That is all there is to them. Nothing at all about subject and content, about a distinctive nature that leads and indeed pushes us into such talk. No matter what is taken to be essential to them, which of course is their causal connections, they are just neural events in certain causal connections. It is imperative to note that they are not made anything more than that by the proposition about variable realization or replaceability. It doesn't add anything more about *their* own nature, constituents, or properties. Nothing at all.

Will it be said that that remark about nature, constituents and properties is obscure and doctrine-ridden? No doubt, and rightly. But such talk will have to be clarified in accordance with the sound idea that a thing's own nature, constituents or properties do not include the thing's uniqueness or want of uniqueness in all or any respects. To discover that something is replaceable by something else is not to discover more of *its* nature. I do not assign an additional property to a screwdriver by adding that its known role could also be performed by something else, say a detached bit of a stapler. No question about a thing itself is answered by way of propositions about its uniqueness or replaceability. There seems even more reason to say this than to say the same about propositions about a thing's relations generally.

I suspect that in the haze of doctrine, many functionalists and their fellow-travellers do not see that nothing is added to their account of our mental events as neural effects and causes by the proposition of variable realization.[6] They mistakenly suppose that by variable realization, by what they might call untying the mental from just the neural, or extending the mental beyond the neural, or indeed making the mental independent of the neural, they have done us a service. They have given some place or recognition to an inescapable conviction of ours about the mental, a conviction that is another part of our ordinary, settled and obscure conception of our mental events, unsatisfactory as it is. That conviction is simply that our mental events have other or more than neural and causal properties. That the given conviction is inescapable and part of the ordinary conception seems to me beyond doubt.

To speak differently, given that this functionalism reduces human mental events to neural events in certain causal connections, it shares the principal character of a family of doctrines including the real identity theory that is the 'nothing-but' materialism rejected by Davidson and almost everyone else. That family of doctrines in-cludes a denial that our mental events have other than or more than neural and causal properties. This makes them *unswallowable*. On account of a related fact, real behaviourism was unswallowable. No doubt strict functionalism taken as an account of our mental events will because of its basic unbelievability follow behaviourism, rightly parodied as the doctrine that my wanting to get my son a book *is* lip and limb movements towards Waterstones, into the honourable past of the philosophy of mind.

The objection of unbelievability, the first of two main objections, does not overlook differences between functionalism and members of the given family of doctrines. I am aware for a start that eliminative materialism may be said to deny, and to intend to deny, the existence of mental events, and that functionalism may be said to intend to *save* them, to offer an account of them, indeed to express our common conception of them. Only for one species of real materialism, eliminative materialism, are our common mental categories like categories in witchcraft – categories that have *nothing* in them in reality. Functionalism and these other doctrines are nevertheless alike, fundamentally alike, in allowing to what we take to be our mental events only some or other neural and causal properties. It is for this reason that functionalism will follow behaviourism into the past of the philosophy of mind.

This will happen, as it seems to me, as soon as the haze clears, despite the fact that it is not easy to construct a fundamental argument against strict functionalism.[7] This is so since it is difficult, perhaps impossible, to find a premise more secure than what we adversaries of this functionalism are asked to prove, that our mental events satisfy the inescapable conviction that they have other or more than neural and causal properties. This is annoying but not much of a weakness of our case, any more than it is a weakness of my belief that I am now in pain that I probably cannot construct an argument with a premise stronger than that belief. Hume, by the way, said exactly the same of arguing against someone who claims to perceive a self in addition to mental events. For Hume, there was nothing more secure than that there is no such perception to be had.

Now consider a second functionalism, not strict. It is distinct from certain other philosophies of mind, indeed many, with different names, only in emphasis. In this functionalism mental events in general are said to have their causal properties as their essential or distinctive properties, and of course also said to have neural or silicon properties or the like. But it is now allowed that *some* mental events may have other properties, taken as needing less emphasis. They may have qualities spoken of in terms of 'a subjective side', or 'qualia', or 'what something is like' or 'what it is like to be something', or 'raw feels'. In particular some of our human mental events may have these additional properties.

This lenient functionalism, as implied, allows for some human mental events that lack the additional qualities. Thus it faces the general objection that in part it has the unbelievability of eliminative materialism and the like. Its careless and curiously disjunctive conception of the other human mental events, which have or may have the additional properties, is in line with the thoughts of various defenders of mental events as ordinarily conceived. That careless conception and the thoughts from which it comes are in my judgement very useful but insufficient. They do not try to characterize directly and in a general way the nature of mental events. Be that as it may, however, the careless conception in assigning certain properties to some mental events is enough to stand in the way of the identity theory commonly included in lenient functionalism as well as in strict functionalism.

3   Functionalism as Incoherent

Consider now a second and more radical objection to strict functionalism, again overlooked by its proponents in their concern with this or that lesser difficulty.

As remarked above, any adequate account of mental events in general must distinguish them from all else. How does strict functionalism attempt this? How does it try to distinguish mental events from others? We are told that at bottom they are events which have certain causes and certain effects. The identification of these mental events then plainly depends on the identification of the causes and effects. It depends in part on the identification of input and output events. For present purposes, we can restrict ourselves to input and output events, and leave aside other inner events.

Which are these input and output events? What distinguishes input events from others, and what distinguishes output events from others? Let us again think of humans. What distinguishes input events, such as an input event involving the glass of wine, from other environmental events that are causal with respect to humans, say one having to do with a flea of mine of which I am unaware? Clearly input events are not all the environmental-causal events. What distinguishes output events, such as the arm-movement towards the glass, from other bodily events which are effects of internal human causes, say the bodily event that is unintended perspiration? Clearly output events are not *all* such bodily-effect events. To speak differently, functionalists are not and cannot be concerned with *all* the causal sequences which run through a body, but only some. They want the ones some of whose inner events are mental. How do they find them?

It is pretty clear how strict functionalism standardly proceeds. What it in fact does, unreflectively, is to take input as exactly environmental causes of *mental events*, with the mental events understood in something other than the causal way. Plainly they are conceived in exactly our ordinary way. For a start, these mental events are conceived as having more than causal and neural properties. They are conceived in terms of a subject or something of the sort and also contents. So with output. That is bodily and other effects of mental events, with those mental events understood in something other than the causal way. It is our ordinary way.

But then strict functionalism proceeds in this standard way on the basis of exactly what it denies, a true characterization of the nature of mental events themselves in terms of something other than their causal relations. It is incoherent in that it proceeds precisely on the basis of what it denies.[8]

Will you say at this point that I have missed or obscured a simple point? Science has regularly been interested in and identified some class of events, say certain hereditary events, maybe having to do with eye-colour. It has taken this class of events to have a cause, and hypothesized about the nature of that cause. Often its nature has been discovered. This is how things went with the gene. Will you say that functionalism does just this sort of reputable thing?

That seems to me a confusion. The scientific procedure is not near to the standard procedure of functionalism. Functionalism does not begin with something analogous to hereditary events, already identified, say what pigeon fanciers call *breeding true*. It begins with something analogous to the gene, which it then uses to identify other events, and which it then claims to understand wholly in terms of those events. It denies that it presupposes and depends on a conception of something analogous to the gene, but, as said, it does use just that conception in order to specify the causal relata. That is not good science but bad philosophy. If the science was analogous, and bad, it would proceed from the hereditary events to the gene, and then deny it used and depended on any other conception of the hereditary events but their being effects of the gene.

Is it necessary that strict functionalism proceeds in its standard and fatal way? Perhaps it can contemplate only two other options. It must (a) pick out a sub-class of environmental-causal events or a sub-class of bodily-effect events by means which make no reference at all to mental events, or it must (b) pick out the sub-classes by means of a reference to mental events which does not render functionalism incoherent.

Perhaps some will be tempted to think that this functionalism can proceed in the first way. They will say something of the following sort. 'Well, can't we just start by specifying a class of environmental causes straight-off, including causes of receptor-events in eyes and ears, and specifying a class of bodily effects straight-off, say limb-movements and speech-productions – and then say mental events are what come in the middle? How does that presuppose an idea of mental events that makes the whole thing incoherent?'

There is a plain reply, that the procedure *does* depend on the fatal idea, at the start. Specifying the sub-class of environmental causes is and can only be done by choosing those that have certain effects, mental events somehow conceived. Necessarily these mental events are conceived as other than just effects of environmental causes. So with specifying the right class of bodily effects. That is how the unnoticed flea and the perspiration get excluded, as they need to be.

Something else does not need to be added, but usefully can be. There is no special or intrinsic character had by some environmental causes and some bodily effects and such that the functionalist can somehow depend on this character to advance his or her enterprise. Special categories of environmental causes and bodily effects do not pick themselves out. One relevant fact here is that it is conceptually and nomically possible that any environmental cause and any bodily effect go with no mental event at all, however conceived. This is so of stimulation of the retinas and of an arm movement in the direction of a glass of wine or my lips producing the sounds in 'Pass me the Marmite, sweetheart.'

If the first option fails, what of the second? Can strict functionalism pick out sub-classes of causal-environmental events and bodily-effect events by means of a reference to mental events that does not make it incoherent? Perhaps you will be tempted for a moment to the idea that functionalism can depend on this conception of mental events: those events to which we ordinarily but mistakenly or wholly unenlighteningly ascribe a certain character. This character will be the one spoken of in terms of 'qualia', 'what it is like to be something', and so on.

This option has several peculiarities, including its own fatal disability. It depends on the thought that we mistakenly or unenlighteningly characterize a certain set of events. But mistakenly or unenlighteningly characterizing a set of events requires that we must already have discriminated them. We must have a conception of them. This cannot be a conception that picks out nothing, or anything. Thus this line of functionalist thought also depends, at one remove, on exactly what it denies, a conception of mental events in terms of other than their causes and effects.[9]

Let me make one final remark here on something implicit in what has been said. If strict functionalism did have no conception of the genus mental events but the causal one, or no conceptions of such species as belief and intention but causal ones, all its propositions would have an analytic nature which they seem to lack – and which, I think, most functionalists must wish them to lack. For a start 'mental events in general are those which have certain causes and effects' would be nothing other than the proposition 'events that have certain causes and effects do have those causes and effects'. Another embarrassment for functionalism and the science it underpins and informs.

4   Mental Realism, Subjectivity, Psychophysical Intimacy

Now some backward glances and remarks in anticipation of a philosophy of mind with fewer problems.

You have been hearing that we have an ordinary but vague conception of our mental events, a conception of their general nature, a conception that includes the clear conviction that they have other or more than neural and causal properties. It is a conception owed to direct reflection on all of them, and in particular to our capability of recalling any mental event just past. (That we can do this is surely beyond question. Whether this recalling was misdescribed by advocates of 'introspection' is a question that can be put aside.) The conception is therefore owed to what we can speak of as *mental realism* – the policy of reflecting directly on mental events in their reality rather than turning away to this or that more tractable fact pertaining to them, such as their causes and effects, or, to glance back, to the logico-linguistic features of sentences about them, or whatever else.

So – when I recall my experience or mental event a moment ago of seeing the croquet lawn, I recall a subjective content or object. It is not the lawn, not part of the world, according to an old and familiar piece of philosophy, since if my visual cortex and a good deal more of my brain had been the same, but the croquet lawn had not existed, I would have had the same experience with the same content. This content or object is for me very certainly not just a bare causal term. It is not something-I-know-not-what in a mechanism about which I know only what affects it and what it affects. Indeed, it seems that contents can exist for me without my knowing their

causal relations. Further, as hardly needs to be added, the content
I recall is for me not at all a neural fact – and hence not something
only causal and neural.

The idea of a subjective content, as remarked earlier, is already the
idea of something necessarily in relation to something else. That the
idea of content is in this way relational is owed to the recallable fact
of something distinct from content but also, as we can say, within
the experience or mental event. It is another component. This other
thing, for various reasons, is not a person. We are tempted, not only
by tradition, to call it a subject. Even initially we can resist the temptation to make more of it than we can discern, more of it than a
property of a mental event. We can have, I think, no view of it as a
causal term, and certainly no view of it as neural.

There is no doubt that such reflections as these rapidly issue in
problems. One group of problems has to do with a content standing
in a second and quite different relation. This is its relation to something else – in the example, a content's relation to the croquet lawn.
Let us speak, in general, of a content's relation to *the world*, and of the
content-world relation. This relation, we naturally say in beginning,
consists in a content's being an effect of and representative of the
world or rather this or that part of it or thing in it. Trying to make
some initial sense of representation, and the true thought that in
standard representation we need to be aware of what does the representing, may result in further reflections on the relation between
content and what was called subject. It may result in the conclusion
that this relation is certainly not one such that the subject is *aware* of
the content – aware of it in the way that I am aware of the lawn. This
is a denial of contents as subjective contents or objects *of awareness*,
which is to say as sense data and the like.[10]

Despite such problems, we can at least begin to characterize the
general nature itself of mental events. And we need to. To flee the
obscurity, to eschew mental realism, is to fail to enter into what has
first claim on the name of philosophy of mind. It is to fail to deal
with its fundamental question. Giving up on mental realism also
makes any true solution to the mind-body problem highly unlikely.
If we have no decent sense of the nature of mind, what will keep us
from mistaken views of its relation to body?

The various sciences which together make up neuroscience may
be said now to have established something to which empirical
philosophers and commonsensical persons have long been inclined,
a general proposition anticipated earlier (p. 23). That is the proposition that every mental event of which we know is *intimately related*

to a neural event: in a kind of necessary connection with it. Just as there are no ghosts, which is to say no minds or persons floating free of bodies, so there are no ghostly mental events either. To speak of a neural event, of course, is not necessarily to speak of anything simple, anything owed to outmoded doctrines of brain localization.

The proposition of psychoneural intimacy by itself rules out some philosophical theories about mind and brain. (It rules out, for example, the central idea of dualist interactionism. That idea is that sometimes an earlier mental event, somehow independent of the brain, causes a later neural event, and sometimes an earlier neural event causes a later mental event as independent.) The proposition of psychoneural intimacy, for good or ill, has had as a natural product the theory, or rather the family of theories, to the effect that each mental event is identical with a neural event. Such mind-brain theories, identity theories, have had a certain dominance which they may now be losing. Not all of them actully succeed in giving a place to the proposition of psychoneural intimacy, but that is not the main point. The main point, as it seems to me, is that they are open to refutation of which you heard in the last paper.

Having also found functionalism inadequate, to say the least, let us turn to what seems to me a superior proposal about the mind-body problem. It is owed to the method or determination of mental realism, the ordinary and essential if unsatisfactory conception of mental events, and the proposition of psychoneural intimacy.

5   The Union Theory

The Union Theory, or the Theory of Psychoneural Union, can be set out pretty quickly, since its first and most basic part has already been introduced and considered. This is the Correlation Hypothesis. This, you will remember, has to do with a mental event and a simultaneous neural event, and their standing in a certain connection. The hypothesis is as follows.

> Any mental event of a given type occurs in any person just
> in case as a matter of lawlike connection a neural event of
> one or another of a set of types occurs simultaneously in that
> individual.

Let me say a few words more of it. What it comes to in part, informally speaking and by way of an example, is that my thought of Woods Restaurant in Bath a moment ago stood in a certain tight relation with a certain neural event, and if another event of exactly that type were to occur I or somebody else would be thinking of Woods in exactly the same way.

The hypothesis relates mental events only to neural events, and for that reason alone is different from the idea of functionalists about the variable realization of mental events not only in our central nervous systems, but in silicon and whatever else. The hypothesis does specify a many-one relation, but this holds between just the neural realm by itself and the mental. It specifies this many-one relation rather than a one-one relation since it appears to be possible or likely that different types of neural events can stand go with but one type of mental event.

There is nothing in any standard explication of nomic relations that stands in the way of such relations holding between mental and neural events, as the hypothesis supposes. Further, although we have not looked at it, there is very impressive neuroscientific evidence for the hypothesis. In my estimate the evidence is over-whelming. Even if philosophical objections to the hypothesis did not seem open to good rejoinders, as they do, the evidence could be taken to overbear the objections.[11] To speak too quickly, if there is a contest between a philosophical doctrine of the mental which stands in the way of its being in nomic connection with the neural, and, on the other hand, neuroscientific evidence that the mental is in nomic connection with the neural, it is the doctrine that must give way.

The second part of the Union Theory has to do with the causation of the simultaneous neural and mental events that fall under the Correlation Hypothesis. Here we get something distinctly different from what we were contemplating in the last paper – something different from the non-mental causation of neural events (p. 27). We get a further and satisfactorily simple representation or explanation of our conviction of mental efficacy, owed to taking a further view of the nature of mental events, and we get an escape from the contradiction that is a sad upshot of the theory of Mind-Brain Correlation with Non-Mental Causation (p. 44).

So far the nature of mental events has been considered without much attention to whether they are in space and whether they take up some space. Descartes said otherwise. But, presumably, if you are not reading these lines in Venice, your thoughts are not there, but, to speak, a little loosely, where you are. Are they not in your head? The answer Yes is not unusual. It is given, of course, by all those philosophers who support real identity theories. But there is something more persuasive than an argument from those theories. The better argument goes by way of the matter of mental efficacy.

In thinking about Mind-Brain Correlation with Non-Mental Causation, we did indeed give a place to our conviction of mental efficacy – by various means, one of them being the idea of personal efficacy. But the theory had a serious problem in the end, the fly in the ointment. Can we now do better for mental efficacy simply by taking mental events to be *causes* – parts of causal circumstances – for later mental events and actions? Was my feeling a moment ago that this room was a little stuffy not actually and exactly a cause of my then thinking of opening the window and then my doing it? Is that not a more natural and persuasive proposition than most other propositions in this neighbourhood, certainly including all philosophers' propositions? Is it not an instance of a kind of axiom about the explanation of later mental events and actions?

Let us suppose mental events themselves are causes – causes *as* mental events. But it seems that there are no causes that are not things in space. The number 5 itself, as distinct from thoughts and representations of it and sets of 5 things and so on, causes nothing, whatever other relations it stands in. So, if we think that mental events are causes, we also need to accept them as things in space. The two thoughts go together. Having got this far, is it not as reasonable to add that our *ordinary* idea of consciousness and mental events as a matter of subject and content does not in itself exclude their being spatial? Those ideas, if settled, are not so precise as to exclude the idea that mental events are in space. So let us take up the proposition that mental events are in space.

Something follows from it immediately – about whether mental events are *physical*. The ordinary idea of the physical (p. 22) is roughly that physical events come in two categories. They are in space and also are perceived by us, or they are in space and also in causal or other lawlike connection with events in the first category. Physical events are events having to do with sofas and so on and with atoms and so on. We now have it that mental events are in space. We also have it that they are causal – that they themselves cause arm-movements and so on. So surely there is no objection to concluding that mental events are physical?

Do you say that this idea, physicality as against spatiality, *is* excluded by our ordinary idea of consciousness and mental events as a matter of subject and content? That would surely be a mistake. What we are convinced of is that our mental events do not have only *neural* properties – ordinary chemical and electrical properties. More generally, they do not have *ordinary* physical properties. But that is not to say that mental events cannot be otherwise physical.

We are well on the way to abandoning the hypothesis about the non-mental causation of neural events. But what we get will have to have something in it that deals with the contradiction, the fly in the ointment. That is about either one or both of a neural event and a simultaneous mental event being an effect of antecedents of whatever kind. The Hypothesis on the Non-Mental Causation of Neural Events did indeed take only a neural event to be an effect – and the simultaneous mental event to be only a lawlike correlate of the neural event. That was the problem. How could there be a mental event necessary to the neural event if there was something else that guaranteed the occurrence of that neural event?

To get to a solution, consider the water in your electric tea kettle. When you switch on the kettle, the water in it gets hotter and it expands. If it wasn't expanding, it wouldn't be getting hotter, and vice versa. So is there the contradiction that switching the kettle on and so on – say the causal circumstance CC – is sufficient for or necessitates the water being hotter, but the expansion, which is not part of the circumstance CC, is also necessary?

Whatever the science of all this may be, there is a certain good line of thought. It can't be the case that since CC happened the water got hotter but *not* the case that since CC happened the water expanded. You can express that by saying that the higher temperature and the expansion count as a *single* effect. If that is a little surprising, what it comes to is not so. It is that the conditional connections in the world are such that you never get a circumstance like CC such that if it had been missing, only *one* other thing would have been missing.[12]

To return to a simultaneous mental and neural event, they are not only lawlike correlates but are a single effect in the given sense. We can call them a *psychoneural pair*. And so we get to the second hypothesis of the Union Theory.

> A mental event and the simultaneous neural event correlated with it are the single effect of a causal sequence having in it physical events, both neural and mental. The initial events of the sequence are events in the individual at the beginning of consciousness and environmental events thereafter.

Of a good deal more that can be said in support of this, one thing is that it does not give great offence to the idea, certainly a scientific idea, that neural events have neural causes. It allows that at *every* stage or instant of a causal sequence for a neural event, there is a neural cause. What it departs from is the idea that at any stage or instant there is only a neural cause. Rather, it also allows for the possibility of another kind of physical cause, a mental cause.

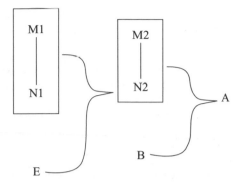

Figure 2: The Union Theory.

The third hypothesis of the Union Theory is that actions are effects of certain causal sequences whose initial events include a psychoneural pair that is the intention to perform the action. Spelling it out fully would take a bit of time and is not necessary. The burden of the Union Theory is in the first two hypotheses.

There is a little model of the theory in Figure 2, again to be understood as the episode of someone seeing some olives, intending to have one, and reaching for one. M1 and N1 illustrate the Correlation Hypothesis, as do M2 and N2 – as in Figure 1 on p. 28. But M1 and N1 are also given as a psychoneural pair, as are M2 and N2 – they make up a single effect. It is also an essential part of the story that M2 itself is a cause of M2 and the action A.

That is a good start on the Union Theory, of which you will be hearing some more.

Notes

1. For enlightenment see one or preferably more of John Heil, *Philosophy of Mind* (Routledge, 1998), Jaegwon Kim, *Philosophy of Mind* (Westview, 1998), E. J. Lowe, *An Introduction to the Philosophy of Mind* (Cambridge University Press, 2000), William Lycan, ed. *Mind and Cognition: A Reader* (Blackwell, 1990), Stephen Priest, *Theories of the Mind* (Penguin, 1991), Stephen Stich, *From Folk Psychology to Cognitive Science* (MIT Press, 1983).
2. David Hume, *A Treatise of Human Nature*, bk 1, pt 4, sect. 6.
3. The term 'the hard problem' is owed to David Chalmers, *The Conscious Mind* (Oxford University Press, 1996).
4. 'Those who study particular sciences and neglect philosophy are like Penelope's wooers, who made love to the waiting women.' Francis Bacon (ed.), *Apophthegmes Old and New* (Hanna Barret, Richard Whittaker, 1625), no. 189.

5. I leave out complications having to do with logical or computational as against causal relations, which change but do not much affect the issue.

6. Perhaps this is true of Kim Sterelny, *The Representational Theory of Mind* (Blackwells, 1990). Others with iron stomachs do certainly see the fact. David Lewis did so in his early paper, 'An Argument for the Identity Theory', *Journal of Philosophy*, 1966.

7. The objection of unswallowability can be said to beg the question, and hence not to be 'an argument'. That shows that there is a role in inquiry for something other than 'arguments', or, better, despite what I say in the text, that 'arguments' can be too narrowly conceived.

8. cf. E. J. Lowe, sect. 4, 'Real Selves: Persons as a Substantial Kind', in *Human Beings*, ed. D. Cockburn (Cambridge University Press, 1991).

9. There is also what may reduce to a variant of the second option, proposed to me by Paul Noordhof. It is that the functionalist can initially identify mental events as those events to which we have direct or introspective access, without saying anything of their nature. This may need more attention than I have room to give it here. So may what may be regarded as a general response to the incoherence objection by Tim Crane in his 'Mental Causation and Mental Reality', *Proceedings of the Aristotelian Society*, 1992, pp. 193–5.

10. We come back to these matters in Chapter 6. For some critical but traditional thoughts on subjective contents and objects of awareness, see my 'Seeing Qualia and Positing the World', in *A. J. Ayer: Memorial Essays* (Cambridge, 1991), ed. A. Phillips Griffiths, pp. 129–51.

11. For a summary of neuroscience for philosophers, probably still sufficiently up to date, see my *A Theory of Determinism: The Mind, Neuroscience and Life Hopes*, or *Mind and Brain*, in each case Chapter 5.

12. For more on this matter, however clear and persuasive, see *A Theory of Determinism* or *Mind and Brain*, especially pp. 163–75. For more on all of the Union Theory, see Chapters 2, 3 and 4 of either book.

Chapter Four

Anti-Individualism v. the Union Theory

The thinking we do that is the most important and often the most salient part of our consciousness is bound up with language. Language, the institution or practice of it, is not something in heads, or not wholly in them, and of course it is not in any single head. Communication, perhaps the first and greatest use of language, is also a fact that is not in any single head. Between heads, importantly, but not in a single one. Meaning itself is in another thing that is in some other category different from my or your brain or weight or hair-colour. Certainly what you mean by your words, in one sense of 'what you mean by your words', is in some other category. This meaning has to be thought about in a way different from what can be called my or your individual or personal properties.

We can struggle to add something about personal identity along similar lines. Who or what you are can be thought of in terms of your role in life, or rather your roles. These are importantly a matter of the expectations and judgements of others, and indeed of a society's conventions. Some of them are written down in laws. To that last reflection can be added a recent political one. According to doctrines of *communitarianism*, we are not the isolated individuals conceived by liberals going about the protection of our individual rights, but in some sense we are to be conceived in terms of our communities.

None of the accounts of consciousness noticed or considered so far pays much attention to these anti-individualist propositions, if any. They are no part of Anomalous Monism, other identity theories noticed in passing, or Mind-Brain Correlation with Neural Causation. They are no part, although there may be a temptation to say otherwise, of strict functionalism. They are no part of the Union Theory, where there is no temptation to say otherwise.

Hilary Putnam of Harvard University did pay attention to an anti-individualist proposition, with great effect. His paper, certainly seminal, is one of two considered below. It begins, you may well think, from the truth that *words mean things* – and that the things are their meanings. There is indeed such a theory of meaning thought to have been assumed by philosophers of great note, including Bertrand Russell. Did it not issue in the problem that troubled him as much as any other: How can 'the present king of France' have meaning if there is nothing for which it stands?

Putnam's paper 'The Meaning of "Meaning"', if it is right, requires the Union Theory and the rest of the accounts or partial accounts of consciousness to pay attention to anti-individualism, to say the least. The same is true of the work of Tyler Burge, of the University of California at Los Angeles. His papers have also been fertile ones. 'Individualism and the Mental', like 'The Meaning of "Meaning"', started something.

Its basis, even if it has Hegel in its pre-history, is what can seem like a home run, maybe a home run that wins the game. If the same piece of language means different things in different linguistic settings, but goes with exactly the same type of neural event, no doubt complex and ramified, how can the facts of consciousness be taken to depend on just that neural event?

Anti-individualism may be important not only as an objection to or refutation of much philosophy of mind. None of the philosophers so far considered has provided us with an analysis or account of the distinctive nature of consciousness itself, or done much in that direction. Anomalous Monism does not really try, some other identity theories futilely deny the need. The doctrine of neuroscientific friends and the Union Theory do not really try. Functionalism can be said to try, hopelessly. Does anti-individualism do better?

---

1   The Union Theory and so on

Remember your reading the newspaper this morning? Suppose that when you were reading the newspaper this morning you had the thought again that Blair's government of Britain, on account of being exposed as having lied about the need for war in Iraq, ought to have been brought down immediately, and then you wished it had, and then you intended to turn the newspaper page to something else, and did. Were the thinking, wishing and intending in your head?

The answer, according to Anomalous Monism, seems to be yes. They were properties of certain events of yours that were also neural. So too were your thinking, wishing and intending in your head, presumably, for the theory of Mind-Brain Correlation with Non-Mental Causation. So too for strict functionalism when it takes the philosophically necessary step of identifying its functional events with neural events. And the Union Theory too locates your thinking, wishing and intending in your head. Thus the Union Theory and the others are in a sense individualist or personalist theories of the mind. They are wrong if a certain group of objections are right.

Other things than individualist theories are also wrong. We have been guiding ourselves in our reflections by certain considerations. One is psychoneural intimacy, which is that there is some kind of necessary connection between a neural event and a simultaneous mental event. Putting aside real identity theories, this is the idea, in part, that the neural event is somehow a sufficient explanation of the mental event. Others of our guiding ideas have been mental indispensability and mental realism. These turn out to be mistakes as well if the group of objections are right. They have had a good deal of philosophical attention. Let us look at them – or rather, for clarity and because life is short, look at the two main ones.

In doing so, we will have in mind the Union Theory, and for a start the mental or conscious event M – which, to keep politics out of the philosophy of mind, we take to be your intending to turn the page of your newspaper. M was the correlate of neural event N. Part of what this comes to is that N was in a way sufficient for M, or necessitated its occurrence. Hence M was in a way necessary to N – on certain assumptions, N wouldn't have happened in the absence of M. Also, as you have just heard, M and N were in a certain sense a single effect. And M, we need also to remember, had a distinctive character, a subjective character different in kind from that of neural events and indeed all non-mental events – that is something that flows from the policy of mental realism. We can try to go further and speculate about the subjectivity of M, a relationship of subject and content somehow conceived, as distinct from a relationship between content and the world.

We have also been assuming something else. It is that M was an individual or personal event. That is, roughly, it was an event within the history of a person, in this case you. Suppose that talk of any event, roughly speaking, is talk of a property or relation being had by an entity for a time. Then our assumption has been, in taking M as an event within your history, that M was a property for a time of but one entity – the person you are, and more particularly your brain or maybe central nervous system.

2   The Surprising Meaning of the Word 'Page'

Let us now suppose further of M, your intending to turn a page, that *it involved the meaning of the word 'page'*. That supposition is irresistible, or can be made so by specifying M further. Needless to say, it is also obscure. Reflection on it will be part of considering the objection to which we now turn.

What is the meaning of 'page'? Consider the conception owed to Hilary Putnam and derived in part from his fertile twin-earth speculations.[1] According to it, a description of the meaning of 'page', and not only of terms for natural kinds, things distinct from manufactured ones and so on, has at least four components. These are as follows:

    i. syntactic markers that apply to the word, such as 'noun',
    ii. semantic markers, such as 'artefact',
    iii. a description of further stereotypical ideas of a page,
        which is to say ordinary or conventional descriptions of
        a page, perhaps of what it looks like and is for, and
    iv. a description of the extension of the word.

That is to say that the *meaning* of 'page', as distinct from a description of the meaning, has at least four components or parts, of which one is extension. Let me call this, which has antecedents in the work of Frege, Carnap and other logicians and sympathizers, the *four-component conception* of meaning.

The first three components are a little puzzling. Into what kind or kinds of things do they fall? The third, and perhaps the first two, are said to consist in 'ideas'. It is remarked that in the parts of the meaning of 'page' that constitute a stereotype (the third and second?) we have the sole element of truth in part of a discarded conception of meaning. It is that part that speaks of a psychological state, a concept or an intension, but also an abstract entity.[2] However, it is not clear how small and indeed what that element of truth is, since 'ideas' go unexplained.

The fourth component is much more important to what follows. Into what kind of things does the fourth component fall? Well, we are repeatedly told, crucially, that the extension of any term consists in the set of things of which the term is true. The answer to the question, it appears, is therefore nothing other than *pages*, all the pages that there are. Let us assume that for a while.

We now have the makings of a first objection which, if it succeeds, will indeed destroy the Union Theory and much else.[3] Stated in terms of the Union Theory, it is as follows.

1. M involved the meaning of the word 'page'.
2. For M to have involved the meaning was for the meaning to be a component or part of M.
3. The meaning of 'page' in turn has as a part or component the set of all pages.
4. Therefore M cannot have been, as assumed, a personal event, more particularly a property of you and your brain.
5. Further, all three hypotheses of the Union Theory seem no less than absurd. N cannot conceivably have been sufficient for M. Clearly M, all of it, cannot possibly have been necessary to N. More generally, psychoneural nomic connection is out of the question. Also, M and N cannot possibly be a single effect. And it would be strange indeed to take all of M as causal with respect to A, your turning to a page.
6. M does not have only the intrinsic and distinctive character assigned to it by mental realism, since in part it is *pages*.

What is to be said of this objection?

3   Replies about Meaning

There is no one thing that is the meaning of 'page'. That is not to say that 'page' is ambiguous or vague, but that the description D 'the meaning of "page"' can be and is variously used, anyway by philosophers. In the story of meaning we are considering, it is allowed that there is a common-sense conception of meaning, which pertains to a certain subject-matter. Hence there is such a common-sense conception of the meaning of 'page'. That is, the description D, of which you will be hearing a good deal, can be used in a common-sense way, of a certain limited subject-matter.

Does the meaning of 'page', so understood, where it may be said to be how the word is used or what is conveyed by it or understood by it, include pages as a component or part? It does not, since the meaning of 'page' so understood will not alter or be decreased if all pages are burned. Also, you cannot *write on* this meaning. That is, we can count on common-sensical speakers insisting, after all the pages are burned, that their lamentations are as meaningful as their apprehensions were beforehand. And we know they never own up to having put notes in the margins of meanings or of any parts of them.

Can the Union Theory make use of this common-sense conception of meaning – what theory doesn't use such notions at some point? – without suffering the embarrassments specified in the objection? Can it escape them, that is, by denying (3) that the meaning of 'page' includes pages? Well, depending on exactly what is taken to be in the common-sense conception, the Union Theory might still be in trouble, related but different trouble, if it allowed as in (2) that the meaning of 'page' was a component or part of M. This component, even if it does not include pages, might for a start be of such a kind as to obstruct psychoneural nomic connection.

But (2) is deniable. The common-sense conception of meaning can readily be taken as to the effect that M, partly in virtue of the meaning of 'page', was about a particular page, but that M did not have the meaning as a component or part. It seems undeniable (1) that M involved the meaning, but in fact very deniable that M included the meaning as a part. The meaning of the word stood to M, perhaps, as the way the gun was aimed stood to the gun.

Consider now developed theories of meaning, having the same subject-matter as the common-sense conception. These assign to the description D – 'the meaning of "page"' – roughly this sense: syntactic, semantic, and perhaps other rules for the use of 'page'. The most important of these rules, to cut a long story short, connect 'page' with a certain set or class of things in the world.

Suppose the Union Theory uses this conception. Do we have reason to think, before more is said, that this conception will embarrass the Union Theory? Well, if rules actually were or if they included print in real dictionaries, and if rules were involved in M as parts, that would again be disastrous. But evidently it is possible to deny both antecedents of the conditional. With respect to the first, rules might indeed be so conceived as still to exist after the burning of all the dictionaries.

These brisk reflections might be granted by an objector of the kind we are considering, certainly at some cost to him. It might hopefully be said, however, that the reflections serve to focus us on what is fundamental to the objection. It is that the four-component conception of meaning, which *does* embarrass the Union Theory, has some unique recommendation. It is when 'the meaning of "page"' is so understood that we get what has a unique recommendation. What is it?

Might it be said that the conception, despite what was asserted five paragraphs back, is the best clarification of our common-sense idea? It is hard to take this seriously, and it is not seriously claimed. The conception is claimed, differently, to be unique in being true to or of something else, or to have some truth-related property, perhaps that it will advance psychology with respect to this other thing. Let me speak just of truth. The claim of truth, given a correspondence or realist idea of truth, does indeed presuppose an identified subject-matter, that of which the conception is true. What is this subject-matter?

It must be safe to say, given what is asserted of it, that the intended subject-matter is this: whatever it is in virtue of which a word means something, *and* what the word means. (The particular subject-matter of whatever it is in virtue of which 'page' means something, and what it means, can also be taken as falling under D 'the meaning of "page"'. Certainly we are free-and-easy in our use of such descriptions as D.) It is not going to be possible, I think, to find a description of the identified subject-matter which is more distinct or distant from the account given of it in the four-component conception.

Let us grant, for purposes of argument, that the four-component conception is true of its subject-matter. Does it then follow that the conception of meaning in terms of rules, mentioned a moment ago, is false or incomplete? This follows if the four-component conception is true and the rules conception has the same subject-matter. But it does not have the same subject-matter. It pertains only to a part of the subject-matter of the four-component conception. It pertains to the subject-matter of the first three components: in short, what it is in virtue of which a word means something. The rules conception may be regarded as coming to much the same as the first three components, in different language.

If it is not truth that gives to the four-component conception a unique recommendation, what then? It might have the recommendation of *relevance*. That is, it might be the subject-matter that has first claim on our attention if our purpose is a certain inquiry, the answering of certain questions. What are our questions? They are those to which a philosophy of mind, in the sense indicated earlier, gives answers. In terms of the example, how is M related to the simultaneous N, what are the explanatory antecedents of M, and what explains A?

But if this is our inquiry, it seems plain that what is relevant is just the subject-matter which is the concern of the rules conception and the first three components of the four-component conception. To say that what is relevant to the philosophy of mind is the limited subject-matter is not to beg any question about any problem of meaning, and in particular not to rule out the four-component conception as a description of its subject-matter.

Nor need the philosopher of mind, in the restricted sense, be troubled by conceding that meaning has to do with more than mental events, that the philosophy of mind does not deal with all the facts of meaning. I can think of no argument to the effect that conclusions within the philosophy of mind are endangered by this. The philosophy of mind, to speak too quickly, has in particular no concern with the truth of mental events, and extension is exactly a matter of their truth. It is of interest to recall at this point that Putnam rightly remarks that only the first three components, and not extension, have to do with the linguistic competence of an individual speaker or language-user.[4]

To glance back, it has been assumed for the sake of argument that D 'the meaning of "page"', being an elastic description, can be used to convey the four-component conception of the meaning of 'page', which is true of a certain subject-matter. It has been denied that that conception or a consideration of all of its subject-matter is necessary to the philosophy of mind as defined, or has a unique recommendation with respect to it. To make that point with reference to the objection, what we have denied is (3) that the meaning of 'page' must be taken to include pages. We have also concluded that if, using the rules conception, we are still in trouble, we can escape it by denying (2) that for M to have involved a meaning was for it to have the meaning as part.

That is not all. Let us reflect a bit more on the four-component conception of meaning, and in particular on extension. We have so far assumed extension to be the set of things of which a term is true, as we are repeatedly told in Putnam's story of meaning. The extension of 'page' is all the pages that there are. That is the foundation of the objection we have been considering. Still, the story of meaning has another theme, indeed a fundamental theme.

This theme has the clear consequence that an extension could not be conveyed to someone in a certain way: by a complete list of things identified only spatio-temporally. There may also be other successful identificatory descriptions which will not convey the extension. Rather, it is fundamental to Putnam's story that the extension of

our natural-kind term 'water' is H_2O, and, to speak quickly, that extensions in general are determined by science. It thus appears that
the extension of 'page' is not merely the set of things of which the
word is true, but a set of things with certain properties, perhaps a
set of things with properties given by chemical formulae, perhaps
properties which are the micro-structure of pages. More briefly, the
extension is now *a set of things with certain scientific properties*.

This is not clear. Consider what has just been said. What is picked
out by the description E 'a set of things with certain scientific properties'? What is picked out by it if what it picks out cannot also be
picked out, as just noticed, by F 'a set of things with certain spatio-
temporal locations', which latter description is true of the very same
things? We must wonder if it is the case that E gives us what can be
called a set of things thought of in terms of certain properties. Does
it then give us a certain thought-of set of things? Does it give us a
property-mentioning rule which limits the use of the word to set of
things?

Those ideas certainly conflict with much of what is said about
meaning and in particular extension. Try another idea then. Is the
extension of a term certain scientific properties of things of which
the term is true? That conflicts with all the usages in the story, to
the effect that a word's extension is the set of things or the stuff of
which the word is true. Further, it is not properties *however identified*
that could possibly be the extension. It would have to be properties
identified and thought of in certain ways – we come back to the
same sort of difficulty as with things.

Putnam's story of meaning, then, involves the proposition that
extension in so far as it is part of meaning is a certain thought-of
set of things or, certainly different and better, a rule specifying a set
of things by way of certain of their properties. The thought or rule,
whatever it is, is not the things. It seems to me he is committed to
the proposition, and moreover that something like it is true. There
is no difference in kind between the first three components and the
fourth component of his view. It is notable that quite independently
of his H_2O theme he at least touches on the idea that what is part of
meaning is not extension in the sense of a set of things.[5]

We have here a further reply to the objection we have been considering, more particularly a further reason for denying its premise
(3) that the meaning of 'page' has as a part or component the set of
all pages. It is not just that the meaning of 'page' need not be understood in the four-component way, and that that understanding has
no unique recommendation, but that if it is adequately understood

in that way, we do not get pages included in the meaning of 'page'. What is said in amplification of the four-component conception transforms it into something that does not at all challenge the Union Theory, and so on.

Is there a general argument, independent of Putnam's considerations having to do with scientific properties, against an extension's being part of the meaning of a word and being just the things of which the word is true? Consider a time t before the word existed. There *did* exist, we suppose, a certain set of things, say undiscovered particles. At this time, that set was the extension of nothing. It was not an extension – not a denotation, referent, or application. This is so since extensions are *of* something, and, what is connected and more important, an extension is a *discriminated* set – what Putnam calls a somehow determined set. Later on, at t1, a mark by explicit definition or other means became the word – for the particles. At that time, there came into existence the extension of the word. Evidently this extension cannot be the set of particles. The set of particles did not come into existence at t1. If the meaning of a word includes extension, therefore, this must be extension where that is other than the set of things of which the word is true.

4   Arthritis in the Thigh

That argument-sketch against Putnam, if something can be made of it, cannot have attention here. Let us turn instead to another objection to the Union Theory and so on. This objection also rests on the idea that mental events are somehow not personal or individual events – not token properties of a person or individual. It is owed to the striking work of Tyler Burge.

We are asked to think of an episode in our actual world W1 and then of one in a possible world W2. In our actual world, we are to suppose, a man at some time thinks he is getting arthritis in the thigh – there occurs mental event M1. We can suppose there also occurs in him the simultaneous neural event N1. His thought is about arthritis, we are to accept, for the reasons among others that he uses the word in it and that he does have various true beliefs about arthritis, such as that stiff joints are a symptom. But his thought that he is getting arthritis in the thigh is false, since in English 'arthritis' means an inflammation of only the joints.

We now imagine the possible world W2, different in that 'arthritis' means an inflammation not only of the joints. The dictionaries say so, and other facts of W2 are consistent with this. The linguistic or social environment is in this way different from that of W1. However, everything else is the same as in W1, including our man's life-history neurally described. At a time he thinks what he expresses by saying that he is getting arthritis in his thigh – that is, there occurs mental event M2. Simultaneously there occurs neural event N2.

In accordance with the supposition about sameness between the worlds, N2 is identical with N1. That is, as we can say, the two neural events are identical in being tokens of the same type. To come to the fundamental point, is M2 of the same type as M1? We are to see that it is not. This thought, which is not about arthritis, is different from the thought in W1, which is. The W2 thought may be not false but true.

These reflections and their conclusion may be taken to refute the Union Theory, on the assumption that N1 and N2 are what it designates to be the neural correlates of M1 and M2. Since N1 and N2 are in the given sense identical, and M1 and M2 are not identical, neither pair M1/N1 or M2/N2 can consist in psychoneural correlates.

More generally, we are instructed that a person's mental events stand in a crucial relation not to personal or individual facts, but to environmental facts of a linguistic or social kind: dictionaries, conventions, standards, institutions, community, minds and activities of others, relations the individual bears to his social environment. The crucial relation is one of some kind of dependency. With environmental change, and no neural change, goes change in mental events. There is in fact a kind of determination, or rather a kind of partial determination, of mental events by environment rather than neural events. Part of their explanation, part of the answer to the question of why they occurred, is environment rather than neural events. If so, the Union Theory and much else is hopeless. Let us look at it all more closely.

5   What the Theory Comes To

One thing so far unmentioned is that this anti-individualism for good reason tolerates the idea that *something* that is mental *is* a matter only of what happens in the brain. Such a mental event is *not* in the dependency-relation with environmental facts. In the case of the actual-world episode, the man does at the given time have an idea that reflects his deviant understanding that arthritis is an inflammation of more than the joints.[6] Theoretical consistency – consistency in

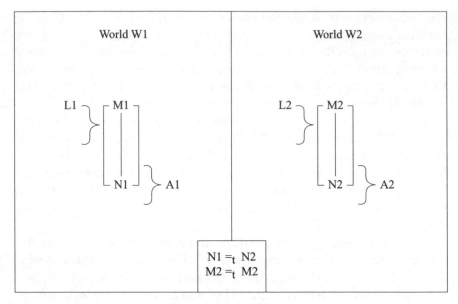

Figure 3: Union Theory.

one's theory – requires that there also be such an idea in the possible-world episode. It too reflects the understanding that arthritis is an inflammation of more than the joints, a correct understanding. We can refer to these two items as *personal mental events,* and label them PM1 and PM2. We leave it entirely open how they are related to M1 and M2.

It will help to have models of the Union Theory's supposedly refuted account of the two episodes and of the very different account given by this anti-individualism. Perhaps it is as true to say that the second model is of my difficulties with anti-individualism.

Figure 3 gives the Union Theory's account. In the actual-world or W1 episode, L1 is our man's *locale,* that particular part of the linguistic and social environment that has actually impinged on him in the ordinary way. L1 is shown as a part of a causal circumstance for the psychoneural pair consisting in M1 and N1. The latter two events are of course in nomic connection, as shown by the unbroken line joining them, and a single effect, as shown by the bracketing. The psychoneural pair in turn is a part of a causal circumstance for an action A1. The possible-world or W2 episode in the figure is similarly represented. Finally, the events N1 and N2 are identical in type ($N1 =_t N2$). So are M1 and M2.

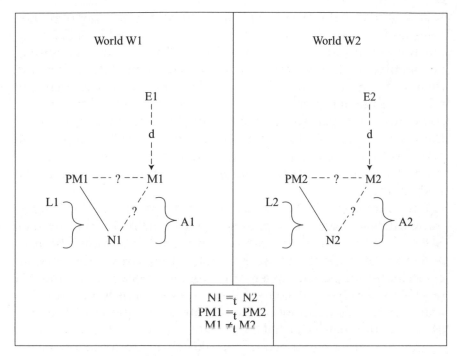

Figure 4: Anti-Individualism.

Figure 4 gives my understanding of the anti-individualist account of the two episodes. Taking the actual-world or W1 episode, the personal mental event PM1 is shown in nomic correlation with N1. It is also in some unspecified relation with M1. This relation between PM1 and M1 could be actual identity, or their being parts of some whole, or anything else. We have it, further, that M1 stands in the crucial dependency-relation d, whatever it is, to the set of environmental facts E1, and in an unspecified relation to N1. With respect to the earlier causal connection, the parts of the causal circumstance other than L1 and also the exact effect are left unspecified, as are the exact parts, other than M1, of the second causal circumstance, for the action A1.

Finally, considering also W2, the neural events N1 and N2 are identical in type, as are PM1 and PM2. But, crucially, M1 and M2 are not – on account of E1 and E2 not being identical.

The dependency-relation d is all-important. It is referred to by a plethora of differing descriptions, often cheek by jowl. What is it? There are a lot of possibilities.

A. It is said that mental events are *individuated* by way of owner, time, and content,[7] and very often said that content is *individuated* partly by environment.[8] Further, individuation by way of something is sometimes distinguished from causation by something.[9] Certainly there *is* a common sort of individuation of events by reference to what does not determine them, where determination of an event by something, as remarked, is for that thing to be the answer or part of the answer to the question of why the event occurred. Most of us will take this to reduce to the proposition that there is individuation of events by what does not cause them and is not in nomic connection with them.

But, to come to a first crunch, the first of a lot of crunches, if anti-individualism were the hypothesis that E1 helped to individuate M1 in the common non-nomic way, it would fail absolutely in its ambition. The anti-individualist models of the two hypotheses could consistently replace the mysterious relation between N1 and M1 (and N2 and M2) by perfectly ordinary nomic connection. Evidently anti-individualism cannot be the hypothesis in question. The very essence of the doctrine is that the two mental events, being different, are not neurally determined or the like. They are somehow partly determined by something else.

B. Is the relation d of E1 to M1 such that a reference to the first is essential to a full description or interpretation of the second? The very first statement of our anti-individualism is indeed that it stresses social factors in descriptions of an individual's mental phenomena.[10] Also, we are told that it is in interpreting a person's words that we need to take account of his community.[11] Further, it is our attribution to a person of a mental event that rests to a fair degree on his having a certain responsibility to communal conventions and conceptions.[12]

This is, so to speak, a linguistic rendering of what can be put more directly. To say that it is impossible to give a full as distinct from an individuating description of M1 without mentioning E1 is to say that E1 is in some relation to M1, and of course it is such a relation, between these latter terms, that is asserted to hold.

But not all relations that must be represented in full descriptions are determinative relations. My action becomes a killing when my victim dies, and a certain bicycle is mine. Neither the death nor the ownership is determinative. Is there a full description of an answer in an examination that does not mention the examiner's classification of it? If there isn't, that does not make the classification determinative of the answer. If relation d were of this undeterminative kind, it would again allow anti-individualism to include what it denies, that is, psychoneural nomic connection.

C. Is light shed by the mention of a person's responsibility to communal conventions in the last passage referred to above? Could the idea be that a speaker in certain circumstances may be held responsible for what he says, which thing is fixed by what the environment makes his words mean? No doubt that is true, but it does not make d into a determinative relation. Also, this idea of responsibility implies a difference between what he says and what he may have had in mind. To talk of *holding* our man in W1 to having said something false about arthritis is precisely to imply what is denied, that he may not have been thinking of exactly arthritis. If he was not doing so, was M1 in fact *identical* with M2, and is anti-individualism deprived of its essential premise and foundation?

D. It is conceivable that a different idea of relation d is conveyed when it is implied that what environment is needed for is our *understanding* of others' mental events, or the explication of them.[13] Perhaps there is an isolable truth here, but we have no reason to think that what gives us understanding is also determinative of a mental event in the required way.

E. Can we then suppose, despite the firm distinction between individuation and causation made above in (A), that relation d somehow *does* involve determination of M1? Other things that are said about the relation might tempt a careless or forgetful reader just to accept that idea. We have it already that with environmental change, and no neural change, goes change in mental events.[14] That is not all. Thoughts are not fixed wholly by neural events, but partly by environment.[15] They depend on environment,[16] and are a product partly of it.[17] They are what they are because of environment and supervene on it.[18,19] They are partly determined by it.[20]

That might indeed suggest that in anti-individualism's model of the W1 episode, what we have is that E1 simply is part of what causes M1 – and the relation between N1 and M1 can be as desired – the first is merely somehow contributory with respect to the second. This causal interpretation of d would make trouble for the model, in connection with E1 and L1, and send us back to the drawing-board.

There is no need for that, it seems. Despite the usages just reported, we are reassured that it is plausible that events in the external world causally affect the mental events of a subject only by affecting in an ordinary way the subject's bodily surfaces.[21] The model is correct in conveying that the only inward causation is from what was called our man's *locale*, which is evidently only a part of his environment. (If, in W1, he had been affected by *more* of his environment, he presumably would have got 'arthritis' right.) Further, we are reassured that any alarmed supposition that the dependency relation amounts to action at a distance by E1, or special forces or anything of the sort, is out of the question.[22] Putting aside the reassurances, we can conclude for ourselves that anti-individualism would simply be incredible if it included causation of my thoughts but not by way of my head.

F. Could it be that the dependency relation d itself somehow depends on the causal connection between L1 and – somehow – M1? 'Information from and about the environment is transmitted only through proximal stimulations, but the information is individuated partly by reference to the nature of normal distal stimuli. Causation is local. Individuation may presuppose facts about the specific nature of a subject's environment.'[23] It is remarked that it is non-intentionally that the sensory intake in W1 and W2 is the same, that input is non-intentionally identical.[24]

Are we to understand that relation d, which certainly has to do with mental events as intentional or representative, is itself a matter of the causal relation involving L1? Again we would have to go back to the drawing-board. But again there is no need. If the dependency relation worked through, so to speak, the causal connection between L1 and M1, the end result would be individualist determination of the mental. There would be no effective difference between the anti-Individualist and Union Theory models.

G. What remains? Is there some determinative relation different from what we have had in mind and for good reason rejected? Well, there may be suggestions to that effect in remarks on individualism as against anti-individualism. 'Individualism is a view about how kinds are correctly individuated, how their natures are fixed.'[25] Is that one proposition or two? Also, individualism is a denial that there is a 'necessary or deep individuative relation' between environment and mental events.[26] It is also a denial that mental events 'depend essentially' on environment.[27]

Can it be that the dependency relation d is one such that E1 in correctly individuating M1 fixes its nature? Does deep individuation also determine? Is one thing's essential dependence on a second a way of the first thing's being determined but not caused by the second? To these questions, I have no answers, but only the response that the dependency relation, if it has a peculiar nature gestured at by these usages, is left unclear, and that if it is made clear, it will surely again make for trouble.

The burden of these reflections, broadly speaking, is clear enough. It is that d is a merely individuative and non-nomic relation, in which case anti-individualism has no reason to deny psychoneural nomic connection, or d is a direct determinative connection, and anti-individualism is unbelievable, or d somehow involves locale and local causation, which is as bad.

The doctrine is a rich one, fully developed, about which only a little more can be said here. The thought-experiment, the reflection on W1 and W2, is the premise from which the conclusion about the dependency relation is drawn. My response has been not in the main to examine the premise, but the conclusion. The failure of the conclusion puts into question the premise. I finish with some remarks, no doubt also made by others, about the premise taken separately. They are no more than opening cards.

It can be allowed that the W1 thinker's utterance of his thought is false, or perhaps presupposes a falsehood, and that this is not so in W2. What might follow from this has been a matter of much philosophical doctrine and dispute. Let me say that there is no easy transition to the conclusion that M1 is not identical with M2, as Burge agrees, perhaps unlike some of his readers.[28] My several reflections that the wine in the cellar is cool do not differ because somebody started a fire in the time between the reflections.

Evidently a difference between M1 and M2 can be made by taking words in them as conventionally understood – as understood in W1 as against W2. This seems of little significance. Mental events depend for their identity on words used as and however the event's owner uses them. What is non-substitutable is uses, words as used. That is not to deny that the interpretations of both correct and deviant uses in a way depends on convention. The truth does not give us anti-individualism.

To consider the anti-individualist model of the W1 episode, it is impossible to suppose that our thinker had two thoughts, the PM1 thought and the M1 thought. He wasn't double-thinking. He had a thought that either did or did not reflect his understanding that arthritis is an inflammation of more than the joints. (That truth about alternatives may perhaps be missed by running together mental events with mental dispositions.) To opt for the second alterntive would be to give no effect to our irresistible conviction that he thought of arthritis or the like in a certain way. We are surely driven to PM1, and its neural correlate.

Given the causation of M1, somehow, by the initial causal circumstance including L1, and the supposition that the environmental relation d is a determinative relation, we appear to have an inconsistency like that in the second philosophy of mind discussed earlier – neural causation and psycho-neural nomic connection. Environment is made necessary to what is already guaranteed.

It is to be agreed, as Burge remarks, that a philosophy of mind must be tested by total plausibility.[29] I think the Union Theory wins over anti-individualism.

Notes

1. 'The Meaning of "Meaning"', *Philosophical Papers*, vol. 2 (Cambridge University Press, 1975), pp. 266–71, 247–52. It has sometimes been supposed that anti-individualism is about natural-kind terms, for no clear reason. My concentration on Putnam's original paper and Burge's series of papers in what follows implies no want of awareness of the equally promising arguments of other philosophers for anti-individualism. See in particular J. McDowell, *'De Re Senses'*, *Philosophical Quarterly*, 1984, and 'Singular Thought and the Extent of Inner Space', in P. Pettit & J. McDowell, *Subject, Thought and Content* (Oxford University Press, 1986). For an acute discussion of these, see Gabriel Segal, 'The Return of the Individual', *Mind*, 1989.
2. Putnam, 'The Meaning of "Meaning"', pp. 249–50, 218.
3. It is suggested by much of what Putnam says (e.g. 'The Meaning of "Meaning"', pp. 220–1, 271) but not everything (e.g. pp. 224, 227). Those who think his reflections should be limited to natural-kind terms can of course change the example.
4. 'The Meaning of "Meaning"', p. 269.
5. 'The Meaning of "Meaning"', pp. 218, 223–4, 245.
6. Burge, 'Individualism and the Mental', *Midwest Studies in Philosophy*, 1979, pp. 92, 94, 95–6, 100–1; cf. p. 78.
7. 'Individualism and the Mental', p. 111.
8. 'Two Thought-Experiments Reviewed', *Notre Dame Journal of Formal Logic*, 1982, p. 286; 'Individualism and Psychology', *Philosophical Review*, 1986, pp. 16–17; 'Cartesian Error and the Objectivity of Perception', in Pettit and McDowell (eds), *Subject, Thought and Content*, pp. 118–19; 'Intellectual Norms and the Foundations of Mind', *Journal of Philosophy*, 1986, p. 697; 'Individualism and Self-Knowledge', *Journal of Philosophy*, 1988, p. 650.
9. 'Individualism and Psychology', p. 16.
10. 'Individualism and the Mental', p. 84; 'Individualism and Psychology', p. 20.
11. 'Individualism and the Mental', p. 84.
12. 'Individualism and the Mental', pp. 90, 114–15, 116; 'Individualism and Psychology', p. 25; cf. 'Intellectual Norms and the Foundations of

Mind', pp. 697–8.
13. 'Other Bodies' in A. Woodfield (ed.), *Thought and Object: Essays in Intentionality* (Oxford University Press, 1982), pp. 99, 98.
14. 'Individualism and the Mental', p. 79.
15. 'Individualism and the Mental', p. 104.
16. 'Individualism and the Mental', p. 85.
17. 'Other Bodies', p. 102.
18. 'Individualism and Self-Knowledge', p. 652.
19. 'Two Thought-Experiments Reviewed', p. 286; 'Individualism and Psychology', p. 4.
20. 'Cartesian Error and the Objectivity of Perception', pp. 122, 125.
21. 'Individualism and Psychology', pp. 15, 17.
22. 'Individualism and Psychology', p. 20.
23. 'Individualism and Psychology', p. 17; cf. p. 16.
24. 'Individualism and the Mental', pp. 77–8, 107.
25. 'Individualism and Psychology', p. 3.
26. 'Individualism and Psychology', p. 4; 'Cartesian Error and the Objectivity of Perception', p. 119.
27. 'Cartesian Error and the Objectivity of Perception', p. 119.
28. 'Other Bodies', p. 110.
29. 'Individualism and the Mental', pp. 92, 97.

Chapter Five

Consciousness and Humble Truths

We all have a grip on the nature of our consciousness, a grip that issues in the ordinary, settled and obscure idea of it. This has to do mainly with what we talk of as subjectivity. My consciousness is somehow a property of me, or a fact pertaining to me, that is unlike my weight, location, or speech-production. This fact of subjectivity has seemed to be mainly a matter of mainly a relation between a subject and a content, or, if such a subject-thing as a self can be left out, as Hume demanded, between something like a bare awareness and a content. The content, for most philosophers, is not the world itself, but something related to the world (p. 70). It consists in representations, images, sense-data, ideas, concepts, feelings, desires, intentions and the like – as those are ordinarily understood.

Our grip on consciousness and the idea of it are certainly strong enough to defeat 'nothing-but' materialism, say the view that mental events have only neural properties as we know them, and also strong enough to defeat what comes at bottom to the same thing, neural functionalism. The latter, of course, is the doctrine that human conscious events are no more than neural events as these are understood and studied in neuroscience, standing as they do in relations to input, other neural events and output. Its stress on the relations does not alter the nature allowed to the conscious events.

The grip and idea have seemed to be enough not only to enable us to reject those identity theories, but also to reflect more hopefully on the mind-brain relation. They have enabled or at any rate helped us, in particular, to pass beyond Anomalous Monism and Mind-Brain Correlation with Non-Mental Causation to what is surely an improvement, the Union

Theory. The same grip and idea served us well in reflecting on anti-individualism.

But it is philosophically unsatisfactory to have only a hold on our consciousness, a kind of ostensive definition of it, and some thoughts of it, given that the thoughts are obscure. We certainly want and we probably need an analysis or articulated conception of the nature of mental events, say as good as our conceptions of the nature of events generally, or of the realm of the physical, or of truth, or of time. Not having such a conception is philosophically unsatisfactory, since inexplicitness and the like always are philosophically unsatisfactory.

Also, the want of a conception leaves neural functionalists in a less desperate position in doubting or denying that our grip on consciousness does establish a difference between conscious events and neural relata. It leaves us in a position that must be less than absolutely confident. We probably also need such a conception, as distinct from just want it, for a related and more general reason. It is not certain that the mind-brain relation can be satisfactorily considered in the absence of such a conception. Finding the very nature of a thing, plainly, may lead you to think differently of its relations.

Contemporary philosophers, as you have gathered, have not tried hard really to satisfy the desire and need – at least by looking directly at the subject-matter. To a considerable extent, this is because they have been put off by something, been unwilling to pay a certain price. One of them, however, has maintained that we do not have to pay the price for what we want. There is such a thing as a philosophical free lunch.

My brief discussion of it below is carried forward in terms of neural functionalism, which may still be the commonest philosophy of mind. The discussion could have been carried forward in terms of Mind-Brain Correlation with Non-Mental Causation, or indeed the Union Theory. If these two views have the great recommendation of not making consciousness into merely neural events, they do not by themselves give an adequate understanding or analysis of it either. They are essentially mind-brain theories rather than mind or consciousness theories. We could have looked into whether they can have an adequate understanding or analysis added to them without trouble. Can they too help themselves to a free lunch? Maybe anti-individualists were moved to their expensive theorizing by their sense of their own consciousness. Can they sit down here too?

---

1   Deep and Murky Water

The history of philosophical attempts to analyse or clarify consciousness in line with our ordinary sense of it has not been a happy one. Some have been attempts to get into deep and murky philosophical water. They have been spiritual in nature, vague 'dualisms', engagements in metaphysics, mainly German. Above all, they have been metaphorical and rhetorical, well beyond the great security of the literal. Truth to tell, they are not well-known to ordinary philosophers of mind writing in English – such labourers as me. More truth to tell, the attempts to get into and come back out of deep and murky philosophical water are not read in your ordinary department of philosophy. We think we know enough to keep away.

The reasonable desire to stay out of this philosophical water, and, just as much, the obscurity of ordinary and metaphorical talk about the mind, and the stuff of novels and literary reflection and so on, has been a principal motivation of the philosophers who have embraced physicalisms and materialisms, and in particular neural functionalism. The main attraction of neural functionalism for philosophers of a certain tenor of mind, among whom I include myself, has been exactly that it stays out of the depths and imagery. Other philosophies of mind, while not denying the problem, have had the recommendation of not really trying to solve it and not pretending to have done so.

In this situation there is a considerable attraction in a particular philosophy of mind. This is one that sees the entire inadequacy of neural functionalism in particular, and hence recognizes the need for something a lot better, something true to our ordinary grip and idea – *and* promises to satisfy the need without succumbing to grandeur or mystery. John Searle, proponent of the best-known and probably the best argument against neural functionalism,[1] makes the promise. He claims we can get an adequate conception of consciousness by attending only to 'humble and obvious truths about the mind' – and, as he should have added in conformity with what else he attends to, certain unobscure philosophical and psychological conceptions and doctrines.[2] These various things make an entirely significant addition to neural functionalism and turn it into something better, the real answer we want. In his book *The Rediscovery of the Mind*, he gives a guide to thirteen of these humble truths and the like.

Can we do better than consider what he offers? And can we go through the list pretty quickly?

2   Physicality and Levels

(1) The first of the thirteen truths is that conscious events are indeed physical events.[3] I take this, of course, to be distinct from the claim that they are exactly the sub-class of physical events that are neural relata. Rather, the claim is that conscious events have a certain general character, fall into a certain general category that has more than neural events in it. Searle is surely right to take conscious events as physical, but what does this come to? What are physical events?

He says that the Cartesian conception of them, in terms of *res extensa*, things taking up space, is too narrow, because electrons are physical and they are only points of mass-energy.[4] Perhaps he suggests, partly as a consequence of electrons so conceived, that physical events are those within the domain of current science.[5] This philosophically popular but unreflective idea makes for trouble. At least it makes for an unnecessary dispute about a possible contradiction. This is so because current science and the contemporary scientific world-view are claimed by many *not* to have conscious events within their domains.

The dispute is avoided by those of us who agree to take conscious events as physical, but make use of the most ordinary conception of the physical, related to but superior to that of Descartes. Here, roughly, physical things are either space-occupants having secondary properties, or space occupants in causal or other nomic connection with space-occupants having secondary properties.[6]

One of the virtues of the conception is its not sharing the indeterminacy of the one tied to current science – as already implied, there is no fixed and agreed demarcation of current science, let alone of the contemporary scientific world-view. Another virtue of the ordinary conception is its not sharing the relativity and transience of the conception based on current science – or, as might be added, the emptiness of a conception tied to completed or final science, things of which we are unaware. Searle, who rightly agrees that conscious events are in space, might better have adopted the ordinary conception of the physical.

But the main point to be made about conscious events being physical is yet simpler. We are, to put the project one way, looking for a
sensible conception of conscious events that makes a difference between them and neural relata. Evidently we do not get even a part
of it in the claim that conscious events *share* something, physicality,
with neural relata. It does not matter how physicality is conceived.
This first truth about consciousness, much insisted on, is of no help
to us.

(2) Do we get the difference when Searle insists on something else,
that conscious events are brain events, events of the brain, caused
by wholly neural events in the brain? When he insists, more fully,
that conscious events are higher-level biological events of the brain
caused by lower-level wholly neural events in the brain? That they
are emergent features in this clear sense?[7] This is in fact the main
proposition of his philosophy of mind, its main claim to uniqueness.

The answer as to whether we get help from the idea of certain
higher-level events is again clear, and can be given quickly.

We evidently do *not* get a difference between conscious events
and neural relata in the specific fact, first, that conscious events are
brain events. So are neural relata. Nor do we get the difference in
the second fact that conscious events are biological, like digestion.
So are neural relata.

And we do not get a difference between conscious events and
neural relata when conscious events are said to be higher-level effects of lower-level neural events, emergent features, as the solidity
of ice is an effect of H_2O molecules in lattice structures and the liq-
uidity of water an effect of such molecules when they are rolling
around on one another.[8] It is plain that we do not get a difference
since just this, being higher-level effects, is true of neural relata and
most of their constituents. It is true, for example, of the transmission
of an action potential down the axon of a neuron. Any textbook of
neuroscience illustrates the fact. There is no surprise in this since
the world is more or less filled up with higher-level effects.

3   Subjectivities and Unities

(3a) We may seem to arrive at a difference from neural functionalism when it is said that conscious events are in a certain category
of things, those that have a special mode of existence or ontology.
What this comes to is that each conscious event is or only exists
as *somebody's* conscious event – for each conscious event there is a

'first person', an 'I', upon which it is dependent. I have this special relation to my conscious events, as you have to yours. This personal dependency of conscious events gives us a first sense in which they are subjective rather than objective.[9]

(3b) It is said to be a consequence of this fact of personal dependency that a conscious event is also in a second sense subjective: it is not equally accessible to any observer. Someone else may not be able to tell if I am thinking of Baden.[10]

(3c) The fact that conscious events, or rather intentional conscious events, are personally dependent or have the first-person mode of existence, is said to have a further consequence, although one not spoken of in terms of subjectivity. It is that my information about the world is perspectival. It may be said to be from a point of view.[11]

(3d) Finally, the fact of the first-person mode of existence is said to involve or have as a consequence that a conscious event is subjective in a third sense. It has a what-it-is-like or what-it-feels-like aspect.[12]

Let us look at these ideas in turn.

How are we to take the point 3a that each conscious event is subjective in the sense of being dependent on a person? What is said is vague. If a person is understood in a standard way, say in terms of one or both of a persisting body and an internally-related sequence of conscious events, then the point will not give us the different account of conscious events for which we are looking. This is so since it is consistent with neural functionalism.

Advocates of that doctrine can and will accommodate the point that a conscious event, as conceived by them, is dependent on a person. They will say, with reason, that a conscious event as conceived by them is dependent on a persisting body. They will take the mentioned relations within a sequence of mental events ('inner events' as distinct from input and output) to be nothing other than a part of their own doctrine.

Might we then take the point as having to do not with a person but with a Cartesian self or ego? Clearly that 'substance-dualism' would be anathema to Searle, who is already enraged by the idea that he is advocating 'property-dualism'. More generally, to turn to a Cartesian self or ego, or to go some way in that direction, would take us outside a ring of unobscure philosophical and psychological doctrines which we are contemplating and to which we are trying to confine ourselves. But if we do not go outside we seem to need to conclude that in this point about personal dependency we get no different conception of a conscious event.

What of the claim 3b that conscious events are subjective in the sense of not being open or accessible in principle to all observers? To whatever extent that is true, it does not help much. Our purpose now is to find an account of the nature of conscious events. Do we get it by way of the epistemological claim? It seems we do not.[13] What we need is not an account of how conscious events are known but an account or part of an account of *what* is known.

As for the claim 3c that my information about the world is perspectival, what this comes to is that conscious events are related to objects by way of only some of the properties of those objects. (Hence the possible alteration of truth-value when co-referring terms are substituted in statements about consciousness.) That consciousness involves a point of view in this sense, but, so to speak, the world has no point of view, is true. But it remains clear, I think, that asserting the perspectival nature of conscious events does not provide and does not carry much promise of a distinct view of conscious events. It is surely no part of neural functionalism that in being conscious of something I am conscious of *all* its properties.

It is the idea or ideas 3d, that a conscious event has a what-it-is-like or what-it-feels-like aspect, associated with the work of Thomas Nagel, that may seem most promising here.[14] One feels that such an aspect is something of which neural functionalism cannot give an account.

But there is a prior question. *Does* the idea of such an aspect make a significant contribution to any *conception* of consciousness? It may be part of what was earlier called our grip on the nature of consciousness, our insufficiently conceptualized recollection of events of it, and it does indeed seem to be no part of neural functionalism. But does talk of a what-it-is-like or a what-it-feels-like aspect contribute anything to any conception of consciousness? I certainly doubt it, for the following reasons.

Searle remarks that we can wonder what it feels like to be a dolphin, but not a shingle on a roof. He would say the same, it seems, of what it would be like to be a dolphin as against a shingle. That, if you will allow me to say so, is to let the cat out of the bag. His remark indicates what seems to be true: that to speak of what it is like or feels like to be something – that is, what it is like or feels like to be anything – is surely to speak elliptically of *what it is or feels like to be anything that is conscious*. It is difficult or impossible to attach any other sense to speaking of what it is or feels like to be anything.

But then the words give no analytic advance. There is circularity. The *definiendum* appears essentially in the *definiens*. Speaking of what it is or feels like to be anything has been heuristically useful in persuading some philosophers in the tradition of Penelope's Wooers (p. 50) actually to return to a subject-matter – consciousness. But it does not offer or contribute to a conception of that subject-matter.

If, incidentally, we direct our attention to what it is like to be a *particular* thing, say a dolphin or a bat, as distinct from what it is like to be anything, there is a further disability. It is that we are then inevitably thinking of distinctions between kinds of consciousness, and not about what we are after, which is the distinction between conscious events generally and other things.

There is one more familiar trouble. If we attach ourselves to the idea of a what-it-*feels*-like aspect as distinct from a what-it-*is*-like aspect, we do not have something about consciousness in general, which is essential. Many conscious events seem to lack such an aspect of feel or feeling. Pure thought seems to lack qualities of the suggested kind.[15]

(4) Consciousness is said to involve two kinds of unity, the first existing at a time, the other existing over short stretches of time. My experiences at a time, say experiences of three objects I now perceive, are parts of just one conscious event. This is said to be the feature of consciousness that Kant spoke of in terms of the transcendental unity of apperception. Distinct from this 'vertical' unity is 'horizontal' unity. For example, it is said, my awareness of the beginning of my spoken or thought sentence continues after the beginning is past. This unity may involve not only the mentioned iconic memory but also short-term memory.[16]

Certainly there are these two facts of unity about conscious events, and they are rightly included in what are called gross structural features of consciousness. It is as clear, I think, that these facts by themselves do not give us a distinct conception of the nature of consciousness. They are facts that can be claimed to be accommodated by *any* conception, and in particular neural functionalism. No doubt there have been philosophers who have moved from reflection on precisely the unities to a distinctive conception, involving a self or ego or the like, but Searle has no inclination to follow them. To follow them, it certainly seems, would take us into the deep and murky water that neural functionalism has the attraction of avoiding.

So we do not get consciousness explained by way of just the unities. As it seems to me, something as disappointing is the case with each of the following mentioned features of consciousness.

(5) Conscious events can be divided up in terms of a finite set of types or modalities, beginning with the five types of events related

to the five senses. (6) Conscious events involve a figure-ground distinction, as shown by Gestalt psychology. They also involve (7) a pervasive familiarity, (8) overflow, which has to do with the way in which thoughts spill over or connect with other thoughts, (9) a centre and a periphery, which has to do with selective attention and levels of attention, (10) boundary conditions, concerning the spatio-temporal-socio-biological location for me of my conscious events, (11) mood, and (12) a pleasure-unpleasure dimension.[17]

In each of these cases, as it seems to me, it is left open to neural functionalists to fit the fact or facts into their account of the mind. For the most part these are familiar facts. In them, we do not get what is needed. Is there more hope in something else?

4   Intentionality

(13) Searle distinguishes ersatz conceptions of intentionality from attempts to get hold of the real thing, whatever that may come to, and effectively despatches the ersatz conceptions. That is, he takes it that the intentionality – or representativeness, aboutness, meaningfulness, or directedness – of the contents of conscious events cannot be described just by asserting that there are causal relations between them and things in the world, including sorts of relations proposed in some doctrines of anti-individualism. The enterprise of trying to *naturalize* intentionality – trying to reduce it to no more than neural facts, bare causal relations having these facts as effects, and perhaps external or environmental facts working in some other way – is futile.

But what is it, then, for an event to be intentional? Certainly many philosophers seem to have supposed that a good account of intentional content will help, maybe more than anything else, in characterizing conscious events. There has been a whole intentionality sector in the industry of the philosophy of mind. Searle is surely among these philosophers, despite a discordant thought of his to which we shall come. To his credit, he is not among those other philosophers who appear almost to suppose that there is nothing more to the problem of consciousness than the problem of intentionality.

He says at one point that the attempt to naturalize intentional content fails on account of leaving out its subjectivity.[18] It is not clear which of his particular facts of subjectivity, so-called, is in question.

Do we get an account of the intentionality of content by way of seeing, to look back to proposition 3a, that each intentional conscious event is subjective in the sense of being dependent on a person? Well, this cannot give or promise an account of intentionality that is distinct from the ersatz conceptions. The situation is the same as the one noticed earlier in connection with personal dependency used directly (as distinct from via intentionality) in the hope of finding a conception of conscious events.[19]

Do we get an account of the intentionality of content by way of seeing (3b) that each conscious event is subjective in the second sense of not being equally accessible to any observer? This epistemological point seems to go no way towards characterizing the nature of intentionality.

Do we get intentionality characterized in a fundamental way via the fact 3c that intentional conscious events are perspectival or have a perspectival shape? I cannot see how. The familiar fact in question is agreed on all hands. From the point of view of a theory of intentionality it is pre-theoretical. All accounts will take themselves to accommodate it.

Do we then get somewhere with respect to intentionality by way of the proposition 3d that intentional conscious events have a what-it-is-like or what-it-feels-like aspect? The answer again seems to be no, for various reasons, several of which were in view earlier, when this third subjectivity was looked at in the hope of coming directly to a distinctive conception of conscious events. Another thought here might also have been mentioned a moment ago in connection with propositions 3a and 3b. It is the fact that *all* conscious events are taken (dubiously) to have the subjectivity in question, but not all conscious events are intentional. Hence there can be no hope of explaining intentionality by reference *just* to this subjectivity, if that is the idea.

The project of characterizing intentionality in other than the ersatz ways, as a means to characterizing conscious events, does not seem much advanced either by the doctrine that intentionality is normative: that intentional notions set standards of truth, rationality, consistency, and so on.[20] Supposing that the doctrine of normativity is acceptable, it nevertheless seems not to help us. The doctrine offers further facts about a supposed fundamental fact, that of intentionality, of which we still lack an explanation. The same sort of disappointment seems inevitable with respect to a second and more developed doctrine, that intentional content depends on what is called *background*, initially identified as certain capacities, abilities, and general know-how.[21]

Let us at this point consider the discordant thought anticipated earlier. It is the insistence that we cannot study the intentionality of content, whatever this comes to, except by studying consciousness, that intentionality can only be understood by way of its relation to consciousness, that intentionality is dependent on consciousness.[22] As will be clear, this recommendation reverses the order of inquiry we have just been contemplating. That is, the discordant thought is that we come to a conception of intentional content by way of already having a conception of consciousness.

So the recommendation goes against the strategy we have been contemplating. *Explanans* and *explanandum* are reversed. Do we have to choose between these strategies? Well, although this is puzzling, perhaps we need to become less traditional or one-directional, less worried about circularity,[23] and allow the possibility of two-way traffic: (a) somehow or in some way the subject of intentionality is enlightened by the subject of consciousness and (b) somehow or in some way the subject of consciousness is enlightened by the subject of intentionality.

But if we try to start out in the way lately recommended, by contemplating (a) that we can find out about intentionality by turning to consciousness, we face the annoying difficulty that has emerged in this discussion, that we seem to lack a conception of consciousness. Furthermore, if we make our way through the bundle of propositions (1, 2, 4–12) that we have about consciousness, and which have not yet been considered in our endeavour to clarify intentionality in the desired way, it is hard to be persuaded that any of them is of use. I leave this exercise to you, reader.

Let us return to (b), trying to clarify consciousness by giving attention to intentionality. We could not get going since we lacked a good account of intentionality, and one was not to be found in what was said of the connection between intentionality and subjectivity. What will now come to mind, no doubt, is recourse to a large account of the intentionality of mental content given by Searle in his book *Intentionality: An Essay in the Philosophy of Mind*.[24] Here we get an account of the intentionality of mental content that is in ways dependent on a prior account of the derived intentionality of language.

This account of mental events, to be brief indeed, takes an intentional conscious event to be a matter of (a) a content, which fixes (b) a truth condition or other 'condition of satisfaction', and of (c) a psychological mode, such that the event is a belief, a desire, or whatever, which mode determines (d) direction of fit – in the case of a belief, the belief must fit the world rather than the world be changed to fit the belief.

This account is perhaps the best of its kind. But what is its kind? Well, it sets out what can indeed be called the logical properties of intentional conscious events. But it is hard to resist at least hesitation about it as a distinct account of the fundamental nature of intentionality. Perhaps this is best expressed by way of the thought that it is unclear what it is in the account that is inconsistent with a neural functionalist or naturalized reading of it. It seems Searle takes it that it does contain such a fact, but what is it?

Could it possibly contain such a fact if it does not concern, as Searle explicitly allows it does not, the 'ontological status' of the events in question?[25] He says he gives that status elsewhere. He says he gives it in something that did not enlighten us and could not delay us. That was proposition 2, that conscious events are higher-level biological events of the brain caused by lower-level neural events.

However, I shall not press the questions, since there is no need to do so. There is no need in our present endeavour – finding a characterization of the nature of conscious events. This is so since, as already remarked, and as is very widely thought, not all conscious events have the property of intentionality. It is a fact too often put aside in the contemporary philosophy of mind. Its importance for us now is simply that there was in fact little hope in contemplating that we could explain conscious events by way of the property of intentionality, and reflections on that property. There are paradigmatic conscious events which surely lack the mysterious property, notably sensations and moods.[26]

We shall be coming right back to the subject of intentionality in a later chapter of this book. But we have now come to the end of a guide to thirteen humble and obvious truths about the mind.

5   Conclusions, Outrageousness Postscript

It is true, I think, that consideration of the thirteen features or groups of features of consciousness, and what is said of them, is likely to increase one's ordinary confidence about the nature of consciousness, to tighten one's grip on it. The procedure, partly because it includes good reminders, strengthens the conviction. This is no little achievement.

But, to come to the first principal conclusion of this paper, reflection on the ordinary truths about the mind and certain relatively unobscure philosophical and psychological conceptions and doctrines does *not* give us a distinct conception of the nature of consciousness. We do not get a conception which is distinct from neural functionalism.[27] Rather, we get things consistent with it, or, in the case of the what-it-is-or-feels-like aspects, something not useful. We have no sufficiently conceptualized ground or major premise, so to speak, for arguments against neural functionalism. None of the thirteen features of consciousness gives us the needed conception.

As we have seen, this is so in particular with what Searle most often relies on in summarizing his views: (2) the feature of consciousness that conscious events are higher-level biological events of the brain caused by lower-level wholly neural events.[28] So too with what is said of subjectivity, intentionality, and so on. It is evidently as true that we do not and cannot get a distinct conception from the sum of the thirteen features.

Searle and a few like-minded philosophers are certainly not like the drunk he mentions, brother to the functionalist and cognitive scientist, who loses his car keys in the dark bushes, but looks for them under the streetlight because the light is better there. Searle and like-minded philosophers look in the right place, but, being worn out by trying to get the drunks into the bushes, and perhaps being a little attracted themselves to the streetlight and the activity under it, leave the keys in shadow.

A distinct conception of consciousness will be informed to a yet greater extent than Searle's reflections by our experience, our common possession of consciousness. A distinct conception will also be owed to a determination not to succumb too soon to the proper demand for literalness, clarity and explicitness. Hence it may not miss the reality on which we have a grip, and which needs to be respected in our reflections on the kinds of subjectivity mentioned above as well as unity, intentionality, and so on. Such a conception will not recoil from mystery, but attempt to dissipate it. It will not avoid deep and murky water but try to get something clear from it.

Of the remaining matters that can have consideration here, one has to do with the question of the relation between consciousness and the brain, traditionally known as the mind-body question. This has not been our main concern here – we have been mainly concerned, rather, with the question of the nature of consciousness. But evidently accounts of the nature of consciousness may contain or entail answers to the mind-body question. It is common to judge accounts of consciousness by way of their upshots for the mind-body question. In particular it is taken to be bad news for an account of consciousness if it entails what can be called dualism.

Searle notices, as we have ourselves, that the terms 'dualism' and 'monism' or 'materialism' or 'identity theory', and variants of them, are no longer of much use.[29] One reason is that typical 'monisms' are in ways property-dualisms. Another is that some 'dualisms' are no more dualistic than typical 'monisms'. He also strenuously insists that his own view can only be mistakenly or misleadingly characterized as *either* materialist or property-dualist. What is to be said of this insistence?

Certainly he is right to object to the names 'property-dualism' and 'materialism' for his view in so far as the names carry the implication of a possible division of what there is into two domains, the domain of consciousness and the domain of the physical, such that nothing is in both domains. Rather, to recall the first of his thirteen propositions, conscious events *are* physical – the domain of consciousness is included in the domain of the physical. He is also right to disavow the name 'property-dualism' if it carries implications of support for particular doctrines of introspection, privileged access, or inward observation and so on which he rejects.

He is as right to resist the name 'property-dualism' if it carries the implication that the view so named nevertheless somehow requires or countenances more 'substances' than particles in fields of force, or that consciousness is 'stuff' in a particular sense which he disavows. He is yet more right to resist the name 'property-dualism' if is taken to imply the once modish idea that the mind-body problem is insoluble, which of course he does not believe.[30] Finally, he would be right to say that his main proposition about two levels of events does not make him into any kind of dualist. What matters is whether the characters or natures of events at the two levels are different.

All of that is worth insisting on, given the deplorable tendency in the contemporary philosophy of mind to conduct argument by sticking on undefined labels. But none of what he insists on takes away from two other things that are true.

He initially and thereafter declares himself to be against reductionism, and this declaration is in part the insistence that our conscious events have properties other than those assigned to them by neural functionalism.[31] Plainly, if this had turned out really to be the demonstrated burden of his view, we would have had a reason for speaking of the view as property-dualist. This conclusion is unaffected, by the way, if we take up a way of speaking of these matters closer to Searle's usually preferred one, and thus get rid of events. Then the reason for speaking of a property-dualism would simply be that the view was that there are wholly neural-causal properties or features of the brain and there are properties or features that require another characterization.

But of course there *is* more to be said than that he declares himself against reductionism. It is one thing to announce and insist that conscious events in themselves are not merely neural relata. It is another to give a conception of them that bears this out – a distinct conception of them. Our inquiry issued in the conclusion that Searle fails to provide this. None of the features 1–13 gives us such a distinct conception, and neither does the sum of these features. Thus the account actually given is consistent with neural functionalism.

My third principal conclusion is therefore that the view as actually set out, or as it turns out under examination, is *not* property-dualist in just the sense in which in effect it is announced to be. There is a difference between the headline and the story. This is perhaps the main explanation of the conflicting responses to his view that Searle reports.

It seems clear – a fourth conclusion – that the distinct and adequate conception of consciousness which I have mentioned will in intent and in fact be correctly describable as entailing something or other like a property-dualism. That will not make it different from some contemporary 'identity theories', including Davidson's. Like them, also, it will in certain senses be quite as correctly describable as 'monist'. What is most important is that the adequate conception will not be unswallowable. It will not be among the theories without a future.

A postscript. Is the prospect of a distinct and adequate conception of consciousness, if not the prospect of something unswallowable, nevertheless the prospect of something outrageous? I suspect that it will seem so to many, and I admit to sharing something of their feeling.

It is the prospect of a view to the effect that there really are two different kinds of events that occur in our heads. There are two different kinds of events that are physical in the ordinary sense and hence involve space-occupants. Or, as we can as well say, there are two different kinds of physical properties of our brains. One kind of events or properties involves only neurons and the causal relations fundamental to neural functionalism. The other kind of events, events of consciousness, are such that each involves what may initially be spoken of as a subject-part and a content-part. It needs to be admitted that if such a view is not clarified by describing it as having to do with *conscious stuff*, it is not travestied either.

I shall not now try to do a lot to alleviate the outrageousness, but only make some remarks. Several of them echo things Searle has to say about the conception of consciousness he promises but does not produce.

One is that it can seem that it is only such a conception that is true to our experience, true to the grip we have on consciousness, true to what we know when we do not withdraw in apprehension from the subject. Secondly, such a conception depends on no dubious doctrine of introspection, but only the indubitable fact of recollection of our passing episodes of consciousness. Thirdly, it really does need to be kept clear that the events or properties in question are conceived of as physical in a strong sense, the ordinary sense. They are not other-worldly.

Fourthly, nothing stands in the way of their entering into the explanatory web of nomic or lawlike connections. More particularly, nothing stands in the way of their being nomic correlates of wholly neural events, and of being causes or anyway causal and also effects.

Finally, it seems to me remarkable to say that conscious events so conceived are inconsistent with the scientific world-view. Neuroscience has long been engaged in precisely the study of nomic connections of a kind between neural events and conscious events – between neural events and the events on which we have always had a grip and of which we can hope for a distinct and adequate conception.

Notes

1. For Searle's Chinese Room Argument, a signal contribution, see 'Minds, Brains, and Programs', *Behavioral and Brain Sciences*, 1980.
2. MIT Press, 1992, p. 17. All page references below in these Notes unless otherwise indicated are also to *The Rediscovery of the Mind*.
3. pp. xii, 13, 14–15, 28, 54, 91, 100.
4. pp. 25, 86.
5. pp. xii, 3–4, 9, 85–91, 118.
6. See my *A Theory of Determinism: The Mind, Neuroscience, and Life-Hopes* or *Mind and Brain*, in each case pp. 87–9.
7. pp. 1, 14, 90, 111–12.
8. p. 14.
9. pp. 16–17, 19, 20, 55, 70, 94.
10. pp. 16, 21, 94.

11. pp. 70, 95, 131.
12. pp. 117–18, 132.
13. I take it Searle might agree that we do not, since he is very firm about distinguishing ontology from epistemology. See p. 18.
14. 'What is it Like to be a Bat?', *Philosophical Review*, 1974, reprinted in Nagel's *Mortal Questions* (Cambridge University Press, 1979). See also Timothy Sprigge, 'Final Causes', *Supplementary Proceedings of the Aristotelian Society*, 1971.
15. Do we get, in what is said of a feels-like or is-like aspect of consciousness, a feature of it made explicit that cannot be accommodated by neural functionalism? (See Note 5.) It seems to me that we do not. Given the circularity, insistence that a feels-like or is-like aspect cannot be accommodated by neural functionalism reduces to what we began with and allowed to be philosophically unsatisfactory: that our grip of consciousness, our insufficiently conceptualized relation to it, persuades us of a difference between neural relata and conscious events.
16. pp. 129–30.
17. pp. 128–9, 132–41.
18. p. 50.
19. See above, pp. 90–1.
20. pp. 51, 238.
21. Ch. 8.
22. pp. 18, 84, 227.
23. p. 83.
24. Cambridge University Press, 1983.
25. *Intentionality*, p. 14.
26. Incidentally, the point that consciousness cannot be elucidated by intentionality since not all consciousness is intentional is distinct from the earlier point that intentionality cannot be explained just by subjectivity since not all consciousness is intentional but all is subjective.
27. As implied in much of what has been said, I take it that the Chinese Room argument and also a further good argument to the same end in Chapter 9 of *The Rediscovery of the Mind*, despite my admiration for them, require reinforcing by the provision of a positive and full account of the nature of consciousness.
28. This account of the mind-body relation, by the way, is open to several objections. One is its seeming, despite Searle's good intentions, to suffer from the curse of much of the contemporary philosophy of mind, which is epiphenomenalism. See *A Theory of Determinism* or *Mind and Brain*, pp. 99–102.
29. pp. 2, 4, 14–15, 25–6, 54–5.
30. His objections (pp. 100–5) to arguments for the insolubility of the mind-body problem do not seem as efficient as they might be. One argument for insolubility, assigned to Thomas Nagel, is that if matter explains consciousness, there has to be a necessary connection between the two, but in fact there is no conceptual connection. The objection to that is simply that the explanation depends not on a conceptual but only a nomic connection. Causal connection isn't conceptual. A second argument for insolubility, derived from Nagel and assigned to Colin

McGinn, is that consciousness is stuff of which we are aware through introspection, and the brain by contrast is something of which we are aware through perception; as for an explanatory link, we could have no way of being aware of it – there is no third kind of awareness. The objection to that piece of enticing thinking, although evidently there are others, is that there is no need at all, if I am to explain C by B, for me to have the same kind of awareness of both C and B, and no need at all for me to have an explanation of the explanation. With respect to the second point, I don't fail to explain C by B (having shown that B is a causal circumstance or nomic correlate for C) because I have not filled out the story. All I need to do is establish the truth of a certain conditional statement about B and C. We would have no explanations, anywhere, if every explanation had to be explained in the given sense. See *A Theory of Determinism* or *Mind and Brain*, ch. 1.

31. There can be no doubt that Searle is officially opposed to the reductionism exemplified by neural functionalism – whatever actually happens in the course of his book. (See pp. xii, 28, 112, 116, 116–18, 169, 199.) Hence, incidentally, his saying that 'the mental is neurophysiological at a higher level' (Note 3, p. 253; cf. p. 161) is at least misleading. It does not go well, to take one example, with the anti-reductionist line that 'The neurophysiology does indeed admit of different levels of description, but none of these objective neurophysiological levels of description ... is a level of subjectivity' (p. 169). Subjectivity, as we have seen, is taken by him as fundamental to consciousness.

Chapter Six

Seeing Things

It was back near the beginning of this book, in the discussion of the thinking of neuroscientific friends, that it was remarked that we can try to do a good deal of philosophy of mind without trying really to analyse or explain consciousness. In particular we can think of operations in or of consciousness, and in or of the brain, without seeing the general nature of consciousness. We can carry on without really analysing or explaining the ordinary, settled and obscure idea we have of consciousness or mentality. We can get through thoughts on the consciousness-brain problem too, but not without being at least nagged by the persistent problem, the prior problem.

This hardest problem has certainly not been solved during our progress, or even much advanced. It was not solved or much advanced by the alarming supposition lately made explicit, that conscious events are in the category of physical events, and physical events in heads, but are not the events of our neuroscience. This want of a solution, common as it is, *must* be a shortcoming of any thinking about consciousness, the mind, mind and brain, the causal or other explanation of the occurrence of mental events, their relation to the world, the explanation of action or behaviour.

As you have heard, it is at least difficult to believe that light is shed by functionalism, however elaborated in cognitive science, from which we have kept a perfectly proper philosophical distance, or in what in the end is the oddity of anti-individualism. Nor is light shed by a bluff confidence in humble truths and the like. With respect to that last hope, on reflection it is a remarkable idea that what all of us find puzzling or baffling can be seen clearly by remembering this or that common fact or collection of such facts. That is a Wittgensteinian proposition, perhaps, and none the better for that.

The following paper is like all of the rest of this book in trying actually to give an analysis of consciousness itself, necessarily a literal analysis. The paper is a first attempt. It restricts itself, like a good deal of what comes after, to what seems to be fundamental to consciousness, which is perceptual consciousness – our being aware of things around us by sight and our other senses. There can be little doubt that perceptual consciousness not only preceded other consciousness in the development of our species, but also is prior in other ways, say in the early development of a human being, however complex that story. The facts of priority hang together, somehow, with the fact of fundamentality. It is hard or impossible to resist the idea that a real analysis of perceptual consciousness will put us well on the road to an understanding of all consciousness, the various problems about it.

With this paper, and more so with those to come, there is less need for introduction. If this inquiry has gone on decently up to now, you know where you are. Or anywhere you know where you are according to one fairly common or even very common orientation, if maybe one with attitude as well as belief in it. But that is another story.

The paper struggles persistently with matters of which you do not need to be told, all of them contributing to our uncertain sense of our consciousness. It has to do, first, with any event of perceptual consciousness involving a seeming relation of something like a subject to a content. It has to do, secondly, with the relation or relations of a content to an object or the world. It has to do, thirdly, perhaps not so familiarly, with the relation between these relations. It turns out, so to speak, that the world intrudes on these reflections.

This paper is not now the success, even the flawed success, that it once seemed to me to be. It could be OK anyway. It has the recommendation of following that policy noticed early on, mental realism, reflecting on mental events in their reality rather than allowing oneself to be distracted (p. 59). It is the opposite to the drunk's policy of not looking for the keys in the bushes where they are, because the light is bad there. It may be better than what follows it in this book. Sometimes earlier thoughts are best.

1   Subject and Content

Consider my experience of seeing the long lawn out the window, suitable for croquet. On another occasion, if my visual cortex and more of my brain were the same, but there was no lawn, my experience would nevertheless be identical, wouldn't it? So we are told. If so, no part of my experience when I see the lawn, and in particular what is commonly called its content, is actually identical with the lawn. That is the argument from illusion, as it has traditionally been known, and its conclusion. Is a different proposition not merely a commonsensical temptation?

Is content abstract, then, not in space and time? Is it, as many say, *propositional*, by which they partly mean not in space and time? That cannot be true of the content being considered here. Nor, by the way, can this content be 'inexistent', as Brentano said,[1] if that means what it sounds like. This is so since content as it is being understood, and as it is relevantly understood in the philosophy of mind, is *causal*. It is part of the causal explanation of behaviour, thereby not being an anomaly in terms of natural selection. It is also an effect of such things as a croquet lawn. Both facts require that it be spatio-temporal. There are no causes and no effects, or, if you like, no standard causes and effects, which are out of space and time.

There is a related point. Nothing that will be said in what follows is intended to involve taking my experience of seeing the lawn as other than physical. There are common conceptions of the physical that tie it to present or future or completed science, and thus have clear disabilities of several kinds. A satisfactory conception, to my mind, which does make physical items *possible* subjects of science, takes them by definition to be either occupants of space and time that are perceived, or occupants of space and time that are causal with respect to occupants of the first category – those that are perceived. Atoms and forces come into the second category. So does all of my experience.

This is fortunate, since otherwise it would not exist in the only clear sense I know. This is not to say experience is neural. It is not to say so even if it is true, as it seems to be, that all my mental properties are properly regarded as properties of my brain and central nervous system. They might be funny properties of those things. They would not be the first funny properties to turn up in the history of science and philosophy.

What else can be said of content? To speak of a content, surely, is already to suggest something else about an experience – that it did not involve only a content. The idea of a content is surely the idea of something in relation to something else. That is not the contingent truth that a content is in relation to *something else*, as perhaps all things are. The idea of a content, rather, is a relational idea, an idea of a thing related to something else, like the idea of a passenger.

Not to depend entirely on the conceptual point, and indeed to leave it in a way open by using 'content' loosely, is a visual experience's having involved more than content established in what can be called an empirical way? Is it established, that is, by our immediate recollection of such experiences? Consider any two which we would ordinarily regard as different – say my experiences of seeing the lawn and of seeing the portrait on the wall.

It seems there is a certain respect in which the two experiences are more or less the same. It is a respect, as needs to be added, in which all my mental events of whatever kind are more or less the same. Moreover, each of the two more or less identical items involved in the two experiences is unitary or featureless, quite unlike the respects in which the experiences differ – that is, quite unlike those properties which are their contents. Each content, far from being unitary of featureless, typically has many features.

You may say of these two considerations, one conceptual and one empirical, that at best they do not establish that a content stands in relation to something else which is *another part* of an experience. You may say that the related thing is a person. Suppose you say, further, choosing not to pay any real attention to my remark about a content's seeming to be related to something that is unitary, that a person consists in one or both of a persisting body and a sequence of mental events. The sequence is such that all the events in it are related in certain ways, above all in that many are anticipations or memories of others.

It needs to be allowed that the content of an experience is related, and may perhaps be understood as being related, both to a body and to a mental sequence. The relationships to a mental sequence, some of those to which functionalism restricts itself, hold or may hold if the content is anticipated or remembered.

It is unpersuasive to say that a visual experience recollected a moment later is understood *only* as having its content in relation to or dependent upon a body. Also, it seems even more unpersuasive to say of the content of a piece of intellectual imagining that it is understood as body-related at all. However, it *is* understood as being in another relation, and surely all contents are in just this respect alike. Is this just the relation to a mental sequence?

The idea that we take contents as related only to mental sequences runs up against a third consideration. Consider a first and entirely forgotten or a last and entirely unanticipated mental event in the life of a person. It is hard to resist thinking that the content of this mental event is to be conceived as being in relation to something else. *Ex hypothesi* this is not other mental events. This further consideration seems to me pretty forceful. Also, there *is* the thought, which pertains as much to the previous idea about a content's being related to a body, that what a content goes with is somehow unitary or featureless. We are not so well supplied with intuitions in this inquiry that we can afford to discard that one.

The several considerations, to my mind, come close to showing that my experience *involved* more than a content. The third consideration, about a first and forgotten or a last and unanticipated mental event, comes close to showing that my experience, my mental event, *had as a part* something other than a content. To say it 'shows' this, however, is to presuppose that we have a wholly settled conception of *an experience*, about which the plain discovery in question can be made. This is doubtful. It seems to an extent open to decision whether something other than a content is part of an experience. What is needed is a decision as to how to use 'an experience', the extension of the term. I shall so use it that something other than a content is indeed part of an experience. Nothing much depends on this, but it will certainly accord better with things to come than would talk of two entities.

In sum, then, the way in which visual experiences typically differ and are many-featured gives us their contents. The different and many-featured property of each of most of our visual experiences *is* its content. As for the property that is more or less the same in each of our otherwise different visual experiences, and is unitary, this can be referred to as its *subject*. In my view all mental events can be spoken of with some reason as a matter of subject and content. That is what mental events are. The nature of the mental, of consciousness, consists in this internal duality. It is what is misdescribed or underdescribed, incidentally, by related characterizations in terms of 'qualia', or 'what something is like', or 'what it is like to be something', or 'raw feels'. It is remote from what is usually gestured at by the word *dualism*, if only because both content and subject are physical.

The term 'subject' is very rightly suspect. I use it for a while in place of others which perhaps are about as good. I might have spoken just of *the experience* and its content, or been a bit more lyrical, perhaps by way of the idea of *mental space* and what it contains, or tried to expand on the image that content is *not inert*.[2] My use of 'subject' is not to be taken as conveying more than what has already been mentioned. A subject is not a self unless a self is taken to be no more than a uniform part of a mental event which is like a part of other mental events which typically are otherwise different. It is worth remembering that a subject within one of my experiences is taken as only more or less the same as the subject within another of my experiences. Whatever the fact about subjects may be, this is not to assert either qualitative or numerical identity. Nor is it to assert persistence.[3]

What is the relation of my visual experience to its object, the lawn? What is the relation, that is, of my visual experience to the world? Surprisingly it seems sometimes to have been confused with a relation between subject and content.[4] It is, rather, that relation expressed by saying that the experience was of the lawn, or that I was aware of the lawn. At least in part that is to say that the lawn was among the causes of the experience. In what we are likely to call another part, the relation consists in the experience being somehow representative of the lawn. More particularly, it was its content that stood in these two ways to the lawn.

There is no doubt about the fact of representation here, no doubt that there is some fact or other that can have such a name. Certainly something could not be an experience without being of something, and it could not be of something without being of something in particular. Something could not be an experience of seeing *the lawn* if it was in no sense representative of the lawn, or, to speak in different ways of the same fact, it was in no sense true of the lawn, in no sense featured as the lawn is featured. It might be an experience caused by them, but it could not be an experience of them. Part of what makes an experience an experience of this rather than that is that it represents this rather than that.

All of the reflections so far issue in, indeed will come close to foundering on, a number of problems. They are the concern of the rest of this paper. What more can be said of and with respect to the nature of the content of an experience? What is the nature of the so-called subject? What is the relation between them? Above all, what is it for an experience to be representative of the world? How do answers to these questions bear on one another?

2   Content and World – Relations of Representation

Suppose we try to think of the content of my experience, so far as it is representative, as being something like an image. It has a property related to the isomorphism of my actual retinal image – the image being shape-related to the lawn. It cannot actually *be* an image since, it seems, the idea of content itself as actually green and dendritic seems to be against our sense of the idea. Or suppose we think of the content as involving conventions, as in the case of a word or statement. Suppose we think of its being representative in a mixture of these two ways.

Long before we get into doctrinal battles beginning in these vague suppositions, let alone try for some detail, there is a something to be settled. For plain and everyday representation, the kind of representation on which we really have a little grip, we need to be aware of what does the representing. For this plain representation where it involves an image, say a portrait of someone, I need to see the image. For representation where it involves a written word or a statement, I need to be given the word or statement. In both cases I need a representation which is itself an object of awareness. I need a representation which is an object of awareness in exactly the way in which the lawn is the object of awareness of my experience.

Do we have such a thing *within* my experience of seeing the lawn? Some philosophers, most notably in the tradition of the representative or sense-data theory of perception, or the related theory of phenomenalism, have supposed so. In ordinary seeing, they have supposed, what I am aware of in this way is ideas in a certain sense, or sense-data, or percepts, or qualia of a kind. By one short description, these philosophers suppose there are *subjective* things that are objects of awareness in the way we ordinarily take the lawn to be the object of my experience. These are objects of awareness but ones that are not public, not open to several senses, and not such as to exist unperceived or outside of awareness.

The trouble is that there are no such things in ordinary perception. We know something of what it is to be aware of things in this standard way. In the case of the lawn, to repeat, it is for there to be a content that is an effect and a representation of the lawn. With respect to my experience of seeing the lawn, it contains no subjective thing such that it is an effect of and represents some other subjective thing. That is not to say my experience had no part which was its content. It is to say its content was not an object of the given kind of awareness. The only object of what we can henceforth call *standard awareness* in connection with my seeing the lawn is the lawn.

This confidence about there being no subjective objects of standard awareness in visual perception rests, as Hume ought to have said, on every person's experience. The claim that there are subjective objects of standard awareness is nothing other than a claim about our *experience* in seeing something. It is a claim to which nothing other than retrospection of experience is most relevant. None of us, just after seeing something, recollects a subjective item which is the effect and representation of *another* subjective item. To speculate that we are standardly aware of subjective objects can only be owed to vagueness about what it is for there to be such awareness of something.

This confidence about there being no subjective objects of standard awareness in perception is not reduced by the tradition of argument that has at least sometimes been aimed at establishing their existence. To take a recent example, it is no good saying that I do not see or do not have sensory awareness that things, say the lawn, are public, touchable, and exist unperceived. That is true, or so we can grant. But it does not follow that I do not see or am not visually aware of what has those properties. It thus does not follow either, to get to the end of this argument for the representative theory, that I must perceive or be aware of subjective objects.[5] Above all, to stick to the point with which we are concerned, it does not follow that there are subjective things that are objects of awareness in the way that the lawn is ordinarily taken to be the object of my experience.

Will someone insist at this point that I *am* in fact in the standard way aware of the *content* of my experience? That can only be insistence that I am aware of the lawn, since it is the only thing I am aware of in this way. It can only be a matter of changing a definition, the definition of the term 'content', and hence the subject-matter. Our subject-matter is a perceptual mental event, not in part what I have been calling the object of that event. Should someone now reply that in her conception a mental event may *include* the croquet lawn, she is welcome to her different subject-matter. It is not ours. Further, if one aim of her enterprise is the explanation of behaviour, her subject-matter contains otiose parts. The lawn is no doubt part of the history of my perceptual mental event, in my sense, but it need not come into the explanation of my actions, any more than the explanation of an event by a causal circumstance or full cause requires an explanation of the causal circumstance.

To return to our question, what *is* to be said of the representative character of content? If we are not standardly aware of anything to do the representing, no analogue of seen picture or heard word, should we give up what was said to be beyond doubt, that content is in some way representative? It seems we cannot. I need an answer to the question of what it is that made my experience an experience of the lawn, and something about representation seems essential as part of the answer.

3   Non-Mental Representations

Many philosophers of mind, as we know, have the very estimable habit of fleeing mystery. Should we follow them? Should we take the course of not trying to think about some sort of non-standard awareness of content, which is mysterious, and turn instead to a representation that is not an object of any awareness and moreover is not mental at all? We can look to neuroscience for such a representative thing, or to various models of the mind and perception. Certainly there are things which are spoken of as non-mental representations. They are spoken of in several terminologies, one having to do with a kind of *information*.[6] One such thing is the real image on my retinas. Shall we say that my experience's representing the lawn comes to no more than that it was caused by the lawn, and the causal sequence in question included a non-mental representation of the lawn, or more than one such representation?

On reflection, there is a pointlessness in this. What is the attraction of a retinal image when we are looking for something non-mental to which to give the name of being a representation? What is it about a retinal image that gives point to talking about it as a representation? If we do not like retinal images in this role, and choose differently, what is the attraction of some configuration of neural events which in a sense preserves information about the lawn? *Ex hypothesi* I do not see the retinal image or the neural configuration, register its outline, see it as something, take it for something, interpret it, use it to refer to something, or stand to it in any other relation which goes with ordinary representation, representation by either image or word.

If we put aside the inclination to half-think in these mistaken ways of the non-mental representation, it is clear that its attraction is just this: each of its parts, features, properties or whatever is an effect of a part, feature, property or whatever of the object of perception, in my case the lawn. It is not just that the non-mental representation thought of as a whole can be traced to the object as a whole, but that each bit of the representation can be traced to a bit of the object. Non-mental representation stands to the object as the *impression* in the wax stands to the seal. Hence, for what it is worth, just as it is possible to say that the impression is true to the seal, so it is possible to say that the non-mental representation is true to the object.

What this comes to is the idea, to which we shall return, that the second of the two relations in which content stands to object, the representational relation, is to be found in the first, the causal. But if this is what the relation of representation is taken to be, there is indeed a pointlessness in turning to non-mental representations. This is so because there seems no objection to taking content itself as standing in just the same causal relation, or rather causal relations, to the object. That I am not standardly aware of a content, that there are no subjective objects of such awareness – evidently this does not entail that the lawn does not stand to the content as the seal stands to the impression in the wax. There is, with respect to a certain bit of my content, the bit of the lawn near the maple tree, and so on.

There is an additional and stronger reason for not turning away from the content itself to retinal images, neural configurations or anything else. To some, I think, the question of the nature of perceptual content is unimportant. This is so partly because their general concern is the explanation of behaviour. Further, however, they suppose in an unreflective way that an explanation can be provided in terms of objects of perception, such as the lawn, and non-mental representations. The general concern is one we must all share. No account of the mind can have attention which includes no explanation of behaviour. But what of the opinion, that we can get to such an explanation without paying attention to the nature of perceptual content?

The recommended enterprise has no chance of success, if success consists in a full explanation of behaviour. This is so since the enterprise begins from epiphenomenalism – which doctrine is *not* supported by or assumed by neuroscience, as is sometimes supposed. Epiphenomenalism is one of the few things about us that really does seem false. Among criteria to be satisfied by accounts of the mind, one is the criterion of mental indispensability. My experience of seeing the lawn is an indispensable part of the explanation of my subsequent linguistic behaviour, my remark on it. *It* is a cause of the remark. That is not to say, exactly, that a full explanation of behaviour must include a satisfactory account of the nature of experiences, and in particular their contents, that we need to go on puzzling about them forever. What it must include is a reference to them. Still, there is not much security in a kind of mere gesturing at a part of an *explanans*.

That is not the only additional reason for attending to the question of the nature of perceptual content. We may actually want to know that nature, independently of our interest in the explanation of behaviour. I do, and, to be bold, I say everybody does, or anyway every philosopher of mind. Those who seem to be uninterested in what is sometimes called the ontological question are better described as put off because they see no hope of getting an answer, or simply are attracted to a research-area which intersects with a part of contemporary science. It is easy to sympathize with them, but not easy to join them.

4   Representative Contents as Impressions

To glance back, we began by assuming that a content stands in two relations to its object, or the world, a causal one and a representative one. The assumption in its second part was taken to require what we do not have, subjective objects of standard awareness. We then contemplated non-mental representations. But these have no greater worth, whatever it is, in preserving the idea of representation, than content itself. Their relevant character, their character of being impressions, can presumably be had by content itself.

That contents are impressions, further, like the fact that anything else is an impression, is no more than the fact that they are certain effects, no more than the fact that perceptual objects are their causes. The question to which we come, then, is this: Does a content really stand in but one relation to its object, that of being caused by it? To put the question differently, can we explain the representativeness of content just by its being an impression?

In fact the move is attractive. If we escape being mesmerized by talk of representation, and ask ourselves what real relations *could* hold between a lawn and a spatio-temporal content, what answer is tolerable other than causation? But can we make this move only if we also try something else? It seems so since a content's being an impression is not sufficient to explain representativeness. There are two objections to supposing that being an impression is sufficient.

First, it is plain that there is some fundamental and relevant distinction between the content of my experience and other effects of an object, say the effect of the lawn that is its photograph, or the effect it has on the subsoil, even when those effects are impressions, as in the two cases mentioned. It is a difference that drives us to say that experiences are *of* things, and intend by that word more than that the experiences stand to the things as impressions to causes.

More particularly, the difference puts us under pressure to say content is representative where that somehow comes to more than saying that it is the impression of the object. As you will gather, it seems to me that we would also have been under this same pressure if we had persevered with only non-mental representations. It is not just that there is a pointlessness in turning to non-mental representations, and that it gets us into epiphenomenalism. Impressions of whatever kind are not enough.

There is a second objection with the same upshot. What we are contemplating is that the content of my experience, simply in being an impression of the lawn, is in virtue of that sufficient fact a representation of the lawn. It seems this cannot be right, as others must have noted. The content is *also* precisely an impression of my retinal image. Morever, it is an impression in the given sense, to speak quickly, of every cross-section of a certain causal line linking the lawn and the content. But we are trying to explain a relation just to the lawn. What the content represents is just the lawn.

Is there an overlooked argument, by the way, that content's being an impression is not even necessary to representation? It consists in the seeming fact noted at the very beginning. There is a conceivable situation, it seems, where my visual cortex and so on is the same, my experience is indistinguishable from my ordinary experience in seeing the lawn, and there is no lawn. In this extraordinary case there would certainly be the fact of representation. Some will say quickly that *ex hypothesi* the content is not an impression. Well, it is not an impression of a lawn there and then. Can we make it an impression of an earlier lawn or whatever? I shall not linger over this now, and not abandon the idea that representation involves causation.

5   Help from Subject and Content, and Unmediated Awareness?

What must come to mind is the idea that we try to shed light on what we have been calling the representative nature of content by reflecting on the relation of this effect to something other than its cause. We have already supposed that content does stand in another relation. The content of a visual experience is somehow related to another part of the experience, given the name of the subject. A visual experience shares this character with all mental events.

Putting aside for a time our motive for looking at this relation, what can be said of it? To take a bit further what has been said already, it seems in some way impossible that there could be a content without a subject. Also, it seems as impossible that there could be a subject without some content or other, sensory or otherwise. A mental event consists in a certain duality. At a first approximation, it consists in the interdependent existence of subject and content.

To discern only this, however, is to think of no more than a kind of necessary connection which also joins things in the non-mental world. To take the subject-content connection as nomic or lawlike, which presumably it is, is not yet to have any distinction between it and, say, the connection between properties of a gas. If I recall subject and content in my thought a moment ago of Baden, or in my sensation in my knee, there is more to it than the necessary connection.

Shall we try to conjecture at this point that the relation between subject and content is one of standard awareness? That the content is the subject's object of standard awareness? What is to be said against the conjecture is not exactly what was said earlier, that I, a person, am not aware in this way of a subjective object in seeing the lawn. A subject is not a person, and it is conceptually possible that persons are not standardly aware of subjective objects but subjects are.

The present conjecture is to be abandoned, however, for essentially the same reason as with the earlier one. It introduces into our mental lives more than we can find there. To subject and content-as-object it adds a middle term. Also and differently, it introduces an awareness relation into the analysis of the same kind of awareness relation – the latter exemplified by my awareness of the lawn. Finally, if we were to take awareness to require something like a person, which we have not, the conjecture would call for a series of homunculi. We need not pursue that.

Does the relation of subject to content nevertheless have something to do with awareness, some fact that can have that name? Shall we take the course of saying that subject stands to content as content stands to object? That is not in accord with what we have bravely discerned, an interdependence of a certain kind between subject and content. It is not part of what was discerned that a *particular* content is necessary to the existence of a subject. But if subject stood to content as content stands to object, then precisely that content would be necessary to the subject-as-content.

To take the given course would also commit us to taking subject as representative of content – taking it to be the case that subject is image-like, word-like, an impression, or some such. That would not be in accord with what we have either. A subject is unitary or featureless. Further, in accordance with our very first conclusion about content's being related to something, making the subject into a content itself would give us another subject, and so on.

We may feel moved at this point to turn to the idea of a kind of awareness different from the standard kind with which we have been concerned. Shall we say, and try to give a certain sense to saying, that in my experience of seeing the lawn, *there is unmediated awareness of content*? That would be precisely not to say that there is any representation of content. On this view there is nothing, in so far as this awareness of content is concerned, as distinct from content itself, which is image-like, word-like, or an impression. The content itself is *given* or *presented*.

The idea under contemplation is that in my experience of seeing the lawn *there is unmediated awareness of content*. That, as you will notice, is to say less than that *a subject is in this way aware of content*. My reluctance to make the seemingly more precise claim is partly a fear of misconception about a self and so on, and partly apprehension about homuncularism. But there is a better if related reason. To make the seemingly more precise claim would be to presuppose that we have more of a grip on a subject than we have, a better idea than we have. That is not all. It seems all too possible that in speaking of unmediated awareness of a content we refer as effectively to the very same fact as we do by speaking of a subject and a subject–content relation. I am inclined to think that is true. Something close to the point was anticipated earlier.[7]

What we are contemplating is that my experience of seeing the lawn included a content that was an impression of the lawn, and, to choose one way of speaking, that there was an unmediated aware-ness of this content. Do we in these considerations have the hope of an analysis or explanation of the representative nature of content?

It was objected above, against taking content as representative to be no more than the fact that it is an impression, that content is an impression of many more things than just the object of the expe-rience. Can we deal with this by supposing that what is required, for something to be a representation, is that there is unmediated awareness of it as an impression of something in particular? Is it the case that what makes the content of my experience representative is just that there is unmediated awareness of it as an effect of a particular cause?

The speculation, whatever else is said of it, might be taken to involve us in another, that my experience of seeing the lawn was in part *a belief*, that the experience included the unmediated belief that a content is an impression of a particular object. That seems to be wrong. The experience of seeing something, although it evidently can give rise to belief in the existence of an object, is not itself one. Various illusions give one reason for this conclusion. I do have a visual experience of lines of different lengths in the Muller-Lyer illusion, but I do not believe that they are of different lengths.[8] Might it be argued that in such a case my experience nevertheless includes *some* belief about the cause of an impression, say the belief that two lines on the page, of whatever length, are causal? If so, consider instead a certain thought-experiment.

Suppose I am now in an extraordinary situation. I know that during each of the next ten minutes I will either be facing the window and seeing the lawn in the ordinary way, or facing the wall and subjected to such cortical stimulation that my experience is indistinguishable from my experience of seeing the lawn in the ordinary way. I also know now that I will have no way of telling, in any minute, whether I am facing window or wall. If I do know these things now, or even just believe them, I will at no time during the ten minutes believe that there is a lawn in front of me, or that they have a certain effect. I will at all times have the same experience but I will at no time have the belief we have been contemplating. It is hard to see any objection to the conclusion, so to speak, that seeing is not and does not include believing.

So we cannot suppose that my experience of seeing the lawn includes *believing* the content to have been caused by the lawn. If unmediated awareness is part of the story of my seeing the lawn, there must be some other characterization of it. Does it include *a datum that is not a belief*? That is baffling, but actually has the right ring. Suppose we were able to get a characterization. Would what we then had, unmediated awareness of a content as an impression of something in particular, be sufficient for representation?

Any inclination to say yes must be reluctant. Since the content is in fact an impression of many more things than the lawn, why should there be awareness of it as an impression of the lawn in particular? The idea seems to involve some supposition having to do with what might be called *a chosen interpretation*. The content is regarded as an effect of one part of its causal history as against others. Is the story not too complex? Does it not make too much of seeing the lawn? Is there not too much going on? Might it not be said that what has been called into existence – awareness-as – must be doubtful since it requires an explanation which we cannot give?

Let us leave these unsatisfactory reflections on representation for a time. Can we hope to get further ahead in the end by looking at our subject-matter very differently? In any case, we can feel a compulsion to do so.

6 The Givenness of the World

The tangled story we have been contemplating is that my visual experience consisted in an unmediated awareness of a content, which awareness was not a belief but was of what might be called a datum, and this awareness somehow involved the content taken as a particular impression, an impression of just the lawn.

The story can for a time seem not only unsatisfactory and tangled but in part plainly false. If I think of my experience of seeing the lawn a moment ago, I can recoil from this talk of awareness of a peculiar content as a particular impression. I can feel impelled to say that *the lawn* was given or presented. What was given or presented was no mental thing or fact, but the lawn. If I can manage, as it seems I can, to mingle with an ongoing visual experience the question of what it is that is given or presented, the answer to which I can feel impelled is that it is precisely the object of the experience.

It seems that if our goal is really to characterize visual experience, and in particular to get hold of the fact of representation, we cannot ignore this impulse. It is an impulse that has been fundamental to resistance to phenomenalism, resistant to the foisting of sense-data on us. We are against phenomenalism, those many of us who are, not only because some phenomenalists have had in mind standard awareness of subjective things, and thus overpopulated the mind. We are against it because it offends against the impulse to take ourselves somehow to be given or presented with, to possess or encompass, exactly the objects of our experiences. Phenomenalism continues to offend if it is improved by having unmediated awareness of purely personal items put in the place of standard awareness. It continues to put each of us in solitary confinement, each of us alone in a personal cell.

Whatever the fact of the subjectivity of consciousness comes to, it does not come to this. The fact of subjectivity, whatever it is, must be a thing consistent with the impulse that we are in touch with things, or rather, that they are in touch with us.

It seems entirely unsatisfactory to suppose that *our conviction of the givenness of objects*, so to name it, is to be written off as just owed to a mistake. Hume began this tradition, with the proposition that the vulgar, and indeed all of us when we are not engaged in philosophical reflection, mistakenly *identify* content and object.[9] Our natures are so constituted that we go in for this life-long blunder. The difficulty with this is that when we do have a clearer view of things, and see that the content of an experience cannot be identical with its object, we do with respect to ordinary circumstances persist in the conviction.

That is not the only unsatisfactory response to the conviction of the givenness of objects. There are two more.

First, it is unsatisfactory to resist the question, the seeming contradiction, raised by the conviction. We resist it by saying that the conviction about objects is a matter of subjectivity or first-person nature or of the *having* of a visual experience, while the awareness-of-content story we have of the experience is from an outside perspective – from the perspective in which we take our experiences themselves as objects. In fact, as it seems to me, despite so much that is said of self-consciousness, it is only from the outside perspective that we have *any* view of our experience, and from this perspective we have *both* views, one in terms of the awareness of content, one in terms of the givenness of objects.[10]

Second, there can surely be no gain in supposing with William James that our conviction of the givenness of objects is somehow owed to there being a relation between content and object wholly different from anything so far mentioned.[11] This would be that there really is one *ur*-item, a neutral thing, such that we can choose to regard it as object or as content – as having either properties we assign to lawns or properties of contents. This comes to saying that philosophical idealism is possibly true. The supposition of idealism, it seems to me, destroys the relevant part of our conceptual scheme, destroys too much of our conceptual scheme. That is, if we try to take the ur-item to be content, we face the disaster that it is not of anything. It is not an effect of and representative of anything. Idealism doesn't merely subtract the world from what there is. It also subtracts experience itself.

The conviction of the givenness of objects can indeed give rise to thinking that the story about visual experience consisting in unmediated awareness of a content as an impression is plainly false. In fact the conviction must lead us not to abandon but to alter the story. Givenness isn't *another* relation. There isn't another independent story to be told of my experience of seeing the lawn. We need to enlarge or amend the story we have been contemplating in order to make it consistent with the conviction of the givenness of objects.

The conviction is that content does not get between us and the world, but is access to the world or delivers it to us – content isn't opaque, but transparent. It seems that we can give more sense to such talk by rewriting it into three related propositions.

7   Contents as Transparent

The first is a denial of the idea that visual experience involves *any awareness whatever, of any kind, of content*. Content is simply not any kind of object of awareness. In particular, we need to put something else in place of the idea of unmediated awareness of content. Consider just having the thought of something, perhaps my having a thought of Baden as it was. What I think about is that village. In thinking about it, am I aware of, in any sense, anything but the village? As others will have said, it seems not. The thought occurs. *It* is not something of which there is then any awareness. So with the desire for a glass of wine, or a pain. Here too I just have it. Given what has been said, should we not regard the content of my experience of seeing the lawn, despite its evident difference, as being of a related character?[12]

That is something, but not enough. Altering our ideas in this first way removes something of the barrier we have put in the way of the world's being given to us. Content no longer has exactly a nature or role which pre-theoretically we assign to the world. But, to succumb to another metaphor, it seems possible to say the world is still located *behind* content. Despite what we are now supposing, object remains *behind* content.

I admit being attracted to a once-familiar and and obscure proposition in order to try to accommodate our resistance to what is conveyed by the metaphor. *A visual content is a presentation of an object, a presentation of the world. In visual experience I have unmediated awareness of the object. To have a visual content is to be directly aware of an object*. This cannot be to understand a visual content and the having of it in terms of a seeming presentation of objects or anything of the sort. This cannot be just more of ideas, sense-data, qualia and so on – so-called subjective items. A visual content presents and thus presupposes objective reality.

For visual experience generally, such as the ordinary case of my seeing the lawn out the window, something like this seems right. Something like this seems right for almost all of our experience, which surely should strengthen our resolve. But you will of course remember the extraordinary case with which we began, and to which we returned. It seems I might have an identical experience without the lawn. It is such a fact which has led very many philosophers away from what they have been tempted to, which is the obscure and radical view that what happens when we see things is that they really are presented to us. We don't *see things*, where that is a matter of awareness of merely subjective or personal things, but rather we see *things*, where that is a matter of objects being presented, our having direct awareness of them.

Evidently there is a choice to be made. Each of two courses we can take is frustrating, but, to my mind, one is more frustrating than the other.

We take the first course by being struck by the extraordinary case and then reasoning traditionally as follows – embracing the argument from illusion. There is something the same in the extraordinary case and the ordinary case, and in the extraordinary case there is no lawn. Hence what is the same must be something subjective. We then end up with the maximal frustration of solitary confinement in our subjective cells – even if they are cells to which our relation is no longer conceived as any kind of awareness. We end up in phenomenalism, a futile struggle against our conviction of the givenness of objects.

The second course takes us actually to be presented with objects in the ordinary case, allows that there is something the same in the extraordinary case, and commits us to explaining how there can be presentation of objects in the extraordinary case. The enterprise, anticipated earlier (p. 115) is perhaps not so absurd as it seems at first. We *can* suppose something other than that there is *no* presentation of objects in the extraordinary case. We can suppose that there is what can be called a distorted presentation. What are the objects? We shall certainly have to do some hunting. We can look at the large category of ordinary objects which includes earlier lawns.

This sort of enterprise does have precedents. We are subject to many of what have been called illusions in the tradition of phenomenalism: the distant tower looking small, the elliptical coin, the bent stick in water, the Muller-Lyer lines, the tepid bath which is warm to the cold hand, mirages, the wax dummy seen as a person. In all or many such cases, there is the distorted presentation of an object. Is it impossible to say that in the extraordinary case, where there is no lawn, the difference is that there is more and different distortion, including temporal distortion?

Here is a reinforcing thought. At any early point in these reflections, we rejected the idea of standard awareness of subjective objects. That overpopulated the mind. We have lately abandoned unmediated awareness of subjective objects. We are left with the occurrence of content, which is something like the having of a thought, and content's being an impression of object. That seems to leave out everything in the way of awareness, and that cannot be right. We do need something like the presentation of objects. Also, and quite as important, we need something which has certain properties, say being green and dendritic.

The third proposition in our conviction of the givenness of objects is the existence of the world. We are in fact convinced that a general scepticism about its existence is impossible. It is notable that all of us, however successful we take ourselves to be in acting on it, are under the impulse to *refute* global scepticism. This accords with the slight account we now have of visual experience, even if visual experience does not consist in belief.

It will not be forgotten that the main reflections in this faltering paper have been mainly directed to explaining the representativeness of content. Is there now more hope? It would be agreeable to think so. Evidently the additional hope would have most to do with the second proposition within the conviction of the givenness of objects. But it is plain that I have failed to say anything positive and useful of content conceived as a presentation of an object, content as involving direct awareness of object. What might charitably be called other loose ends remain. The world's being presented, direct awareness, is somehow a matter of what was first spoken of as the subject-content relation. But how? There is the lesser question of what, in visual experience, is to be put in place of belief.

Let me return for just a moment to the two objections to the idea that content, whatever is to be said of what was called the subject's relation to it, is to be explained as just an impression.

There is the small consolation that we can distinguish content from other impressions of the lawn, say its photograph. This we do by saying that content is an impression of which it is also true that it is *had*, in the way that a thought is had, and so on. Sadly, this *having* and what goes with it is obscure.

As for the objection that content is an impression of more things than the object, it does again seem that we have no hope of explaining particular representativeness by reflecting on just the causal line from object to content. It cannot be, so to speak, that an end itself of a causal line gives greater importance to one of its previous stages as against others. The only hope is in reflection on the having of content and the new story that goes with it.

Notes

1. Franz Brentano, *Psychology from an Empirical Standpoint*, eds O. Kraus and L. McAlister(Routledge & Kegan Paul, 1973), p. 97.
2. I draw the line before we get to 'act' and content. An act, presumably, requires an inner agent – of which thing, like Hume, I have no glimpse.
3. My confidence in these propositions about a subject was reinforced by a chapter in Alastair Hannay's *Human Consciousness* (Routledge, 1990). Perhaps my confidence was not so determined as his when he writes 'that there is a subject side is unquestionable' (p. 65). But his admirable scrutiny of views more audacious than mine, some of them exhilarating, did much to persuade me that there is the subject of a subject. No doubt there is room in philosophy for a kind of inductive argument which has as its premise the existence, as distinct from exactly the truth, of a sizeable body of philosophical views.
4. In connection with the two relations, subject-content and content-object, although he does not speak explicitly of the first one, Searle writes as follows in *The Rediscovery of the Mind*: 'One can never just be conscious, rather when one is conscious, there must be an answer to the question "What is one conscious of?" But the "of" of "conscious of" is not always the "of" of intentionality.' (p. 84; cf. pp. 130–1) That brevity, if that is what it is, is misleading. The 'of' that has to do with a relation between subject and content is *never* the 'of' of intentionality, which has to do with the relation between content and object. Every conscious event involves something which prompts use of the first 'of'. Only many conscious events also or in addition involve the second 'of'.
5. See A. J. Ayer, *The Central Questions of Philosophy* (Weidenfeld & Nicolson, 1973), pp. 80–1. The argument is considered, maybe dealt with, in part of my 'Seeing Qualia and Positing the World', in A. Phillips Griffiths (ed.), *A. J. Ayer Memorial Essays* (Cambridge University Press, 1991).
6. F. Dretske, *Knowledge and the Flow of Information* (MIT Press, 1981).

7. See above, p. 109. Hannay's reflections on a subject in *Human Consciousness* do, I think, involve the hope I have been considering, that representation can have light thrown on it by ideas with respect to a subject. Perhaps a possibility of progress exists in what he has to say of a system of concepts or rules which form a subject's experiential repertoire (p. 77). As the rest of my paper indicates, I cannot myself see a clear way forward.

8. Tim Crane, 'The Non-Conceptual Content of Perception', in *The Contents of Experience: Essays on Perception*, ed. Crane (Cambridge University Press, 1992).

9. *A Treatise of Human Nature*, bk 1, pt 4, sect. 2.

10. cf. J. J. Valberg, *The Puzzle of Experience* (Oxford University Press, 1992).

11. *Essays in Radical Empiricism* (Longmans Green, 1912).

12. I have struggled to say something useful of the distinctiveness of perceptual content in 'Seeing Qualia and Positing the World' (see Note 5).

Chapter Seven

Consciousness as the Existence of a World

You can get fed up with putting up with problems, including philosophical problems. You can get fed up not because the problems become boring, although they can, but because your attempts to deal with them remain arguable or assertible but less than satisfactory. At the end of the last chapter but one, to take a good example, we arrived at the proposition that our conscious or mental events are events in heads, physical events, but not the neural events of our existing neuroscience.

The proposition, if it can seem forced upon us, is a little outrageous, partly because it is a kind of science-fiction. This sort of thing is indeed the stock-in-trade of some of the current science of consciousness – for example the wonderful bit that proposes to dispel the mystery of consciousness by adding to it the greater mystery of a self-contradictory interpretation of Quantum Theory. Science-fiction is not philosophy. Philosophy, surely, should not be dealing in funny properties, even if a situation of extremity can call up a moment of braveness in their defence.

Moreover, the idea that mental events are as-yet-unknown physical events in heads is unsatisfactory in innocently assuming that those physical events will not have the disability of the physical events we know. If the conception of consciousness in terms only of the neural events we know leaves something out, will some future conception in terms of other physical events not have the same disability? They'll be in the same heads. They'll have *something* to do with transmitter-substance and action potentials, won't they? Maybe a lot.

That is not the only worry about the proposition of funny events. You can slow down and consider a certain question, with a certain effect. Is your consciousness, whatever it is, *in your head*? Is your consciousness, whatever material or events it consists of, *in there*, like the transmitter-substances? If you are like the rest of the world, or the sample of it known to me, which includes neuroscientists, you will at least be reluctant to answer Yes. Whatever the source or reason for the reluctance, it certainly does exist. You may say your reason is that consciousness doesn't seem to be the sort of thing that can make the answer Yes comfortable.

So much for one example of a proposition you can get fed up with. There are other responses to problems, a lot of them, that are not entirely comfortable. No doubt you have a few on a list, but there is no need to survey all the possibilities now. They have something in common. They can tempt you to try to turn the whole subject around, or turn yourself around, or anyway to relocate something in the subject, or see something as something else. There is the chance that if you do, old problems and unsatisfactory responses to them may disappear, whatever comes into view in their place.

But it is not just that we can and should get fed up with responses to a problem that are nagging or worse. Sometimes in doing philosophy we can and should be struck by something different. We should let ourselves be struck. In this present inquiry of ours, we can and maybe should be struck by something different in answer to another clear and more general question. It has been part of our struggle up until now even if it was not made explicit. 'What is my consciousness right now like?' That is the question, but there are also closely related ones. 'What is the nature of this fact that I'm in or that pertains to me – if I put aside distractions, can't it be got into focus?' Or, to settle for a less audacious question, 'What, anyway, *seems* to be the fact of my consciousness now?'

That is enough introduction to the paper below, and, for the moment, to what goes with this paper, the rest of this book. The paper and the rest of the book depend very greatly on what has preceded them – the unsatisfactoriness to one extent or another of other views of consciousness, neural functionalism above all. It is not too much to say that this unsatisfactoriness is at least half of the argument for the theory of *Consciousness as Existence*. But the theory does not really grow out of the past. For good or bad, it is a new start, at any rate to those of us not at home in the history of philosophy.

It was foreshadowed in the paper you last read, unknown to the author. But 'Seeing Things' turns out to have been a departure-lounge, not the first stage of some travelling, maybe flying.

---

1   Leaving Consciousness Out, or Trying To

The difference for present purposes between ourselves and stones, chairs and our computers is that we are conscious. The difference is fundamental. Being conscious is sufficient for having a mind in one sense of the word 'mind', and being conscious is necessary and fundamental to having a mind in any decent sense. *What* is this difference between ourselves and stones, chairs and our computers? The question is not meant to imply that there is a conceptual or a nomic barrier in the way of non-biological things being conscious. It may happen one decade that the other-minds problem – the problem of proving that others or other things are conscious – will shoot up the philosophical agenda. It will get a lot of attention as a result of a wonderful computer attached to perceptual and behavioural mechanisms – which thing will in the end be taken as conscious, rightly. Our question is not what things can be conscious, but what the property or nature of consciousness is.

Conscious or mental events, as we know them now, are in some kind of necessary connection with neural events. This fact of psychoneural intimacy, which is consistent with what has just been said of the possibility of non-biological things being conscious, provides the best argument for the real identity theories of consciousness with which we have been concerned. These take the property of consciousness to be a neural property, or, as we can say instead, take conscious events to have only neural properties. The objection to these theories seems to me not that they make conscious events physical, exactly that. What disposes many of us against real identity theories is of course that our experience of conscious events, the having of them, leaves us thinking that they have a property or nature other than the properties or nature had by wholly neural events – transmitter-substance properties and so on. Real identity theories leave something out.[1]

They seem to leave out not something elusive, or something diaphanous, or something peripheral, but the reality of our mental lives. They leave out the most immediate of all the facts we know.

Hence almost all of us feel that psychoneural intimacy must be accommodated by a means other than asserting that conscious events have only neural properties. All other identity theories, the lenient or arguable ones such as Anomalous Monism and also the Union Theory, all of which bear the slight burden of also being called property-dualisms, raise the very question we are considering. They allow that consciousness brings in something non-neural. What is it?

Conscious or mental events as we know them also have causal roles. That is, they stand in many kinds of necessary connections with input and output. Some desires stand in necessary connection with things that have been perceived and with the subsequent behaviour of acquiring things. Some pain stands in necessary connection with certain sensory stimuli and with avoiding things or getting away from them. There are also distinctive connections in the case of perception and thinking. Here is a respectable and daunting subject-matter in itself, the standard connections to and from mental events, worth the diligence invested in it by many cognitive scientists.

The basic fact, conscious events being characterizable as many kinds of effects and causes, is also used to provide the argument for functionalism and philosophical cognitive science. These doctrines, as you know, are distinguished by taking conscious events in general to be nothing more than the many kinds of effects and causes. But, I remind you, stones, chairs and our computers, considered in themselves, also involve standard events that are kinds of effects and causes. More relevant, you may think, are also certain events in *us*. There is the event of, say, my own unnoticed little gain in weight, which never comes to my mind.

How did functionalism and philosophical cognitive science even separate off irrelevant events, in particular irrelevant events in us, from mental events? Nothing is more essential to the doctrines. We need to know what they are talking about. Put differently, what *is* their general conception of consciousness? Giving us such a thing is exactly what they are supposed to be doing. They are not supposed to be assuming we know, gesturing, going on as if we already have the answer to the large philosophical question, the one in hand.

You may be made uneasy by such scepticism about what a lot of philosophers take to be unavoidable good sense – you may be made uneasy by what the scepticism could lead to. Your concern will not be reduced by hearing that what is missed out by the theories we have glanced at is the reality of consciousness or subjectivity, which things are certainly not really clear. Are we departing towards some thinking that is going to be permanently elusive, maybe best discussed with the aid of faded doctrines of mind traceable back to old Vienna? Not merely humanistic rather than scientific but all too humanistic? Thinking that is too close to metaphor and maunder?

You may uneasily suppose, differently, that the picture in the offing, given my physicalism avowed at the start, will be of our heads having two kinds of properties or events in them, the first being neural and the second non-neural although physical. Properties of the second kind are perhaps not rightly to be abused as ghostly stuff or material, but they are bad enough. The idea is that there exist properties or events which, although physical and in the causal and nomic web, are not akin to neural kinds now accepted, but properties or events whose actual discovery would transform or conceivably overturn neuroscience as it is. If this idea is something you may be driven to contemplate (p. 100), it is surely much too strange and adventurous.

Maybe you can be reassured in advance. That is, I hope it will be possible to maintain what is unquestionable, that conscious events have more than neural properties and particular causal relations, and do so *without* adding to the kinds of properties or events we already know to be in our heads. Those are the kinds allowed in contemporary neuroscience. Further, since conscious events will be taken to involve more than what goes on inside heads, I hope the view will not add to the kinds of properties and events we already know to be outside our heads. Those are roughly the kinds allowed by ordinary experience and contemporary science.

What is needed is not more things, but a different way of categorizing, conceptualizing or looking at the ones we have.

2   The Existence of a World

The difference between me now and a chair in this room, it can be said, is that for me a world exists, and for the chair a world does not exist. Or rather, as I prefer to say, *my consciousness now consists in the existence of a world*. The rest of this paper will have to do with understandings of this seemingly metaphorical sentence. It is owed to contemplating consciousness directly, despite its obscurity. This policy of mental realism unsettles some philosophers in the current philosophy of mind, since they are averse not only to dualisms which no one should contemplate,[2] but also to the seeming mystery that is the fundamental question of the nature of consciousness.

But you, if you are in a way stronger-minded, may share the hope that the sentence points in the right direction, does indicate the nature of consciousness. That is, the sentence may express more than one proposition, and the hope is that one of them, certainly a literal one, will really shed light on the nature of consciousness. It seems to me that trying to dissipate this mystery is better than recoiling from it.

The sentence can naturally be taken for another one. It is that *all* of my consciousness now, including any thoughts unprompted by this room, maybe some day-dreaming, consists in the existence of a world. Perhaps we can on some later occasion get to an account of consciousness generally, or all of the consciousness of one person, which is pointed to by that sentence. But let me limit myself here to something else, my *perceptual* consciousness now – my consciousness in so far as it consists in my seeing, hearing, and so on. So what we have is that *my perceptual consciousness now consists in the existence of a world*. Let us think about only this, and trust, as seems reasonable, and in accord with several philosophical traditions, that perceptual experience is the base of all consciousness, and that on some other day an understanding of it will be used to explain the rest.

Thinking of my perceptual experience now as consisting in the existence of a world needs to be distinguished from and may be more promising than another piece of mental realism, a well-known one. In this, to revert to it, my perceptual consciousness is characterized as part or most of *what it is like to be something,* or *what it feels like to be something.*[3] As you know, what strikes me as wrong with these locutions if they are intended seriously, as being on the way to a general understanding of consciousness and of course not just about differences between conscious things or states, is that the *analysandum* is right there in each of the *analysans.*

The locutions surely presuppose and depend for their understanding on what some supporters of them assert, that there is not something that is what it is like to be a stone, chair, or computer, and of course not something which is what it feels like to be one.[4] Does the familiar piece of mental realism not come to this, then, that my perceptual consciousness is characterized as part or most of what it is like *to be conscious,* or *to feel conscious?* This is of no use to us, no analytic help.

But does the sentence I am promoting, 'My perceptual consciousness now consists in the existence of a world', share a quite different disability with talk of what it is like or feels like to be something? (I postpone for a little while the very large question of whether it shares the first disability, being no analytic help.) You may grant that conceiving of my perceptual consciousness as amounting to the existence of a world points at something, indicates the nature of something. But, you may say, that thing, as in the case of talk of what it is or feels like to be something, is only the *phenomenology* of consciousness. It is only consciousness as it seems or appears to be, not the reality of it. This objection may amount to one of several things.

It may simply be insistence on a real identity theory or strict functionalism and philosophical cognitive science as the truth about consciousness. Asserting that something is illusory is commonly no more than or little more than asserting that something else is the whole story. Or perhaps what we have is an identity doctrine lightly amended by something about *qualia*. The latter over-worked items, I take it, are elusive differences between kinds of perceptual consciousness.[5] They are 'feels' rather than contents, or more of the nature of 'feels' than of contents, and very evidently not the character of all of consciousness.

These amended and lenient doctrines, as you will anticipate, have not been sufficiently amended to satisfy me and many others. They too leave out an explicit and general account of what is fundamental about consciousness. As you will gather, my sentence about the existence of a world is not an assertion of the existence of qualia. No doubt they exist, but they are not the general nature of perceptual consciousness.

If the phenomenology objection fails when taken in this way, is there a better way? Is there a better reason than the given doctrines for dismissing my sentence as only talk of the appearance of consciousness?

Well, the dismissal may be misleadingly expressed, but be intended as conveying that there is some other fact about consciousness more important than anything conveyed by the sentence – say the relation of conscious to neural events, or the causation of consciousness, or the role of consciousness in the explanation of behaviour. There is also the truth already indicated, which strict functionalism and philosophical cognitive science wonderfully exceeded, that kinds of conscious events, say desire, pain and thinking, and sub-kinds of them, are differentiated by their causal connections, and could not be characterized adequately without reference to those connections. But surely none of this, although it involves disagreements about what is important, amounts to the proposition that the general conception of consciousness we are contemplating is of only the appearance of it, not its reality.

In fact this proposition, if taken literally and not as a misleading expression of other things, seems to presuppose a falsehood. It is that we can attach sense to talk of *a reality-behind* or *a reality-underneath* with respect to consciousness itself. Things, say stones, chairs, and computers, may of course be otherwise than they seem, but that is not a distinction *within* consciousness. The distinction presupposes consciousness, our having different views of things, but what it has to do with or is about is the chairs, stones and computers.

If we stick to consciousness, is it not the case that *all* there is, in so far as it itself is concerned, is what is being misdescribed as an appearance? Is it not the case that all there is, in so far as consciousness itself is concerned, is what is pointed to by my sentence and perhaps related ones, and also, despite its disability, by talk of what it is or feels like to be something? Consciousness, after all, is what we *have*. And what we don't have in this sense isn't consciousness. Also, we don't have *it* in two ways. Certainly we can't get behind or under or beyond consciousness itself by introspection or recollection and bring back a hidden part of *it*. There isn't any other experiential access to it than the single one we've all got.

The only conceivable other access, so to speak, would be a theory about *it*. But, so far as I know, we haven't had any philosophically successful theory about it, the reality of it, as distinct from about its causation, explanatory role, other relations, kinds of it and their differentiation, secondary features of it, and so on. The theories that do seem to be about consciousness itself, having to do with aboutness or intentionality, cannot be regarded as successful. None has come to the fore.

A final thing is worth adding – something implied by what has just been said. If there are ways or techniques of bringing things into consciousness, perhaps dispositions of ours of which we have been unaware, these are not a different access to consciousness itself. As for those very dispositions, often called the subconscious or the unconscious, evidently they are not *in* or part of consciousness. No doubt they are neural. To repeat, what we don't *have* isn't consciousness, and we don't have it in more ways than one.

So much for the objection that my sentence points at only the phenomenology of consciousness.[6] Let me now make a start on the inevitable objection postponed a little way back – that the sentence about a world is of no analytic help.

Saying that my perceptual consciousness now consists in the existence of a world, if this is understood in certain ways, will indeed be of no help. For a start, it cannot usefully come to just this, that my perceptual consciousness consists in my seeing, hearing, and otherwise sensing what exists around me spatio-temporally. If the sentence is taken this way, it will be useless, a really overt instance of the *analysandum* turning up as the *analysans*, the *analysans* being no advance on the *analysandum*. We already understand perceptual consciousness to be seeing, hearing and otherwise sensing spatio-temporal things. That is the ordinary content of talk about percep-tual consciousness. That is what we are trying to improve on.

This objection of uselessness, of course, is likely to come up for a particular reason. Perceptual consciousness, according to the sen-tence, is *the existence of* a world. Furthermore, it was first said above that the difference between me and a chair is that *for me* a chair ex-ists. Both those sentences can indeed be taken to suggest that the idea is that perceptual consciousness is more than a world – it is the world's *existing*. Or the world's *existing for me*. And, the thought continues, all that *that* can mean is that the consciousness consists in a world's being seen, heard, and so on. Well, that is not the hope. There is some heuristic advantage in saying, as I shall sometimes persist in saying, that perceptual consciousness is the existence of a world – that might just wake us up to something we have been missing or mislaying or looking at in only one way. But no more is being suggested than is also suggested by saying, simply, that *perceptual consciousness consists in a world*.

There is something else to be put aside. We would not get anything useful by interpreting my sentence as taking perceptual conscious-ness to consist in awareness of what we call subjective or personal things – representations, sense-data, or the like. This would amount to giving the particular account of perceptual consciousness. That is the representative or sense-data theory of perception or phenom-enalism. My reason for saying that giving this account would not help is not that to do so would be to impose on the sentence a theory supported only by doubtful arguments, although this is surely true, and my thinking so will inform some later comments.

The reason we would get nowhere is that in this interpretation of the sentence, what we would have is that perceptual consciousness is *awareness*, if in an obscure sense. But it is indeed awareness that we are trying to understand. 'Awareness' in the obscure sense is not synonymous with 'perceptual consciousness', but it is too close for comfort. We would get no understanding of perceptual conscious-ness itself by being directed away from certain objects of it, objective ones, and towards other supposed objects of it, subjective ones.

This reason for not imposing the representative theory on our sentence is equally a reason for not imposing on it direct or naive realism, the theory that grows out of what was mentioned a moment ago, the ordinary content of talk about perceptual consciousness. The theory is to the effect that perceptual consciousness consists not in the awareness of subjective but rather of objective things. Let us say that such things, unlike representations and sense-data, are public, which is to say perceivable by more than one person, and are perceivable by more than one sense, and also exist unperceived.[7] Plainly this different theory, first of all in speaking of awareness, also contains the problem. We need to approach the problem on our own.

3   A Mental World?

It happens near the start of our lives that each of us does what each continues to do afterwards, distinguish herself or himself in a particular way from all else, all other things and persons. Each of us comes into possession of the fact of something unique and persistent in a life, certainly not a body, or all of a body. Each of us comes to have some kind of sense of something like a subject, self, person, or other uniqueness – a sense of oneself, as we can uncommittedly say. This claim can be true, of course, without our having a respectable theory of consciousness or relying on daring philosophical theories of the self. We do not have to swallow Descartes in order to have senses of ourselves or of something apart from other things.

More will be said about a subject later, but let us for the moment rely on what we all have – in order to state the first of five considerations bearing on what has been said so far and seeming to point in a particular direction, an unhappy one.

1. The particular subject each of us senses enters into the existence of a world, a person's perceptual consciousness as I understand it, in a certain way. The essential thing for now is that this state of affairs could not exist in the absence of the subject. The particular subject is somehow a necessary condition of the state of affairs. It is so because it is in some manner a part of it. But that is not all. In the absence of the subject, there would not exist anything of the world whose existence is what perceptual consciousness consists in.

Such a dependency on a particular subject is not true of three larger worlds. They are different. The first is the one that is *physical* in the sense mentioned earlier (p. 22). This is the world, of which much will be said, that is spatio-temporal and has perceived properties or is spatio-temporal and is in nomic connection with things that have perceived properties. This world of two levels does not have the mentioned dependency. The part that is perceived is not dependent on any particular subject. And the part that isn't perceived is also not dependent on any particular subject – this part doesn't enter into perceptual consciousness at all.

There is the same want of dependency on a particular subject with a second world, with which we shall also be concerned. This is one lately in view, the *objective* world. It has in it things perceivable by more than one person, and perceivable by more than one sense, and such as also to exist unperceived. Evidently it shares a feature or two with the physical world as defined. Finally, there is the same want of dependency on a particular subject with a third world, also in view earlier. This is the world of *things in current or anticipated science*, an indeterminate world to say the least.

Let us call these three worlds mind-independent worlds. The label is not to be taken very seriously, however. The worlds in question may only be *relatively* mind-independent. That one or more of them is coloured is rightly taken to have something to do with our shared perceptual and conceptual history, what you can call the fact of humanness.

Let me make it clear at once that speaking of these various worlds, a world of perceptual consciousness and three others, is not to be taken as indulgence in any sort of ontological extravagance, or even in large and seemingly inflated talk about possibilities of change in *one* world. My talk is not an assertion of the reality of all possible worlds, or even the contemplation of possible worlds. It has nothing to do with those items.

In the primary and most ordinary sense of the word, there is but one world. Of it or of some of it, we have different conceptions. What falls under a conception is, in my secondary sense of the word, a world. My endeavour in this paper, as will become plain, is to see relations between several conceptions and worlds, and to recommend one conception and world in connection with consciousness.

2. There is also another dependency that needs to be attended to. If I take my perceptual consciousness now to consist in the existence of a world, this necessarily is a world that also has a second dependency, seemingly different in kind from the one on a particular subject. It is impossible for me to resist the conclusion that the correct understanding of the fact of psychoneural intimacy mentioned at the start is not the strict identity theory but the theory that consciousness is in nomic or lawlike connection with neural certain events, events with only neural properties. Although the story of the Union Theory gets complicated, part of it is that my perceptual consciousness has a dependency on, has a kind of nomically necessary condition in, my own simultaneous neural events (pp. 61, 23).

So the world that is my perceptual consciousness, for this second reason, cannot be the physical world as understood, or the objective world, or the world indicated by science.

3. There is something else, another part of the story of lawlike connection between consciousness and simultaneous neural events. A neural event, we have it, is not only a kind of necessary condition but also a nomic correlate of a conscious event. That is, although the conscious event is not an effect of the neural event, it is true that given the occurrence of the simultaneous neural event, the conscious event necessarily happened. In a traditional terminology, the neural event was not only a kind of necessary condition for the conscious event, but also a kind of sufficient condition. We can say the neural event was a guarantee of the conscious one.[8]

Of course these considerations having to do with the brain, together with what should be added about dependencies in the other direction, of brain on consciousness, go against such doctrines as Anomalous Monism in their denial of the existence of psychoneural laws (p. 7). But allow me to take psychoneural lawlike connection for granted. If it does not exist, by the way, that will certainly be bad news for neuroscience, since standard neuroscience certainly presupposes it.[9] Should that fact not give pause to any philosopher of mind who wants to keep an eye on science? And on the part of science most relevant to mind, which certainly is not physics? To stick to my subject, however, we have in the neural guarantee a third reason for supposing the world which is my perceptual consciousness certainly cannot be identical with the physical world as understood, or the objective world, or the world indicated by science.

What you will already suppose, very likely, unhappily for me, is that the world in which my perceptual consciousness is being said to consist must be *a mental world*. An *interior world* or a *mind-world*. It is what the dictionary calls the totality of my thoughts and feelings, or all of a class of them. Certainly you need a particular subject for one of these. Maybe such a world *is* a subject. It is such a world, too, that has a person's neural events as a kind of necessary and sufficient condition. And you will say, very truly, that if this is what the speculation about perceptual consciousness comes to, we are back in the *debacle* of having the *analysandum* in the *analysans*. To say that my perceptual consciousness consists in a mental world would be no help at all. But in addition to the three dependencies, another reason or two are likely to occur to you for your disappointment or maybe *Schadenfreude*.

4. Is it not implicit in what has been said of my world of perceptual consciousness, most notably about dependence on a subject, that this

is a *private* world? Is it not the case that what is being postulated, despite the rhetoric, is no more than a multitude of worlds each private to their owner? Well, part of the answer is yes, in a way. You do not have access to my perceptual world. That seems to me no deep proposition, incidentally, nor one that necessarily will be true of those who come after us. There seems no conceptual impossibility or incoherence in the speculation that in some future decade one member of our species will have replicated in her head the neural events of someone else, and so by guarantee have access to what otherwise would have been only the other person's experiences.

Still, the point remains that a world of consciousness is in this way private. This, at least in an ordinary understanding of them, is not true of any of the three mind-independent worlds. The objective world is explicitly said to be perceivable by more than one person.

5. Finally, although it may seem that no more needs to be said in support of the supposition that a world of perceptual consciousness is a mental world, there is the idea that a world of perceptual consciousness, because of the three dependencies, does not exist unperceived. The point is worth separating out from (1) the necessity of a subject to a world. But unperceived existence is an explicit feature of the objective world, and of one part of the physical world, and it is fundamental although implicit in what was said of the world indicated by science.

One burden of five considerations, then, is that the worlds I am promoting, the worlds of perceptual consciousness, are different from and not identical with any of three other worlds. Is there another burden – that the worlds being promoted are no more than mental worlds? And hence that we get no useful understanding, certainly no analysis, of perceptual consciousness? Just talk? Just the rhetorical line that my perceptual consciousness now consists in a mental world?

4   My World of Perceptual Consciousness and the Perceived Physical World

I wonder. There are troublesome facts.

The world in which my present perceptual consciousness seems to consist is surely spatial. That chair over there is bigger than that other one, and to the left of it, and I can measure the distance between them. It's not a *representation* of the first chair that is bigger than a representation of the second, and it's not representations that are relatively positioned in that way or the given distance apart. So with time. In this world of my perceptual consciousness, one thing happens before, simultaneous with, or after another, and things come out of the future into the present and then go into the past. It's not *thoughts* of them that do this. Nor, thirdly, does this world have in it only sense-data or ideas or whatever of other properties of things. It has in it the solidity and brownness of the chair. You can sit on things in this world.

In short, despite all that has been said, it seems this world at least *resembles* something else we have noticed regularly on our way. It seems to resemble *the physical world in one of its two parts*: spatio-temporal things that are perceived as against spatio-temporal things in nomic connection with the perceived things. Having arrived at this proposition about resemblance, fundamental to this paper, it is my aim in what follows to clarify and defend it, and, above all, to draw a proposal from it. As you will gather, the proposition about resemblance is not the weak one that the world of perceptual consciousness has in it *representations* of what is in the given part of the physical world. The point, strongly if dangerously put, is that both worlds have chairs in them.

Let me pass by what I hope is the battered idea that the troublesome facts and the proposition of resemblance are just a matter of the phenomenology of perceptual consciousness, not the real fact of it. Let me also put aside for a while (1) the dependency of my world on a subject, and attend to something else. It is the second consideration going against the resemblance, the fact that my world is dependent on my neural events. However much it may seem to have chairs in it, not representations of chairs, must this neural dependency not destroy any talk of real resemblance between my world of perceptual consciousness and the perceived physical world? And must any lingering hope not be finished off by the third consideration, that this world of consciousness is no less than guaranteed by my neural events?

Several things need to be recalled or taken on board at this stage, and in particular in connection with the second consideration. One is that it is no part of what has been suggested that *only* the worlds of perceptual consciousness exist. There *is* the unperceived part of the physical world, and the objective world, and the world indicated by science. It has certainly not been doubted that these conceptions are true of what there is, or anyway of some of what there is. Something of their sort is undeniable.

Also, these conceptions evidently overlap to certain extents, and will overlap with other more or less mind-independent conceptions of what there is. Let us now focus on one fundamental overlap. It is asserted or implied in at least two of these conceptions that part of what exists is not perceived, not in perceptual consciousness. It will be convenient to have a name for this. Let us have one last world, the *world-in-itself* or noumenal world, but leave out any implications from the past, notably the doctrines of Kant and Plato. Think of the world-in-itself, if you like, in scientific terms, perhaps as a world of particles in fields of force, or of course as spatio-temporal events in nomic connection with spatio-temporal events that are perceived.

The principal role of the unperceived part of the physical world as we have understood it is to do some explaining with respect to the perceived part. That is also the principal role of the world indicated by science. We carry over this idea, of course, to our world-in-itself. What we then get is that my world of perceptual consciousness, while having a dependency on my neural events, also has a dependency on the world-in-itself. The world-in-itself, we can say, if obscurely, is somehow constitutive of my world of perceptual consciousness.

One secondary consideration here is that my neural events do not come out of nowhere. If they are in a way the necessary conditions of my conscious events, they are also effects of something else. Each neural event is the upshot of a causal sequence, every stage of which is a causal circumstance or kind of causally sufficient condition for what follows. Of what initial causal circumstance is my neural event at some time an effect? Well, some will simply say the world-in-itself. I have in mind particularly those who take the world-in-itself to be a world of science, and in particular of physics. But, to be more cautious, it must surely be that there is a causal circumstance for my neural event in which the world-in-itself plays at least a large part.

These propositions are of importance to us. We are considering the argument that since my world of perceptual consciousness is dependent on my neural events, has a kind of necessary condition in them – it must be merely a mental world, and not something that importantly resembles the perceived part of the physical world. Is that a good argument if my world is *also* dependent in the way outlined on the world-in-itself? It seems not to be.

I say so because the perceived part of the physical world, as we ordinarily understand it, has the same sort of dependency. We do not subtract the chair from the physical world, and, so to speak, put it *in the mind,* on account of our common and shared contributions to it, elaborated in philosophy and science since the seventeenth century. This contribution, a contribution of none of us in particular but of the fact of humanness, has to do with our perceptual apparatus and our conceptualizing and so on, and in particular the physical chair's general neural dependency. The relationship between the physical chair and the chair-in-itself gets in the way of putting the physical chair in the mind. This consideration against identifying my perceptual world with a mental world does seem persuasive.

Why indeed should the particular neural dependency of my perceptual world degrade it into being 'mental' if much the same fact, a general fact of the same kind, does not degrade part of the physical world? In both cases the second dependency, on the world-in-itself, makes for an *independence* that is lacked by what we have been calling a mental world.

What of the third consideration, that my perceptual world has not only a kind of necessary condition in my neural events but also what was called a guarantee? My neural events are a kind of sufficient condition for my world. Is that not a disaster? If my neural events stand in this relation to that chair over there, how can it be other than in my mind?

I certainly grant that our conception of the perceived part of the physical world does not include the proposition of psychoneural correlates, of any particular neural guarantee for what is in this part of the physical world. But, as it seems to me, this is not essential to my line of argument. It *is* part of our conception of the given part of the physical world, as just noticed, that the world-in-itself is in some way necessary to it. There is, as we also know, this same dependency with respect to my perceptual world. The world-in-itself is a necessary condition for my neural events, the correlates of my conscious events.

Evidently this provides *a* response to the argument that if my world of perceptual consciousness is guaranteed by my neural events, it must be merely a mental world and not something that substantially resembles the perceived part of the physical world. The world-in-itself is necessary to the guarantee.[10]

What of the fourth consideration, about privacy? Does what has been admitted as to the privacy of my perceptual world stand in the way of claiming that it substantially resembles the part of the physical world? Well, what has been admitted is that in a sense you do not have access to my perceptual world. Such a thing could happen in the future, but it is not a possibility now. That does make a difference between the two worlds. But it is not a difference of much size, is it?

The fifth consideration was that because of the three dependencies my perceptual world is something that does not exist unperceived, but that unperceived existence is an explicit feature of the objective world, and fundamental if implicit in what is said of the world indicated by science. And, most relevantly, as was remarked (p. 138), it is an explicit feature of the physical world – that part that is spatio-temporal but only in lawlike connection with what is spatio-temporal and perceived.

My remark, since we were then reflecting on differences rather than resemblances, left something out, maybe a little heuristically or even deceptively – the part of the physical world we are now interested in above everything else, the perceived part. It is *there* that we need to look for likeness or the lack of it to my perceptual world. Does *this* stuff, the perceived part of the physical world, exist unperceived?

What does it mean to ask if anything exists unperceived? It is the question, presumably, of whether any properties can be assigned to a thing when it is unperceived. What property is assigned to the perceived part of the physical world if it is said that it also exists unperceived? That is not very clear to me, but perhaps the answer is that it is capable of being perceived. Can any properties be assigned to the items in my perceptual world when they are not in it? That is, taking my perceptual world to be a large temporally discontinuous particular, can any properties be assigned to an item in it in the times when this world is not in existence?

Well, there seems to be a good deal to say. In brief, this item too has a capability – of being in my world when my world reappears. This fact is tied up with another, the item's relation to the thing-in-itself. Further, if this is a different fact, my chair when unperceived by me remains spatio-temporal.

One final remark here. My perceptual world was casually described a moment ago as a discontinuous particular. Like a club, and a lot of other things, it pops in and out of existence over time. That idea, it might seem, itself stands in the way of asserting any important resemblance between my world and the perceived part of the physical world. Still, something can be said. The latter thing is, as we can say, 'a world as perceived' or 'a world as experienced'. In that case, it too is a discontinuous particular. It is not dependent on any particular subject, but it is not there when we are *all* asleep, and parts of it are not there when they are in *nobody's* experience.

This fifth consideration about unperceived existence gets us into deep or anyway troubled waters. Let us emerge from them with only the proposition that the consideration does not easily defeat my claim about resemblance, and turn back to what was passed by, the first consideration, about my perceptual world and a subject, self, or person.

Here too, as elsewhere, there certainly is a difference between my perceptual world and the perceived part of the physical world. It is perhaps the signal difference. The perceived part of the physical world has no dependency on a *particular* subject. But the extent of the difference between the two worlds will depend on how we try to understand the subject, the fact of real subjectivity with respect to my world. I seem to have no full and satisfactory understanding of the fact. But, since the matter of a subject is bound up with the matter of perceptual consciousness, there is the consolation of being able to say something. Something can be said too of the idea that it is possible to come to a tentative conclusion about perceptual consciousness without being able to say more of a subject.

One thing that can be said is that the view of perceptual consciousness being contemplated allows for a literal understanding of some common philosophical talk about a subject: that it is or involves a point of view, a view from somewhere rather than nowhere, a perspective. There is one of those, *literally*, in the world of my perceptual consciousness. It is the point of view from where my head is. This is a little blessing – an escape from metaphor, the besetting problem of the philosophy of mind when it does not abandon its mission.

Furthermore, it is possible on the view we are contemplating to start to explain what was remarked on earlier, that a subject is not only a necessary condition of perceptual consciousness in the sense of somehow being a part of it, but is such that the state of affairs would not exist at all in its absence. The explanation is that a point of view, literally speaking, is constitutive of the state of affairs. There could be no understanding of it which left out a real point of view. It is all a matter of the way things are from here, where my head is.

The view we are contemplating of perceptual consciousness gives some promise of a satisfactorily naturalistic conception of a subject. In so far as it does that, we get some *consonancy* between my perceptual world and the perceptual part of the physical world. I also pass by the role not of a particular subject but of subjects in the perceived part of the physical world. And the role of conceptualization. These help too.

5   Consciousness as Existence

Let me sum up the comparison now completed between my world of perceptual consciousness and the perceived part of the physical world. My world has dependencies on (1) a subject, myself, and (2, 3) on my neural events. It is (4) in a way private and (5) is said not to exist unperceived. This is enough, certainly, to make a difference from the mind-independent worlds and in particular the perceived part of the physical world.

However, and to be brief, my world of perceptual consciouness is spatial, temporal, and has chairs in it. That tells in the other direction. That is a large similarity. Also, there is more to be said about the perceived part of the physical world. This is at least akin to my world in its neural and thing-in-itself dependencies. In the matter of unperceived existence, it is not all that far from my world, and it can be said to be consonant with my world's dependency on a subject.

These propositions, in my submission, amount to an important resemblance between the two worlds. That is to say that my world *cannot* be regarded as just what was called a mental world – a totality of thoughts and feelings of mine. More particularly, my world is not being conceived in a useless, pre-analytic way. On the contrary, what we have, by way of the resemblance with part of the physical world, is an articulated and relatively rich conception. My perceptual consciousness, my world of perceptual consciousness, is an articulated state of affairs.

I own up to doubts about the details of all this, and a residual worry that some inconsistency has gone unnoticed. But not enough doubts and worry to stand in the way of my main proposal in this paper. It is in part that in thinking about the mind and what exists, we have been stuck with two categories. These are, in the most general terms, the relatively mind-independent worlds and mental worlds. It is not only philosophers of the mentally-realist kind who have been stuck with not only mind-independent but also mental worlds. Philosophers sceptical about mental worlds, indeed with some reason disdainful of them, have nevertheless not escaped them, but write more and more books trying to accommodate them.

To come to the very nub, what we need, in order to deal first with perceptual consciousness and thereafter somehow with all of consciousness, is a new category: worlds of perceptual consciousness. They take a good deal from both mind-independent and mental worlds. We do not need new kinds of properties or events. We need this different way of looking at what we have got. Or, to remember my doubts, and to be properly hesitant, we need *some* new way like this, something along these lines.

We need some view of perceptual consciousness *as existence*, or, if you like, existence as perceptual consciousness. We need an idea to the effect that for something to be conscious is for a world to exist, although certainly not a world wholly dependent on it. This, in my submission, is what we have missed out in being anchored in the two categories of mind-independent and mental worlds.

Is there not much to be said for this different category?

For a start, the category is not factitious. Our worlds of perceptual consciousness, in fact, are the *only* worlds that are not worlds of theory. They are not got by inference or speculation, however well-founded or even coercive the inference or theory. They are epistemically and perhaps conceptually prior to all other worlds, notably the objective and scientific ones. It is not clear, since the idea of ontological priority is more difficult than sometimes supposed, that they are not ontologically prior to the rest.[11] There is reason for trying to make clear the inviting idea that they are not less but *more* real.

Does the category of worlds of perceptual consciousness offend against a commitment to physicalism, taking the latter to be a commitment to the physical world and the world indicated by science, and perhaps the objective world, and at least a scepticism about mental worlds? The answer is that what has been proposed arguably *is* a kind of physicalism, certainly akin to physicalism. One reason is that our worlds of consciousness, despite being different, are approximate to the perceived part of the physical world.

Notes

1. Do you remain in doubt about this central proposition? Unwilling to abandon the clarity and simplicity of real identity theories? It may be that you are under the influence of a certain tendency in the recent philosophy of mind. We are predisposed in a materialist direction by a certain means. Let me again take Papineau's *Introducing Consciousness* (Icon/Totem, 2000) as my example. We are sometimes told in the book that our subject is 'the felt nature of consciousness' (p. 8). This is said to be exemplified by the pain of having a tooth drilled without an anaesthetic and the look of a red rose (p. 3, p. 61). Our subject, we

hear again, is the fact that 'conscious states *feel* a certain way', 'the *feelings* involved'. (p. 7, p. 21) We are concerned with 'something about experience' – conceivably as distinct from experience itself (p. 14). So is our subject an *aspect* or *property* or *side* of consciousness generally? Better, a class of aspects, one kind of ways in which conscious states are different from one another? It can certainly sound as if this is our subject. It's feels and looks. It's the side of consciousness directly or indirectly owed to sensation and perception, including dreams. It's what a lot of the recent philosophy of mind speaks of as *qualia*. But the real subject of *Introducing Consciousness*, of course, is *not* just an aspect or the like – but the nature of consciousness, the fundamental fact of it, as the title of the book rightly announces and the author definitely says in most other sentences. Still, the ambiguity as to subject lingers. What it does, with innocent persons who haven't sorted it out, is to predispose them in the direction of materialistic doctrines said to be about consciousness but which seem to almost all of us to leave it out. The innocent persons half-suppose it's not so bad if the doctrines have trouble with or actually just leave out an *aspect* of consciousness, which indeed they do – this allows the doctrines to be OK about what really matters, the very nature of consciousness. Well, the innocent need to see clearly that what the doctrines seem to leave out is the real subject-matter, indeed the only subject-matter on the agenda. Feels and looks *is* definitely a side-issue of course, because they aren't all of any conscious state, and because there are perfectly good conscious states that don't include any feels or looks at all, anyway any distinctive ones. There aren't any feels or looks discernible by me when I just think that neural functionalism is a mistake. Thinking in general, pure thinking taken by itself, doesn't have feels and looks worth mentioning. Its reality for us is something else. That reality, shared with all consciousness, is what the materialist doctrines are supposed to be capturing for us.

2. The most numbing of these dualisms, perhaps, well beyond ghostly stuff, is to be found in *The Self and Its Brain* (Springer, 1977), by the philosopher of science Karl Popper and the neurophysiologist J. C. Eccles. To conscious and neural events a Self is added. Also known as the Self-Conscious Mind, it is not tied to the brain but is its proprietor, somehow free-floating and magnificent. Maybe in its infant stage it chooses which hemisphere of the brain to light on. All this is aided by the research of Benjamin Libet et al., to my mind remarkable in not distinguishing things. The relevant part of the research is to the effect that a conscious sensation occurs on its own, before the brain catches up with it. See my 'The Time of a Conscious Sensory Experience and Mind-Brain Theories', *Journal of Theoretical Biology*, 1984, and 'Mind, Brain and Time: Rejoinder to Libet', *Journal of Theoretical Biology*, 1986.

3. Thomas Nagel, 'What is it Like to be a Bat?', in his *Mortal Questions* (Cambridge University Press, 1979). See also Timothy Sprigge, 'Final Causes', *Supplementary Proceedings of the Aristotelian Society*, 1971.

4. John Searle, *The Rediscovery of the Mind* (MIT Press, 1992), p. 132.

5. Thomas Nagel, 'Qualia,' *The Oxford Companion to Philosophy* (Oxford University Press, 1995).

6. I cannot resist adding something, a comparison. For you to be conscious or aware of this room now, we have it, is for the room somehow to exist. Is there any better phenomenological answer so-called? Think of the immaterialist family of answers that what it is *like* for you to be conscious of this room now is for there to be a thing or substance and stuff out of space, but somehow still in your head. Really? Will anyone say that that is what it is like to be aware of the room? Think of another family of answers. What is it *like* for you to be conscious of this room now is for there to be a neural instantiation in your head of a computational or functional sequence. Or an electromagnetic field. Or, God help us, what your consciousness of the room seems to you to be is a generating in your head of macroscopic quantum coherence, with Bose Einstein condensates combining and microtubules microtubuling. These answers to the phenomenological question are of course taken directly from two families of views as to the very nature of your consciousness. They are in fact the *best* phenomenological answers those views can give. Those views are not strengthened by abandoning themselves, so to speak, by allowing that consciousness doesn't seem to be what they say it is, and then telling some *ad hoc* tale about mistakes we supposedly make in or about our own experience, our taking attitudes to it or getting confused or whatever.
7. The distinction is taken from A. J. Ayer, *The Central Questions of Philosophy* (Weidenfeld & Nicholson, 1973)
8. This is a good example of something we will be coming back to, something about which it turned out to be possible to have useful second thoughts – in Chapter 11.
9. *A Theory of Determinism* or *Mind and Brain*, Chapters 1 and 2.
10. As remarked in Note 8, this is not the end of this book's story.
11. 'Dependence', *Cambridge Dictionary of Philosophy*, Robert Audi (ed.) (Cambridge University Press, 1995).

Chapter Eight

The Theory Embarked On

The theory of the nature of consciousness to which we have come is one that goes against cranialization and instead conceives of perceptual consciousness as a state of affairs outside the head. Admittedly it is an unconventional theory, a radical one, if no more radical than behaviourism once was, and of course the materialisms that preceded it. The theory's unfamiliarity ensures that it disconcerts those who are still hard at work in the philosophy of mind and the science of consciousness of the twentieth century, and not raising their heads.

Their problem, of course, is that their orthodox theories of consciousness are not believed by anyone else, notably by philosophers outside the philosophy of mind. Nor are they believed, I suspect, by those very labourers themselves not raising their heads from their computers. Rather, so to speak, they take the theories on board in order to get on with things. This is a policy well-known in the history of science. It has very notably been the policy with Quantum Theory.

Does the theory of consciousness as a kind of existence of things have an antecedent in the the anti-individualism considered a few chapters back? Well, Putnam's doctrine of meaning did indeed get mental events partly outside the head. Burge's doctrine of meaning, much more difficult to encapsulate and indeed resistant to exposition, does somehow make meaning a matter of enviromental determinants of it that are not the ordinary ones. More than that, there is some difference between merely personal mental events, as we called them, which are events tied to brains in the ordinary way, and what are actually presented as proper mental events, which are not so tied, and whose location in heads is perhaps less certain.

Still, it is difficult to see that the theory of consciousness as an existence shares any more with the two anti-individualisms than the uneasiness, and more than that, of asserting that your consciousness is in your head. The theory on which we are embarked looks back to a natural beginning not in the philosophy of language, but in our experience. It begins naturally in the seeming nature of the fact of perceptual consciousness – things in some way existing outside you in space and time, and then in the proposition that perceptual consciousness, like consciousness generally, is something to which a distinction between appearance and reality, talk of phenomenology, does not really apply.

The line of thought on which we are embarked does indeed leave a lot behind. Near the start of this inquiry into consciousness, when we were considering the thinking of some neuroscientific friends (p. 21), we began contemplating the subjectivity of consciousness as a matter of three things: subject or something of the sort, content, and object or world. We subsequently struggled with the relations between them.

Now that trinity has been subverted and made into one thing – anyway in connection with perceptual consciousness. The relations have thereby been done away with too, of course. Out of a trinitarianism has come a unitarianism. Is this much more than a step too far, maybe a massacre not to be seriously contemplated despite the impossible alternative? Well, you've got the book in front of you. Read on.

1   Naturalism and Subjectivity

The question of what it is for you to be aware of your surroundings, perceptually conscious, is still given the answer of neural functionalism. According to this functionalism limited to our human species, which leaves out theories, hopes and dreams about computers, being perceptually conscious consists in effects and causes that are neural. Typical ones come in between predecessors that have to do with seeing and successors that have to do with moving.

There was also another answer to the question of what is for you to be aware of your surroundings. that was that your consciousness is physical properties in your head, somehow subjective in involving two connected things, properties not now known in neuroscience but properties that will be discovered in some future neuroscience. This answer can come to seem a desperate one. And it is all too possible to anticipate that such new properties would still be taken as leaving a lot out, in fact leaving out consciousness as much so as current neuroscientific properties.

These two views, to remember another honorific term in the recent philosophy of mind, do have the good recommendation of *naturalism*. This is sometimes understood, but cannot be well understood, as belief only in things that are allowed to exist in science – whatever things – along with a commitment to scientific method. This characterization of naturalism is uninformative – it gives only a signpost to the things rather than tells you of their nature. It is also an uncertain signpost, if only for the reason that psychology is within science and there is uncertainty about what is within psychology. Also, at best, the characterization is vulnerably tied to a current time-slice of science.

A better philosophical understanding of naturalism is belief in only physical things, and in fitting methods of inquiry, of which scientific method is at least the dominant one. As for the physical things, given what has just been said, they must not be weakly identified as the things allowed in science. Let us continue to understand them in something like a standard and traditional way. There are two categories of them, those taking up space and time and having perceived properties, and those unperceived but taking up space and time and standing in causal or other lawlike connection with the perceived things. Sofas go into the first category, atoms and a good deal else into the second.

We now have something from neural functionalism and the answer about future properties of some kind of physical subjectivity. We have another account of perceptual consciousness, a start on a speculation that looks at the thing very differently. Something new certainly seems necessary in the face of our persistent philosophical failure to get agreement, outside of groups and coteries, on the nature of perceptual and other consciousness. We need a change.[1] This particular different account is close to naturalism but not actually within it.

The new account is that what it is for you now to be aware of your surroundings is for things somehow to exist. To speak a little grandly, what it is for your to be perceptually consciousness now is for a world somehow to exist, a certain changing totality of things. Mine now consists in things in this room and outside the window.

The theory of consciousness as existence makes perceptual consciousness into a state of affairs that is akin to the state of affairs that is the perceived physical world. It is spatial and so on. But this state of affairs, given in answer to the question of what perceptual consciousness is, is also different, and thus has what is surely a tremendous recommendation. It gives clear, strong and acceptable sense, at last, to talk of subjectivity. That really distinguishes it from the two naturalisms, and needs to be lingered over.

My being conscious, as you heard at the beginning of this book, is not a thing or fact about me or pertaining to me like my weight, location, or the events of giving my name when asked. My consciousness involves a subjective thing or fact. It seems to involve both a subject or awareness or the like and also something else, content. My consciousness is somehow different from the world of objective fact. More was said or conjectured along these lines about subjectivity later on in the book, notably in 'Seeing Things'.

The theory of consciousness as existence makes perceptual consciousness into a certain reality, but this does not get in the way of the theory also making it subjective in a sense that has the merit of being crystal-clear. If it is surprising that a realism about consciousness, a near-naturalism, can also give us real subjectivity, surely the fact is that it can.

In the theory to which we have come, my consciousness is subjective in that there is a fundamental difference between my perceptual consciousness and yours. Still more important, there is a fundamental difference between either mine or yours and, in Nagel's phrase, a view from nowhere.[2] There is, in terms of the account of perceptual consciousness as existence, a fundamental difference between your world of perceptual consciousness and mine, and, more important, between either of them and the perceived part of the physical world, not to mention the unperceived part.

In the theory to which we have come, simply, your consciousness is the existence of a world that is *other than the physical world*, the world that does not have a dependency on anyone in particular. No world of perceptual consciousness is identical in its contents with the perceived part of the physical world – or of course the other part. Your world of perceptual consciousness is exactly *not* the physical world. What it is, to repeat, is a totality of different things in space and time. It is prior to and a constituent or the like of the physical world.

In short, the fundamental fact of subjectivity, whatever else is to be added, is the existence of subjective worlds, no less subjective and no less distinct from the physical world for being spatio-temporal and propertied – for being real in roughly that sense.

More or less the same remarks can be made, obviously, about differences between subjective worlds and what were distinguished as the objective world and the world of science (p. 136).

2   Subjectivity and the Mind-Body Problem

Does this great strength of the theory go with a great weakness? To return to the two naturalisms, they do indeed have a great recommendation themselves. It is in fact the recommendation that governed and directed most of the philosophy of mind at the end of the twentieth century and almost all of the science of mind or consciousness then and since then. The recommendation has to do with the mind-body problem, the problem of the relationship of consciousness to the brain, and, more particularly, of events of consciousness to neural and other physical events. We think of the problem in two ways, (1) in terms of physical events in our environments and also neural events giving rise to or contributing to or being in lawlike or nomic connection with consciousness, and (2) in terms of conscious events giving rise to or contributing to our behaviour, this being physical.[3]

Neural functionalism, regarded as a proposal about the mind-body problem, and of course limited to human minds and bodies, is that a conscious event is a certain causal relatum or effect-cause whose other properties are only neural. It cannot be, as loose talk of variable realization sometimes suggests, that there are *two* distinct events in question, a neural one 'realizing' the other one. The relationship between the event as neural and the event as conscious, further described, is that the event as conscious is an effect-cause that it might still have been if it were not neural. The other account of perceptual consciousness, finally, was that it consists in properties in the head that are physical but not neural – not part of current neuroscience and not certain to fit into it. They can be regarded as in lawlike connection with known neural properties.

The two accounts, considered in terms of the mind-body problem, share a certain recommendation. It is that they put conscious events as they conceive them, on the one hand, and, on the other hand, physical events, into relations that are not baffling. More precisely, to come to the fundamental point, causal and other lawlike relations between these two categories of events, which relations indubitably exist, are not left baffling or made baffling.

In the two accounts, these relations hold between replaceable causal relata and other neural or otherwise physical events, and physical events yet to be discovered and other physical, perhaps neural, events.

This is of course the strength of naturalism, a matter of the comparison with mental-world or other ethereal accounts of consciousness. These latter accounts, given their vagueness, certainly do not make conscious events into things of which it can be seen that they can be causes or effects of, or in other lawlike connection with, physical events. But the success of the naturalistic accounts is also their failure. What they do, in the course of making conscious events causally and nomically acceptable, is to divest them of their seeming nature and their reality, above all their subjectivity. Conscious events are, so to speak, left solidly neural or physical, but not solidly conscious.

What of the mind-body problem and the theory of perceptual consciousness as existence? It is a theory, so far, having to do only with *perceptual* consciousness and what it is causally or nomically related to. The question is that of whether a world of perceptual consciousness can be unbafflingly in causal or other lawlike connection with physical things. We know it has another recommendation, indeed more than one, but can it be as unproblematic in this essential way?

To reflect on this is to come to a crucial question. Does an unproblematic cause have to be *spatio-temporal and somehow propertied*, or does it have to be *physical* according to the definition with which we have been working? I take it that it is clear only the former is required. To revert to an original crux in the philosophy of mind, the great problem of Descartes' account of the mind was that he put it out of space. What destroys the account, to speak plainly, is the idea of effects and causes that are nowhere, of course having causes and effects that are somewhere. The account of perceptual consciousness as existence is entirely different.

I allow that we have an inclination to require our causes and effects to be physical, but what is this requirement? It seems to me that it is an epistemological requirement having to do with certain contemplated or confirmed or true causal statements – all those having to do with other things than consciousness. What is taken as needed is other and more than a subjective basis. What is needed is a basis having to do with perceivers generally, not just one of them.

But that is not a requirement on causal and related connection itself. All that is needed for such connection is something in space and time and somehow propertied. Certainly two things do not have to fall into any other single classification or category. There are many cross-category or cross-classification causal connections.

A great recommendation of taking perceptual consciousness as existence, then, is that it is unique in allowing both for real subjectivity and also for comprehensible causal relations. The near-naturalism of the account allows for the causal relations, along with them, other things we have to have.

3   Historical Theories, Brains in Vats

Evidently the theory is different from each of the two historical theories of perception noticed earlier (p. 134), these being analyses of seeing, hearing and so on that give little attention to the matter of consciousness, or indeed by-pass it entirely. Direct or 'naive' realism is to the effect that in perception we are aware of only physical objects. The representative theory of perception and phenomenalism are to the effect that what we are aware of is objects internal to the perceiver – ideas, sense-data, percepts or the like.

The account of perceptual consciousness under consideration has to do with neither physical objects exactly nor of course with ethereal and cranial objects. Rather, it has to do with spatio-temporal and propertied constituents of ordinary physical objects – with things, so to speak, that are the material out of which we construct the physical and other worlds. These things are subjective in the fundamental sense that they themselves are not physical objects – rather, they have a dependency on or are related to one perceiver in particular, and so on. If these are important distinctions between the account in hand and the historical theories, there is a yet more fundamental distinction.

It is implicit or explicit in the tradition of direct realism that consciousness or awareness of physical objects consists in a perceiver's baffling relation to them. One thing is clear, however. This relation or fact of perceptual consciousness is not itself taken as being the existence of the physical objects or, more relevantly, the existence of spatio-temporal and propertied constituents of such objects. Direct realism is not the theory of perceptual consciousness as existence. Rather, the assumption or story is roughly that a chair satisfies conditions of being a physical object, and thereafter it may or may not be perceived by you, within your awareness. Little or nothing is said of this conscious awareness.

It is harder to be clear in this connection about the internal objects of awareness in the representative theory of perception. They too, however, seem to be taken as distinct from awareness of them. They are what is different with respect to different episodes of perception, as against what is the same. The fundamental distinction of the account of perceptual consciousness being considered, then, as against the two historical theories, is that for you to be perceptually conscious *is* for a world or totality of things in a way to exist.

Still, the account is in part similar to direct realism – perceptual consciousness is made a matter of something not in the head. It will thus be apparent that it is open to something very like the long-running objection to direct realism, this objection also being an argument *for* a representative theory of perception. The long-running objection and argument is essentially that in perception we cannot be aware of physical objects, since hallucination, where there are no such objects, is indistinguishable from perception. What we must therefore be aware of in both cases is objects internal to ourselves. The argument from illusion, or, you can say, the argument from a brain in a vat.

The related objection to the account of perceptual experience as existence will be that such experience cannot consist in the existence of propertied things in space and time because something indistinguishable from such experience could be had in the absence of such things. It is conceivable that you, or a brain in a vat, thanks to the ministrations of neuroscientists, could have an experience indistinguishable from one you are having now, but in the absence of the right propertied things in space and time. There are similar objections to doctrines of anti-individualism about mental events.

It has been my opinion that the best defence against all such objections, which certainly are troublesome, must be an attack on the views being argued *for*, representative theories of perception. The objections, as must not be forgotten, are commitments to, or at least contemplations of, representative theories. It seems that a certain attack on such views can now have more weapons, if not more logic, given our greater knowledge of the processes issuing in consciousness. Also, we may now have a better grasp on the question being answered by representative theories and direct realism, and its distinction as a philosophical question. Let me explain.

At the heart of representative theories of perception is the idea of an inference, from some premise or other, to a conclusion about a physical thing. We begin with an internal object of awareness, a sense-datum or the like, and we end up with belief or the like in a chair. But of course there is no sign of any such carry-on in the phenomenology of consciousness. To which truth it is replied by defenders of the representative theory, of course, that the inference, and also the awareness of the inner thing, are not conscious. That necessary defence must give rise to a fatal rejoinder.

We are now much better informed of the process that issues in your perceptual consciousness of the chair. To actual retinal images we add much about neural structure and activity in the visual cortex, and so on. No direct realist and no advocate of perceptual consciousness as existence is committed in the slightest degree to any scepticism about the science, of course. Rather, we draw on it to make what is surely the fatal rejoinder that the representative theory of perception, having taken its subject-matter *out* of consciousness in order to defend itself, is no more than a kind of impressionistic version of this scientific story or some last part of it.

The scientific story, and the philosophical impression of it, are evidently not an answer to the philosophical question asked, historically or now, about perceptual consciousness. That question, as now seems clear, is the question of the so-called phenomenology of consciousness, better expressed as being the question of the real nature of consciousness. True to a deep impulse of philosophy, it is a question of at least an epistemological cast, about our conscious acquisition of belief and knowledge.

The answer to it *cannot* be anything like the representative theory of perception. *That*, to defend itself, necessarily removes itself from the discussion. The answer to the question of the nature of consciousness *can* be the account of perceptual consciousness under consideration. But, whether or not it is, to stick to the point, the objection from hallucination needs to be regarded for what it is, advocacy of an impossible theory. It is thus not a true objection but a difficulty to be dealt with.[4]

4   Something Left Out?

What we have is the idea that for a person to be perceptually conscious is for a certain world to exist – in part, for certain relations to certain things to hold, in particular the several dependency-relations. One term of these relations is said to be a person or the like. But a more precise and satisfactory identification of that item can be asked for, and indeed is owed and needed. It would be another disaster, certainly, somehow to identify the item in question as being conscious, say a conscious subject. To do so would be to fall into useless circularity, to make no analytic advance in the endeavour of trying to explain the nature of perceptual consciousness.

It seems that what needs to be said, the short story, is that for a person to be perceptually conscious is for a certain world to exist that is in part dependent on *neural* structures and events of the person. Quite a lot is contained in the longer philosophical story, as you know, about phenomenology, reality, subjectivity, dependencies, privacy and the mind-body problem, but there is no further and independent fact that needs to be mentioned in order to complete the account of what we take as a person's role in that person's perceptual consciousness.

Are you then inclined to object that this account must go the way of the two naturalistic accounts with which we began? That consciousness is left out? Well, it is essential to keep in mind that a person's perceptual consciousness is indeed being conceived as a subjective world. That is, it is precisely not the physical world, despite its being real in the sense of being spatio-temporal and having propertied things in it. Furthermore, this view of a person's perceptual consciousness takes on strength in a certain way.

Naturalistic accounts in general, as noticed in connection with Searle (Chapter 5), try to give a place to ideas of subjectivity and the like. These give little or no satisfaction for a certain reason. Essentially it is that the ideas are applied to a subject-matter, say events with only neural properties, that makes the ideas in question thin and unsustaining. That is, they do little to satisfy another rooted philosophical impulse. The case is different with the account under consideration. Here, so to speak, we have the thing for which the ideas of subjectivity, dependency, privacy and so on were made. Here there is something of the right sort to have such properties – a totality of things different from the things of the physical and other worlds.

Do you persist in objecting, nonetheless, that our prephilosophical conception of consciousness simply is such that one of my so-called worlds of perceptual consciousness could exist, and the person in question not be conscious – not be aware of his or her surroundings? That the account in terms of a world leaves out consciousness? Well, I do indeed deny this – or at any rate do intend to see to what extent and with what effect the denial can be sustained. Being perceptually conscious, according to me, *is* for such a world to exist.

Here are several further reasons to end with.

There do exist what are being called worlds of perceptual consciousness. That is, a certain conception is consistent and otherwise conceptually adequate, and things fall under it. If worlds of perceptual consciousness are allowed to exist, but denied to be any part of perceptual consciousness, what *is* to be said of them? How *are* we to think of them? They can't be left out of our reflections in this neighbourhood, and they need to have a status or role, don't they?

Do remember that no world of perceptual consciousness is the physical world. No world of perceptual consciousness is the world of which we say in an ordinary way, thereby giving it a status or role, that it is the thing of which we are aware. It is possible to wonder how a world of perceptual consciousness could not be what it is for someone to be perceptually conscious.

One last thought here. Some will say that the idea of a world of perceptual consciousness is a *part* of what it is to be perceptually conscious. Suppose that much is granted. What could conceivably be the remainder of what it is to be perceptually conscious? Would this be some ethereal stuff, some gossamer, made somehow consistent with a world of perceptual consciousness? Could such a remainder, if ever got clear enough for serious consideration, be other than a peripheral part of the present story? What need can there be for it?

The story of perceptual consciousness as existence raises still more questions, evidently, but maybe this fertility is no bad thing.

Notes

1. Cf. the resolute hope in Thomas Nagel's 'Conceiving the Impossible and the Mind-Body Problem,' Royal Institute of Philosophy Annual Lecture, *Philosophy*, 1998.
2. Nagel, *The View from Nowhere* (Oxford University Press, 1986).
3. What is in a way a separable constraint on an adequate account of perceptual consciousness, as of consciousness generally, is bound up with the mind-body constraint. It is that facts of consciousness itself must be so understood as to be ineliminable in explanations of our behaviour. Epiphenomenalism is false – there *is* mental causation or mental indispensability, truly so named. Perhaps fortunately, there is little call for a proof of this guiding axiom. As with one or two other bits of the philosophy of mind, there seems no proposition more certain than mental causation, and hence nothing available to be a premise in a proof of it.
4. You may be reassured that more will be said of this, something very different, in the last paper of the book.

The End of Intentionality in Perceptual Consciousness

It is easy to suppose that something is going wrong, has already gone wrong. The line of thought in these pieces of argument, you may suppose, is doing too much violence to our settled conceptual scheme. You may grant it *is* uncomfortable to say that consciousness is something in heads, and that it is *more* than uncomfortable to judge that it consists in the chemical and electrical processes of cell bodies, axons, dendrites, transmitter-substances and the like. But, you may suppose, there is something as wrong with the theory of perceptual consciousness as existence.

You may dig in your heels and declare that your consciousness isn't in your head but it isn't *out there* either. That sounds right too, somehow. But does it sound right because of a bit of forgetfulness? Our subject has latterly been one part, kind or side of consciousness – what can be labelled awareness or experience rather than thinking and desiring. Are you so certain that what it is for you to be aware of your surroundings isn't for things out there somehow to exist? But that is reassurance and encouragement, and a promise of things to come, not introduction to our subject now.

There is another source of scepticism or worse with respect to the theory in hand. It is the declaration that consciousness is *of* something or is *about* something. There must be something true in that, you say. It can't be that consciousness is in no sense relational. Well, I agree. In fact it needs to be granted that there is another criterion for an adequate theory of consciousness – that it gives a place, *some* considerable place, to the declaration that consciousness is somehow of or about things. Any theory that gave *no* assent to the declaration could get no assent to itself.

But is it the case that *perceptual* consciousness cannot be as has been supposed because of the truth in the declaration? Or truth in related declarations? Many philosophers of 'of' and 'about' will hurry to say so. Nothing so clear, they say, as that our consciousness of the world is not just a fact, but a fact of or about something else. Anyway, something or other like that just has to be right. Various propositions of *intentionality*, as it has misleadingly been named by philosophers, can't come to nothing much. There is too much sense in them for that.

---

1   A Good Start but a Blunder?

We ought to have had enough of accounts of perceptual and other consciousness that in fact are denials of it – denials of a reality on which we have a grip. Thomas Kuhn, the philosopher of science, spoke of a period of what he called normal science coming to an end with a paradigm shift.[1] Have we not come to an end of some normal philosophy of mind? Do we not need a new paradigm with consciousness? With that want of humility so natural to the philosophical temperament, I would like to carry forward the proposing of one.

What is it for you in the room you are in to be perceptually conscious at this moment? What is it for you to be aware of your surroundings? *It is for a world somehow to exist.* It is not for *a world somehow to exist – of which you are conscious or aware or the like.* There is no such circular addition to the answer. And what that existence-claim comes to is that a collection of things, reasonably referred to as chairs and the like, are in space and time, have other properties, have certain dependencies, and are not exactly physical. They are, so to speak, what exactly physical things are made out of.

Recall the earlier quick definition of the physical – space-occupiers that are perceived or space-occupiers that are in lawlike connections with space-occupiers that are perceived. To say that something is physical in the first sense is to say that it has a several-sided dependency on *perceivers in general* or some of them, maybe a class of experts, most familiarly a dependency on their perceptual apparatus. Their contribution to secondary properties of things, the founding fact of the tradition of British Empiricism, running from Locke, Berkeley and Hume up to Ayer and beyond, is one large side of this story of dependency. In contrast, to say that your being aware of this room now is for a world somehow to exist – for a particular world of perceptual consciousness to exist – is to say that things are in space and time and have other properties, but have a several-sided dependency on only *you*.

The chairs now in your world of perceptual consciousness are certainly not in your head or mind, or out of space, but are right there in space outside of you. This is perfectly consistent with their having a dependency on the atoms and so on in the other half of the physical world, what we can call the scientific world, which dependency certainly is important to the view in question, as well as the unique dependency on you alone among perceivers.

The existence of the chairs, this state of affairs, is no more mysterious than things existing physically, that other state of affairs. It is in several ways *less* mysterious. The first sort of existence, dependent on one person, is in fact somehow fundamental to the second. As already remarked, we get to or make up or posit the physical world from the material of our perceptual worlds. In short, what we have here are two related ways of conceiving of *what there is,* where by those latter words we can gesture at whatever it is to which we bring our perceiving, conceptualizing, science and so on, something like a Kantian noumenal world or simply the substratum of science.

Taking naturalism as before, as the attitude that we should somehow or in a way restrict our thinking to the physical world, this theory of percepetual consciousness as existence is not exactly naturalism. But it is not far off. It is as good as identical in spirit. This theory about perceptual consciousness could not possibly be regarded as substance-dualism, and is remote from property-dualism as traditionally and now conceived. That is, it does not turn perceptual consciousness into a ghostly thing or ghostly stuff whose natures go unexplained. Although different in its source, it has an accidental affinity with meaning-doctrines of anti-individualism – it might be thought to make sense of them. It may be a basis for an account of consciousness generally – its other two parts. These are reflective consciousness, which roughly speaking is thinking without perceiving, and affective consciousness, which has to do with desire, emotion and so on.

The theory has main recommendations having to do with phenomenology so-called, the reality of consciousness, subjectivity, and the mind-body problem. Does it also have a fatal weakness? Might it be a kind of blunder?

It has been a philosophical commonplace that most of nonperceptual consciousness, and perceptual consciousness as well, has a property or nature that is its *intentionality*, glanced at when we were surveying humble truths about the mind (p. 94). In the philosophy of mind since Roderick Chisholm's book *Perceiving* of 1957,[2] a lot has been heard about intentionality. Many have contemplated that it may be 'the mark of the mental', and taken consciousness as at least a main part of the mental, the remainder being our various capabilities and dispositions. Intentionality is typically introduced by way of certain casual remarks.

1. Conscious events are *of* things.
2. They are *about* things.
3. In consciousness there is something before the mind.
4. The mind has a capacity to direct itself at things.
5. Conscious events are directed at or have reference to things.
6. We do not just believe, or just desire, or just see, but believe, desire or see something.
7. We can believe what is not the case, want what does not exist, and so on.

Do you suppose, on hearing or rehearing these remarks, that you have already been told what intentionality is? That would perhaps be in line with Daniel Dennett's initial and snappy definition of intentionality as simply 'aboutness.'[3] But what it is for something to be 'about' something else is entirely unclear. The word in itself is no more an analysis or explanation of something than are the words 'cause', 'time', 'good' and so on, through the list of large philosophical problems.

Presumably there is something philosophically valuable that has the name of intentionality. This is some more clarified property or character of conscious events, most of them, this property or character being their intentionality properly speaking. Such a property or character is given to us in a philosophical proposition, theory or doctrine, or one of a family of these. This is what we need.

Thus we can take the initial remarks as parts of what has been called *folk-psychology* – what ordinary people believe about the mind. The subsequent propositions of intentionality are not part of folk-psychology. They are in a way on a level with the dualisms, physicalisms, functionalisms, ideas of the subjective character of conscious events in the head, and so forth. This is so although the propositions, theories or doctrines of intentionality may not compete with but may enter into the dualisms and so on. Nearly all of these, save eliminative materialism, have somehow added to their materials at least a recognition of a somehow clarified property or character of intentionality.

The general question in front of us, then, is whether the various remarks, the folk-psychology, indicate or give rise to a truth about perceptual consciousness, anyway some proposition of importance – which proposition has to be part of any satisfactory account of this consciousness. More particularly, do we here find another criterion or constraint with respect to a satisfactory theory of consciousness, including the theory of perceptual consciousness as existence?

Is the criterion one that this theory fails to satisfy, maybe does not come near to satisfying? Is it the case that what has to be added to the theory of perceptual consciousness will be entirely at odds with that theory, destroy it?

It is clear, if you are still wondering about it, that we do not have much of a test of theories of consciousness, if any at all, in the various remarks themselves. For example, there is no challenge in the fact (6) that to see is always to see something – that being understood as a remark in an ordinary unphilosophical tone of voice. What about the remark that (1) in consciousness there is something before the mind, or the remark that (2) the mind has a capacity to direct itself upon things? Does the latter introduce an actual criterion of consciousness, something beyond the truth that seeing is always seeing something? To the extent that the term 'the mind' can be assigned a plain man's meaning, do we get a requirement on accounts of consciousness?

Let us not reflect further on the use of the opening remarks about intentionality. In fact the distance between several of the remarks and the ensuing propositions is not great. Let us assume that the remarks are *some* guide as to perceptual consciousness, as distinct from reflective and affective consciousness, but leave the matter a little unsettled. Let us try to arrive, by way of them, at an analytical or otherwise enlightening product of the remarks, a clear and useful proposition about intentionality, maybe several. Seven candidates present themselves for consideration.

2   Conscious Contents, Unconscious Contents, Intensionality

The first of these candidates, certainly a contradiction of consciousness as existence, is as follows.

Consciousness involves a relation of directedness or reference between something or other, this being unspecified,
and a content or object internal to the conscious event in
question. The event in question takes place in the head of
the perceiver, as must its contained content or object.

This proposition of intentionality does not have in it something
often associated with the matter – this being a mediaeval embarrassment about the content or object existing only in some funny
way, its being halfway between nothing and something. It comes
from and in fact is closer than many propositions to what Franz
Brentano actually says in his famous and often misread paragraph
on the subject:

Every mental phenomenon is characterized by what the
Scholastics of the Middle Ages called the intentional (or
mental) inexistence of an object, and what we might call,
though not wholly unambiguously, reference to a content,
direction towards an object (which is not to be understood
here as meaning a thing), or immanent objectivity. Every
mental phenomenon includes something as object within
itself, although they do not all do so in the same way. In presentation something is presented, in judgement something
is affirmed or denied, in love loved, in hate hated, in desire
desired and so on.[4]

But the somewhat more explicit proposition rather than
Brentano's paragraph is my concern. Evidently it has in it nothing
whatever about objects or contents *outside* the head of the perceiver –
objects or contents of which it is remarked, by other doctrinalists to
whom we will come, that they may not exist. Also, as you will not be
surprised to hear, this first proposition is in accord with the truism
that a relation requires the existence of its terms, and in particular that a dyadic relation requires the existence of two terms. If the
second term in the proposition, the mentioned content or object in
consciousness and the head of the perceiver, did not exist, the token
relation would not exist, and hence the particular event of perceptual consciousness would not exist. But there is no reason whatever
to raise a question of such an inner content or object not existing.

What is to be said of this? It seems out of touch with the initial
remarks as ordinarily understood that (3) in consciousness there is
something before the mind, that (4) the mind has a capacity to direct
itself at things, and that (6) in seeing we see something. According
to them, do I not have before me, direct myself at, and see, *ordinary rooms outside my head*? Folk-psychology is not the doctrine of

sense-data. Even when a supposed external object in fact does not exist, say the fountain of youth in Hampstead, what I seem to get in hallucinating it is not what I as a member of the folk would then describe as a fountain *in my head*. Very definitely this first proposition of intentionality as applied to perceptual consciousness is wonderfully incomplete. Seeing involves *some* relation to something outside the head in question, whether or not the relation is in the consciousness. That is built into the concept of seeing.

We need to object, too, that the relation in this first proposition, inside the head, is left about as metaphorical and obscure as in the ordinary remarks with which we began. Certainly the relation, although *reference* to the content or object is mentioned, could not possibly be one of *representation*, like that between a word or picture and what it stands for. What the account evidently wants to bring in as the first term of the relation is something like *the mind*, which itself, whatever it is, can be no representation or symbol. Also, what *is* this thing called the mind? We are doing philosophy now, not chatting. We need to know.

A further objection will have counterparts with respect to other propositions of intentionality to which we are coming. We have it that an event of perceptual consciousness in a head includes within itself a content or object. The account says nothing of the nature of this item, about whether it is conceptual or not and so on. But leave that. The relevant fact is that the content or object is understood as being *within or a part of the consciousness of the perceiver*. It is as much so as if it were a sense-datum – which, for all we are told, it may be. It would also be within or a part of the consciousness of the perceiver if it were the original sort of thing in the intentionality tradition, the *intentio* of the mediaevals, this being an idea, concept or notion.[5]

But when I am aware of this room now, what is within my consciousness, so to speak, is *the room* – and no other relevant thing. Seeing isn't always seeing double. Seeing isn't seeing by way of using some conscious means to the end, having some image or idea or whatever else. There's no picture or word or the like in the story of my perceptual consciousness now. It's not as if I'm aware of living my life as a life of doing something like watching television. There is no minimizing this objection. The very centrepiece of this first account of intentionality is missing from its subject-matter, from the reality of perceptual consciousness. This account discovers within perceptual consciousness what simply is not there.

Does a scientist of consciousness now say that this last objection is beside some large point? And say that that point is that the content or object actually need not be within or part of the conscious event? Well, that is not at all like the account we have been considering, the one closest to Brentano's paragraph, but of course we *can* contemplate a second proposition, something distant from Brentano's paragraph if related to it.

> An event of perceptual consciousness involves a relation of directedness between something or other, far less elusive than *the mind*, maybe a neural system, and a content or object not internal to the event of perceptual consciousness, but within the head of the perceiver. This content or object has an explanatory role with respect to the conscious event itself.

The objections to the first proposition having to do with incompleteness and an obscure relation also apply to this second one – which is certainly at odds with consciousness as existence. This story of non-conscious intentionality *does* escape the largest objection, since its centre-piece is not known to be missing. The escape, however, is by means of what is hardly less than philosophical disaster. This is not because the account is in a certain way false. No doubt at all – there are *many* things that may be dubbed contents or objects that are within or on the surface of a perceiver and are within the directedness of something else, and are somehow explanatory of events of perceptual consciousness. The most familiar one is a real retinal image. Neuroscience provides a lot more candidates.

The philosophical disaster of this account is, rather, that it is in fact *no account whatever* of the kind promised, an account of perceptual experience itself, this consciousness. It merely changes the subject while pretending to stick to it.

Is there a reason for changing the subject, for contemplating this second account? Could it be that someone's reason, so-called, is just some other account of perceptual consciousness, something that calls for the relocation of intentionality outside of consciousness as we have a grip on it? Maybe hybrid or modified functionalism, having in it the story of inner causal relata but also something about 'qualia', these being a matter of consciousness but not intentionality?

But this is not a defence of non-conscious intentionality, a reason in favour of it. It *is* in effect pretty much the opposed proposition – and thus near to begging the question. We want a *ground* for moving from intentionality within consciousness to non-conscious intentionality, not an assertion of the latter. By contrast, as it seems to me, my objection that the proposition of non-conscious intentionality gives no account whatever of something, as implicitly promised, is not the question-begging assertion of another account.

One of the initial remarks about intentionality was that (7) we can believe in or want what does not exist – and of course hope for it and so on. This plain fact is thought to be catered for in *some* proposition of intentionality. It is not catered for in the first proposition, as noticed, or presumably the second. There is nothing in either proposition about any relation one of whose terms does not or may not exist. The plain fact that we can believe in or want or hope for what does not exist may be turned into something else, as it was by Chisholm.[6] It may be replaced by a fact about language now philosophically familiar, the fact of *intensionality*, with an 's'. This linguistic fact is:

It does not follow, from the use of a referring expression, that the thing referred to actually does exist.

It does not follow, from the truth that someone wanted to find the fountain of youth in Hampstead, that it exists. But the unusual entailment-failure, as is now well-known, occurs with other things than consciousness and the like. It tells us nothing of the distinctiveness of consciousness. I mention this so-called account of intentionality only to put it aside quickly. Even if the linguistic fact turned up only and always with consciousness, of course, it *by itself* would tell us little worth knowing of consciousness itself.[7] It would not be an account of how it was that consciousness gave rise to the linguistic fact. Our subject is not language.

3   Two Relations, a Causal Story

Is there some proposition of intentionality, as distinct from anything else, that does cater for the fact that we can believe in or want what does not exist? Is there some proposition that does involve us in the 'problem', as it is called, of a relation to something that does not exist? Indeed there is. Consider the following fourth candidate, anticipated in passing earlier.

An event of perceptual consciousness is such that a mind is in a relation of directedness with respect to a content or object internal to the event, as before, but there is a second relation between the content or object and something outside the event and the head in question. This second relation may hold between the content or object and something that does not exist.

The proposition, fatal to consciousness as existence if it is true and arguable, is complete in the way that the first two are not. We get outside the head. It faces the objections noticed earlier having to do with the obscurity of the first relation between the mind and internal content or object, and the obscurity of the mind itself – and, as might have been said before, an objection having to do with the probable circularity of recourse to the mind in an account of consciousness. It is also entirely open to the major objection that we have no awareness at all of the supposed content or object. It is just missing. The theory is discovering something that isn't there.

There is also the fact that the second relation, to say the least, is obscure. If it is said to be *representation*, what is that in general? Few philosophical questions are further from an answer. As for the philosophical question of what this sort of conscious represen-tation is supposed to be, as against representation with real sen-tences and pictures, this is a philosophical question often regarded as unanswerable.[8]

That is not the end of the trouble. There is worse. It is no good tripping lightly past the so-called 'problem' of a non-existent term of a relation. This is in fact a simple contradiction. The relation of representation or whatever is indeed presented as a relation. What we are thus offered is a nonsense – the nonsense of the possibility of a dyadic relation with one term, the nonsense of a relation between something and nothing.

Do some of us come to tolerate the so-called problem by con-centrating on the many happy cases where the thing outside the conscious event and the head *does* exist – say the fountain in South End Green rather than the fountain of youth? Can it be supposed that despite the contradiction in the second case, we can have a clear and good account of this relation in the first case? Exactly the oppo-site can be argued. The so-called relation of representation, it seems, is the same in *both* cases. Well then, what is clear about the first case is *not* part of that relation. Exactly what you can't do is depend on what is different about the first case.

Let me be brief about something else, a once hopeful proposition that is best regarded as a part of or serious and exclusive functional-ism and hence something we have put aside. It could, however, be made part of the proposition just considered or of something else. It is distinctive in being a certain attempt to make an escape from the obscurity of the second relation at which we have been glancing, regarded as one of representation, aboutness or whatever. What it does is to suppose that:

> The relation between the internal content or object and the particular thing outside the head is just that the latter causes the former.

This fifth proposition seems hopeless. The simplest reason for saying so is that the internal content or object must be the effect of myriad things other than the particular thing it is said to represent or whatever – it is the effect, for a start, of a real image on a retina. It's not supposed to be about the retina. Complicating the simple causal story has not succeeded, and further attempts, more epicycles, seem unlikely to do better. *Of course* the truth about perceptual consciousness is causal, but it is a different kind of truth. You do not get to it by fiddling with the central causal story in the science of perception.[9]

4   Being Given to the Mind

Before turning to the fullest and best-known account of intentionality, let us consider one by Tim Crane.[10] It has to do with something so far not given much attention, a consensus that while intentionality is a feature of most conscious or mental states, it is not a feature of all of them. It is not a feature of such bodily sensations as having a pain and such moods or feelings as truly undirected anxiety or depression. As is commonly said, they are not about or of anything. The proposition we are about to consider is also different in another way. The previous ones, those that do not change the subject, have at least the smell of the sense-datum theory of perception about them. Here, we get rid of it.

In this exposition, tentative and not doctrinally-burdened, the consensus about bodily sensations and moods not being intentional is at least questioned. The essential first move in this connection, certainly arresting, is simply to detach the supposed fact of intentionality from a mental state's being (1) *of* anything, or (2) *about* anything, or its *representing* anything. The facts that a pain and being gloomy about nothing in particular are not *of* or *about* anything, and do not *represent* anything – these were of course just the reasons that those states were *not* regarded as intentional. Now these states can be intentional. The main plank of the proposition is said to be captured by or expressed in or inspired by what we have treated as a guiding remark, that (6) we do not just believe or desire or see, but believe or desire or see *something*.[11] This main plank is as follows.

What it is for something to be an intentional state is for it to
be given to the mind.

Particular accounts are given of the pain and gloom. With respect to the pain, it is first contemplated that an internal mental object is presented to the mind. However, an alternative acount is preferred, one that takes being in pain to be a case of being aware of something non-mental – one's body, or a state of it, or bodily events in it.[12] With respect to the undirected gloom, what is mainly said is that really it *is* in a way or ways directed. As Sartre held, emotions in general are a mode of apprehending the real world. This is a kind of direct realism about pains and gloom.

So we have these two instances of something being 'given to the mind', which fact is the fact of intentionality. The view is said to be close to previous propositions of intentionality for two reasons. One, alas, is that it involves what appears to be a *relation* in consciousness between thinkers and the objects of their thoughts – despite the fact, as is allowed, that this cannot be true in general. Secondly, the view is true to the idea so far unmentioned that when something is apprehended as the object of an intentional state, it is apprehended in a certain way. This is an idea closely associated with intensionality with an 's'.

This view must prompt a number of reflections. One, of some importance, has to do with the initial remarks, also a matter of consensus, that an intentional state certainly *is* about something or of something. There is also the philosophical commonplace that an intentional state *represents* something. Are these items not pretty much the heart of the matter? The ease with which this heart is jettisoned should go some way to curing anyone of the thought that with intentionality we have philosophical propositions that at least have agreed foundations. To say the least, things are not that clear. And, putting aside foundations, there is not even a decent consistency in what we get. But another reflection is as important.

We have long had philosophical accounts of the various kinds of consciousness – including accounts of seeing and other perceiving, and of sensations like pain, and of being subject to the emotions. Accounts of the latter two things are offered in the doctrine we are considering. A view of seeing and other perceiving is also favoured in the doctrine – direct realism, in line with what is preferred in connection with the pain and gloom. The doctrine's main aim, however, is to characterize a wholly pervasive character of consciousness. The aim is rightly higher than a certain disjunction: consciousness is either such-and-such, as when it consists in seeing and the like, or such and such, with pain and the like, or . . . The aim, rather, is to come up with a *common* character of conscious events, their intentionality.

We have the sum total of that character, I take it, when we are told that in consciousness something is *given to the mind*. Regarded as a philosophical account, this is very safe, because it says so very little. In fact it would fit well into the initial remarks with which we began. Presumably more than a metaphor is intended, but what? My apprehension is that we learn nothing from this account. If it goes beyond the remark that (6) in believing, desiring and seeing we believe, desire and see *something*, where does it go? Is it helped on its way at all by additional unexplained talk of 'directedness?'

The thinness can be made clear in a particular way. Consider the 'of-ness', 'about-ness' and representativeness of other mental states than pain and gloom and so on, those that do indeed seem to have this character, belief above all. Is this what it is for them to be instances of something's being *given to the mind* or is it not? If it is, then we have no *general* philosophical account of intentionality, one that also applies to the pain and gloom. This is the disjunctive failure. But if the 'of-ness' and so on is *not* what it is for something to be given to the mind, then what *is* this givenness? Could it be that what we have here is no more than a generalized direct realism – something pretty unlikely to throw light on consciousness itself, a fundamental character of *it*. In direct realism's talk of direct awareness, it has never analysed awareness, but only asserted it to be direct.

The doctrine under consideration also has in it something else to give us pause. Not only *conscious* states can have things *given* to them. Unconscious ones can. Well then, what is it for something to be *given to* something else if the latter thing is not conscious – if it is, as presumably it is, a neural structure? Do remember, by the way, if you are willing to tolerate non-conscious *representation*, that this givenness of something is specifically *not* its being represented by or to anything.

Let me also remark quickly, as in another case earlier, that if we are giving an analysis of a fundamental fact of consciousness or mentality, and something called 'the mind' turns up in it essentially, we are not a long way forward. Finally, and as important as anything else, there is that matter of a wonky relation between thinkers and the objects of their thoughts. Can you say, in effect, as our philosopher does in this case, that something is *usually* a relation but sometimes is not? That in general intentionality is a relation, but not always?[13] No you can't. At best you face immediate questions. *What* is that thing? One thing that it isn't is a relation.

5   Contents as Experiences

Let us finish this survey by looking a little more closely at what got some attention earlier, Searle's doctrine in his book *Intentionality*.[14] There is too much of it to be encapsulated in a sentence or two, but it is in part that *in your now being aware of this room, there exists some-thing called a content, but no directedness towards it*. Nor, then, is there anything that is directed towards it. What can be said, at most, is that a person has the experience. The content, then, is no object of awareness. It is not a sense-datum, sensum, impression, copy, kind of picture or the like – this doctrine, like the previous one, is presum-ably a version of direct realism as against the representative theory or phenomenalism. The content is not a 'linguistically realized' item either.[15]

Despite not being any of these things, however, it *is* something else. *This content is directed to something*. It *is* a *propositional content* or *representative content*. It may represent an object or state of affairs, as in the case of your awareness of a yellow station wagon or of this room. Or, it may represent without there being any object or state of affairs that it represents.

Several other things are said along these lines of contents in gen-eral. One is that instead of taking a conscious experience to be a relation between a person and the content, it would be more accu-rate to say the experience was *identical* with the content somehow realized. With respect to the representative character of the content, gestured at by what is admitted to be only the metaphor of direct-edness, it is allowed that it is not possible to give an *analysis* of it in simpler terms. Intrinsic intentionality is a ground-floor property of the mind.

Despite this, however, as you have heard earlier, light can be shed on the intentionality of the mind by way of the derived intentionality or representativeness of sentences of language, real pictures, and so on. These latter things, in what is called their logical character as against any of their ontological realizations, are a matter of (i) a truth condition or other 'condition of satisfaction,' (ii) a psychological mode, such that the sentence or whatever is a belief, desire or the like, which mode determines (iii) direction of fit. In the case of a sentence that is a belief, the belief needs to fit the world, rather than the world be changed to fit the belief, as in the case of a command. So with your awareness of this room, and perceptual consciousness in general. To speak of any content being a representation is just shorthand for such 'logical' facts about it.

To return to perceptual experience in particular, it is added that it has what are spoken of as phenomenal properties. Above all, while it is true that your being aware of this room is more or less a rep-resentation, it is more natural to regard it as a *presentation* of a state of affairs – directly of it, immediate, and involuntary. Also, with perceptual experience, it enters into the content somehow that the content is caused by the object it represents. This is 'shown' in the experience. Finally, a perceptual content may involve an aspect under which an object is presented, as in the case of Wittgenstein's duck/rabbit drawing.

Is this account of intentionality a damage to consciousness as existence? The account of it seems to me both impressive and a disaster – being philosophy, it can be both. If it escapes metaphor, scientism and spirituality, it faces some of the same seemingly insuperable difficulties as its predecessors. Also, for a large reason not yet given, it seems in the end to raise a question about itself, a general question about the interpretation of itself.

The exclusion of anything about a relation of a content to anything so vague as *the mind* or the like is of course understandable. But the exclusion is also impossible. It runs up against the seeming necessity that a representation *is* something that is *to* or *for* someone or something. A mark or propositional content or whatever such that there is no possibility of there being a reading or understanding of it by something is no representation. This remains true if representation is reduced to satisfaction-conditions and so on.

It thus seems that eschewing of the vagueness of a *mind* or whatever in relation to the content will not do. An account of that thing to which something is a representation is needed, and no account at all is given. Nor, secondly, is any account given of any relation from the thing to the representation. That is quite as bad, not an incidental failing.

To come on to the other relation, content to object, there is the other old difficulty of there being no sense in talk of a dyadic relation with only one term. There still is a relation asserted, of course, when representation is conceived in the way just mentioned, by way of the several notions – satisfaction-conditions and so on. It is no good saying, as it is said, that intentionality cannot be 'an ordinary relation' since the object or state of affairs at one end of it need not exist.[16] It obviously cannot be a relation *at all*. Ordinary, extraordinary, plain, fancy or of any other kind.

To come on to other difficulties of this account, they involve us in what seems to be a general question of how to interpret it. It may seem in a way clear enough. The content of a perceptual experience is not an object of awareness, not seen, not a sense-datum or the like, and not a linguistically realized item. However, that does not exclude a related possibility – very likely exactly what you have had in mind in contemplating the whole story. It is just that the content is *within* or *a part of* the experience, in consciousness, something reportable without inference.

One reason for this interpretation is that the content, as you will remember, is on the way to being identical with the experience, and that the experience is of course something *had* by the perceiver, something that is *experienced* by the perceiver. It is at least indicative, too, that it is said that such a content, which has a self-referential side having to do with causation mentioned in passing earlier, can be made explicit in a certain form. 'I have a visual experience (that there is a yellow station wagon there and that there is a yellow station wagon there is causing this visual experience.)'[17]

That same conclusion, that the content is within consciousness as a part, can be based as well on the content's having, as you will remember, such phenomenal properties as being a *presentation*. It seems we can tell or indeed are given this difference of perceptual experience from other consciousness. Remember as well that perceptual experience may involve an aspect under which an object is presented. It is certainly worth keeping in mind, too, that Searle's official position with respect to the ontology of conscious events is against reductionism – against, as it seems, their having only neural properties.[18] Further, while he does indeed distinguish his position from phenomenalism or the representative theory of perception, he stresses that for him experiences are *real* in a way that he takes to be denied in some other versions of direct realism.

The burden of all this is that the account we are considering is that in seeing the room we have the content *in* our experience – and, as we know, it is certainly not the object, which is such a thing as the yellow station wagon out there in the world. This is all very well, but there are reasons for hesitation. The situation is close to the one in Searle's philosophy of mind looked at earlier (p. 100). There are reasons to consider a very different interpretation. It is that the content of which we have heard so much is *not* in consciousness.

We have learned in recent philosophy of mind that the language of consciousness is easily degraded. The meanings of terms can be reduced to what is far less than the realities the terms are supposed to be about. This is true of 'consciousness', of course, and 'content' itself, and 'information', but also such other terms as have turned up in the exposition of this doctrine of intentionality, including 'experienced', 'representation', 'aspect' and so on. It does indeed seem unlikely that Searle should be among the degraders, given his role as the hammer of the artificial intelligentsia.[19] But for certain reasons it is not impossible.

One reason of which you heard earlier is that he insists that his doctrine gives the *logical* properties of intentionality, and not the *ontology* of the experiences that realize those properties. The distinction is perhaps sufficiently clear, and it does certainly leave us with the question of the ontology or actual nature of perceptual consciousness. We hear about that in another book we have considered, *The Rediscovery of the Mind*.[20]

We are told there that a reductionist account of the nature of perceptual consciousness is not intended, but it is uncertain how such an account is avoided. To repeat a principal contention of mine, it certainly is *not* avoided by what is mainly said of consciousness, that it consists in higher-level biological events of the brain caused by lower-level wholly neural events in the brain. *That* description, certainly, allows the higher-level events to be wholly neural.

It is not reassuring either that in one place in *Intentionality* where he says his contents are not objects, that there are no internal objects of awareness, he also goes further. 'The visual experience is not the object of visual perception, and the features which specify the intentional content are not in general literal features of the experience.'[21] That does not sound at all like the first interpretation – content in consciousness. Do we need to hear *all* the lines about experience, awareness and so on in a way very differently from before?

Let me notice in passing, on the way to a conclusion about the interpretation of the doctrine, that there is a special difficulty in saying that no analysis is possible of the intrinsic intentionality of consciousness. If this ground-floor property of the mind *does* defy any analysis, how can we know that light is shown on it by the intentionality of language, pictures and so on derived from it? This is not obvious, if only for the reason that there is no sense in which causes have to be *like* their effects.

Let me notice, too, that there is a remarkable difference between derived intentionality and intrinsic intentionality. With derived intentionality we have actually *got* representations – words in English, sentences, pictures, images and so on. When I use your name in saying good morning to you, that representation of you is about as real as you. If we cannot actually find any analogue with intrinsic intentionality, why should it be thought that it can have light cast on it by derived intentionality? How could something so unlike intrinsic intentionality cast any light at all?

I shall not attempt to settle the general question of interpretation that has emerged, opt for one thing rather than the other. Like much philosophy, what we have may be an attempt to have it both ways.

Let me suggest, rather, that we have a dilemma. If content *is* taken to be within consciousness, there is a large problem, and if it is not so taken, there is as much of a problem.

With respect to the first supposition, that contents are within consciousness, parts of perceptual experience – this is false. It is not only false that in perceptual experience we have a content as a sense-datum or other object of awareness. It is *as false* that we have the content otherwise conceived somehow within or as a part of the experience. What I have in my awareness of this room is nothing more than this room. What we get, to speak in Searle's terms, is just the object. We just get the station-wagon itself. That is the so-called phenomenology of it, as noted already with several other propositions of intentionality. So on this interpretation of the proposition what we again get is the imposition of a fiction on what we know. No more needs to be said.

The second interpretation is that really Searle wishes to relocate all that stuff about content *out* of consciousness as we have a grip on it. On his account correctly understood, it is really somewhere else. It is in the neural facts. The proper response to this is the same as before, with another proposition of intentionality, the second we looked at it. It is that we are left with no account at all of perceptual consciousness itself, and no reason for changing the subject.

6   A Mess

So much for this last thinking about intentionality – now let me rehearse our advance through the various propositions or doctrines.

It seemed possible in the beginning that an adequate account of perceptual consciousness needs to satisfy a requirement having to do with intentionality conveyed by a number of remarks, the first being that consciousness is typically *of* something. The remarks in question have issued in a number of philosophical propositions or doctrines of or related to intentionality that can enter into dualisms and the like. We have looked at these propositions of intentionality in order to see if any of them do have to be added to these philosophies of mind, destructively in the case of consciousness as existence.

They do not. They do not satisfy *any* requirement of interest. This is because these propositions are a mess. I have been a little relentless in laying out objections to them, some of which may have been noted by you before. My aim has partly been to reinforce a suspicion or at any rate a tentativeness that should have become a

suspicion – maybe a suspicion or tentativeness less expressed because of the idea that there is no alternative to some proposition of
intentionality or other. In any case, the propositions *are* a mess. Searle
was on the way to a truth, which humanly he did not reach, when
he took only the intentionality tradition before him to be 'something
of a mess'.[22]

The largest reason for my judgement, now familiar, is that what
most of the propositions centrally affirm, a content or object internal
to perceptual consciousness, is a fiction. The appearance and reality
of perceptual consciousness has no such thing in it. The second reason is the nonsense of a relation to an object or state of affairs that
does not exist or need not exist, a dyadic relation with one term.
The third is the vagueness of that to which something is a representation, maybe a mind. The fourth is obscurity about the second
relation, often said to be representation. A fifth, as with Crane, is
the obscurity of some relation or other, givenness, in the direct realism. A sixth, in the case of several propositions, is incompleteness.
A seventh, in two cases, is missing the subject entirely. Finally, there
is the uncertainty about the general interpretation of the fullest account, Searle's, which helps to open it to all of the objections already
mentioned.

One principal conclusion in this paper, then, is that we need to give
up on propositions of intentionality – anything of the sort we have
considered – in connection with perceptual consciousness. Propositions of intentionality have no such future. Another conclusion is
that these propositions do no damage at all to the theory of perceptual consciousness as existence. That is not all. Reflection on the
propositions actually favours perceptual consciousness as existence,
in various ways.

The theory does not exactly follow from, but is certainly suggested
by, there being no content or object within perceptual consciousness.
Might it be that it is only this theory that is both arguable and also
consistent with the fact of the missing content or object?

The theory is suggested too by the nonsense about a relation lack-
ing a term. In perceptual consciousness as existence, there is no such
relation – and thus no relation that can tempt anyone in the direction
of the nonsense. You are right to suppose there are other relations, between a world of perceptual consciousness and the scientific world,
and between a world of perceptual consciousness and a brain, and
between such a world and the perceived part of the physical world,
but no question whatever arises of a relation existing in the absence
of one of its terms. If consciousness as existence has to fit in illusion

and hallucination, which it does, and about which not enough has been said so far,[23] it does not have to do so by pretending that a non-relation is a relation.

There is the very same story with our other reflections on the propositions of intentionality – incompleteness, vagueness about the possessor or whatever of a representation, obscurity about the relation of this thing to the representation, obscurity of the relation of representation to an object, and missing the subject-matter entirely. These shortcomings of philosophical propositions of intentionality – not to mention startling inconsistencies between them – point to something very different, arguably the theory of perceptual consciousness we have been considering.

Let us return briefly to the bundle of remarks with which we began, the folk psychology as against the developed philosophical accounts of intentionality. How does percepetual consciousness as existence stand to that bundle? Also, how much of a requirement on accounts of perceptual consciousness *is* the bundle? Does perceptual consciousness as existence, for a start, accord with the remark that (3) in consciousness there is something before the mind?

Well, you could say that the view actually gets rid of the distinction between 'the mind' and 'something before it' – thereby meaning just the central proposition that to be perceptually conscious is for a world in a way to exist. You could also say, however, that the view gives a certain sense to the remark that in consciousness something is before the mind – that in a perceptual experience there exists a particular world rather than any other. You could say, too, that our existentialism about consciousness does better than did certain propositions of intentionality in accommodating the remark. My own first reaction, however, is one that does not accord too much respect to the remark. It is that it is a recommendation of the view that it gets rid of the mind as a ghostly entity, which the remark seems to take it to be.

So too with the remark that (4) the mind has a capacity to direct itself at things. Of this it can also be said that in a perceptual experience there exists a particular world rather than any other. But I leave to you further reflection on the bundle and the extent to which we have catered for it, and how far we should be constrained by it.

Finally, three general reflections on intentionality from elsewhere.

The first is by the distinguished Brentano and Husserl scholar, Reinhardt Grossman.[24] It is about dilemmas, and begins with what can seem to be one – that in perceptual and other consciousness either the mind is related to what is before it or it is not. The second horn of this dilemma *is* a horn because there is no plausible non-relational account. The first horn is a horn because it leads to difficulties of which you have heard something from me. That is, a relational account must deal with the proposition that we can believe in and desire things that do not exist. Thus what we have is either that there can be a relation to things that do not exist, a weird relation, or certain things that do not really exist do somehow exist – another dilemma.

In the tradition of Brentano and Husserl, I take it, the response to the first dilemma has indeed been that there is no non-relational account of perceptual consciousness. Thereafter a lot of fortitude has gone into trying to make sense of a relation underdescribed as weird, or to make sense of objects that somehow do not and also do exist. As you will anticipate, my response is different. We need not get into all that deep water, since, to go back to the first dilemma, so-called, there now *is* a non-relational account of perceptual consciousness – as a kind of existence.

The second reflection is by Quine.[25] It has to do with both the tradition of Brentano and also his idea, so far unmentioned, that intentionality is not only the mark of the mental but something that cannot be accounted for in physical terms. There can be no account of it that preserves a naturalism. Quine's response in effect is that if there is inconsistency between a supposed fact of intentionality and naturalism, then it is the supposed fact that must be given up. Does this response come to an entire disregarding of the requirement we have been considering on an account of consciousness? Does it come to supposing there is *no* sense or truth in the remark that in the consciousness on which we have a grip something is before the mind? Then it is no tolerable conclusion.

But that does not drive us far from Quine's position. If the choice *was* between something about the mind inconsistent not only with naturalism but also with the near-naturalism of perceptual consciousness as existence, my own inclination would be to give up that thing. That is not the choice we face. It may be a recommendation of taking perceptual consciousness to be a kind of existence that we can satisfy what requirements we need to satisfy in connection with intentionality and still remain philosophically respectable.

The third reflection is Jerry Fodor's, often reported, that '...if aboutness is real, it must really be something else.'[26] What is supposed to stand in the way of taking aboutness to be real? Fodor's answer, and the answer of many, is that it has seemed not to fit into naturalism at all, and particularly has not been open to the hopeless causal analysis mentioned earlier.[27] That is, there is no serious chance of taking *B*'s being a representation of *A* as just the fact that *A* causes *B*.

A response to Fodor is that getting near to naturalism is enough, and certainly that it would be absurd to suppose that intentionality is somehow non-causal. But of course consciousness as existence *is* near-naturalism and *is* a causal account of perceptual consciousness. Aboutness *is* real, and no doubt is more a fact of more of consciousness than perceptual consciousness. But, given our account of perceptual consciousness as the basis of consciousness generally, aboutness really *is* something else than has been supposed. He's right about that.

Notes

1. T. S. Kuhn, *The Structure of Scientific Revolutions* (University of Chicago Press, 1962).
2. Cornell University Press.
3. 'Intentionality', in Robert Audi (ed.), *The Cambridge Dictionary of Philosophy* (Cambridge University Press, 1995).
4. *Psychology from an Empirical Standpoint*, ed. Oskar Kraus, Linda L. McAlister (Routledge & Kegan Paul, 1973), p. 88. For interpretation of the paragraph, in particular in connection with existence-in rather than non-existence, see David Bell, *Husserl* (Routledge, 1990), ch. 1.
5. For introductory sketches of intentionality, see Stephen Priest, *Theories of the Mind* (Penguin Books, 1991), Owen Flanagan, *The Science of the Mind* (MIT Press, 1984), Robert Stalnaker, *Inquiry* (MIT Press, 1984), ch. 1, and Tim Crane, 'Intentionality', *Routledge Encyclopedia of Philosophy* (Routledge, 1998), ed. Edward Craig.
6. *Perceiving*.
7. See my *A Theory of Determinism* or *Mind and Brain*, both p. 71 ff.
8. Tim Crane, 'Representation', *Routledge Encyclopedia of Philosophy*.
9. Cf. Jerry A. Fodor, *Psychosemantics: the Problem of Meaning in the Philosophy of Mind* (Bradford Books, 1987).
10. 'Intentionality as the Mark of the Mental', in *Current Issues in the Philosophy of Mind*, Royal Institute of Philosophy Lectures for 1996–7.
11. 'Intentionality as the Mark of the Mental', pp. 246, 238, 243.
12. M. G. F. Martin, 'Setting Things Before the Mind,' in *Current Issues in the Philosophy of Mind*.
13. 'Intentionality as the Mark of the Mental', p. 244.
14. Cambridge University Press, 1983.
15. *Intentionality*, p. 6.
16. Ibid. p. 4.
17. Ibid. p. 48.

18. Searle, *The Rediscovery of the Mind* (MIT Press, 1992), p. xi ff, p. 1 ff, p. 113 ff.
19. Searle's well-known Chinese Room argument is in 'Minds, Brains and Programs', *Behavioral and Brain Sciences*, 1980.
20. pp. 86–103.
21. *Intentionality*, p. 44, 45.
22. Ibid. p. 1.
23. The matter comes up again in the last chapter in this book.
24. 'Intentional Relation', in *The Oxford Companion to Philosophy*, ed. Ted Honderich (Oxford University Press, 1995).
25. *Word and Object* (Wiley, 1960), p. 221.
26. *Psychosemantics: The Problem of Meaning in the Philosophy of Mind*, p. 97.
27. See p. 168.

Chapter Ten

Reflective and Affective Consciousness

Little needs to be said in introduction to this fourth stage of what I hope is progress. This stage does not immediately leave behind seeing and the like as against thinking and feeling – consciousness as perceptual as against reflective and affective. There is the good reason that the latter two facts of consciousness are to be understood only by reliance on the first. Their nature is to an important extent owed to the nature of perceptual consciousness. It might have happened, I suppose, that there was pure inquiry in the universe or pure feeling, or just the two together more likely, but those would not be *our* inquiry and feeling. It is hard to think these detached things, detached from a perceived world, would be inquiry and feeling at all.

In what follows, after an addition to the criteria of which you know for an adequate account of consciousness, and a different kind of characterization of the theory to which we have come, the next concern is the seeming bundle of activities that make up reflective consciousness. In understanding someone's reflective consciousness, should we think not of an actual but of a possible world?

In fact the bundle does not invite or allow for the kind of view that has been taken of perceptual consciousness. It turns out that there is as much departure necessary with affective consciousness. Both developments are in accord with the additional criterion of adequacy, which has to do with differences between the sectors or the like of consciousness. Both developments are important to a picture of the actual places of intentionality or aboutness in consciousness. Both modify the inclination not to have consciousness inside the head. They moderate our natural resistance to cranialism.

There must be uncertainty in all this. There is also one certainty.

___

1   Inescapable Criteria

Consciousness is a reality, something that exists in an ordinary way. Yours came into existence at some stage of your embryonic development, and it goes out of existence and comes back into existence when you fall into and come out of dreamless sleep. What is it for anything to exist in an ordinary way? It is for the thing to be physical or of the same sort as the physical. That is, the thing occupies space and time, has or is connected with properties somehow perceived, and is in certain relations to other things.

Consciousness is subjective. It divides up into certain sequences, and each of these is different in what it is in it, even when two sequences are related to the same bit of the physical world, or of the objective or scientific worlds. All the consciousness we know about – forget the speculative talk about computers and extra-terrestrials – is also subjective in being in a special relation to one person or organism, some kind of living subject.

Consciousness enters into causal relations. Events of consciousness, whatever their intrinsic natures, are in causal relations with physical events that precede and follow them. Locations of croquet balls cause ideas, and vice versa. This third criterion of an adequate theory of consciousness, by the way, is like the previous two in having various implications, of which the following is one.

The fact that conscious events are in causal relations with physical events has certainly been a problem. Impulses about consciousness, mystifying impulses, have made the causal connection hard to understand. To come to a specific implication of the criterion of causal interaction, a theory of consciousness with the upshot that there really has been *no* mind-body problem at all, that it has all been just an illusion, is at least suspect on this ground alone. I speak of real materialisms or physicalisms, of course.

Consciousness, fourthly, has a seeming nature. In particular, *perceptual* consciousness has a seeming nature. Furthermore, there is every reason for taking the seeming nature of all consciousness simply to be its very nature, the full reality of it. Whatever explains, underlies, shapes, informs or distorts it, whatever employment it gives to those who try to control or improve it, or just poke around under it for the edification of their clients and themselves, all consciousness itself is immediate, something given to us in its entirety. What is not given to us is not consciousness.

But more is to be said than until now of this fourth main criterion of a decent theory of consciousness. Perceptual consciousness itself does indeed have a nature, and a theory must be true to it. But it is one of the three parts, sides or elements of consciousness. Perceptual consciousness is seeing and the like. Reflective consciousness is thinking and the like. Affective consciousness is desiring, feeling and the like. The seeming natures of the perceptual, reflective and affective parts or whatever of consciousness are different despite similarity. Thinking about philosophy is not like seeing a croquet lawn and neither is it like wanting to get to sleep – and the seeing and wanting are also different. So an adequate analysis of all of consciousness, even if general, will preserve the differences. It will pass the test of what you can call differential phenomenology.

The theory of perceptual consciousness of existence is perhaps unique in satisfying or entering into the general satisfying of these inescapable demands. Too many other theories, indeed the main ones, fail to satisfy the last one, and instead make consciousness all too uniform. They also do badly or disastrously with the other criteria.

Something else, close to another criterion, also needs mentioning. This is our reluctance to say that our consciousness is in our heads. We find the question of whether it is at least confusing.[1] The theory of perceptual consciousness as existence is not indefinite about this matter. According to it, what it is for you to be aware of the room is for an extra-cranial state of affairs to exist. This, as you will have noted, is not a certain familiar truth. It is not the truth that our ordinary concepts of seeing or touching, to the extent that there are ordinary concepts, bring in extra-cranial facts – that *seeing* by definition is different from hallucinating. This ordinary truth leaves it possible that the perceptual consciousness itself is in the head – cells, immaterial stuff, or whatever. That is not the different idea we are considering.

Why is it that we are reluctant or confused with respect to the question of whether our consciousness in general is in our heads? Perhaps some of us are inclined to say it isn't there on account of what can be called the immaterialism or 'dualism' in ordinary beliefs about the mind, folk psychology. Differently, some of us may want to say No on account of the fact just remarked on, that seeing and so on necessarily involve a thing seen or whatever. Is it possible to put aside both of these distractions and still want to answer No to the question – straight-off, so to speak?

Well, there is another possible reason for the reluctance and confusion, a possible reason that is uncomplicated and larger. It might be, might it not, that our uncertainty has to do with the three parts, sides or elements of consciousness? Might our uncertainty have to do with the simple fact that the three parts or whatever are different from one another in this respect? Some in the head and some not? There could be some truth in cranialization as well as falsehood.

2   The Sort of Theory We Have

There seems no doubt that perceptual consciousness is fundamental to reflective and affective consciousness. To say a bit more of it, therefore, is also to speak of them. Perhaps the theory with which we have been engaged can be made clearer not by adding more to somewhat formal statements of it, but by more informal means, the first ones being questions and thoughts about its general nature as a theory – the sort of thing it is.

Some have remarked that it makes consciousness part of *ontology*, not the philosophy of mind? Maybe the remark has a use somehow understood. In it, what is the subject-matter of ontology taken to be? *Being* may be mentioned. If that subject-matter includes existing states of affairs, and if the subject-matter of the philosophy of mind is restricted to having to do with a mysterious mental relation of ours to those states of affairs, then the view in question does of course transfer perceptual consciousness from the philosophy of mind to ontology. But that depends, of course, on the chosen definitions. Also, is there any theory of consciousness that is not somehow about states of affairs?

Is the theory of perceptual consciousness as existence a piece of metaphysics? That is, let us say, is it a very general proposition about the nature, constitution and structure of reality – maybe about the right general categorizing of reality? It is indeed, like so much else, including *all* theories of consciousness. Think of neural functionalism. It tells you that a supposed fundamental distinction in reality, between mind and matter, does not exist.

To come to what may be the most reasonable impulse behind such questions as these, is the theory of perceptual consciousness as existence a departure from the customary metaphysics of the philosophy of mind? A departure from the ordinary categorizing of reality in it?

It should be a familiar truth that all of the philosophy of mind, like most of the rest of philosophy and of course science, rests on and is informed by *some* metaphysics in the sense indicated – assumptions or whatever about the nature, constitution and structure of what there is. Indeed consciousness as existence *is* a departure from the customary metaphysics of the philosophy of mind. The proposition before you is that it is a necessary departure for the better.

Another thought about the theory, touched on already, is that it presupposes what some philosophers will hurry to call a Kantian premise. This is that there is a so-called noumenal reality to which we bring our own perceptual and neural machinery – our classificatory machinery. It is my own inclination to think of this reality-underneath as not being beyond or almost beyond our conceiving or classifying, as Kant supposed or half-supposed. Rather it is the unperceived but certainly theorized part of the physical world.

Of this world, the world of atoms, we and it make or construct the perceived physical world, that public world, and we also come to have exactly what you have been hearing of – worlds of perceptual consciousness. We and the reality-underneath make of it a lot of other worlds as well. So it is true that a somewhat familiar line of thought out of the history of philosophy is in perceptual consciousness as existence. But, as you need to remember, no real multiplying of worlds, no creative prodigality in the way of Lewis.[2]

One more informal characterization of our theory will lead us into our main agenda. It is very relevant to what will turn up there. Brentano, as we know, regarded consciousness as consisting in *content* or *object* and something else. The second thing, to which he referred with commendable restraint in his talk of *direction*, was the presupposed self or inner point of view or what you will along these lines. There has been since the time of Brentano a certain amount of philosophical time and energy given to the subject of content – the content of consciousness. One common view takes the content of your present perceptual consciousness to be physical chairs and the like – things in the physical realm as we have been understanding it.

Given this, it is possible to see the view of perceptual consciousness as existence in a certain way. What it does is to reduce perceptual consciousness to something related to what others often more vaguely call its content or object. Consciousness becomes roughly what it is taken to be about by others. Those of sensitive philosophical dispositions, who react badly to talk of reduction, can as well see the view otherwise. They can see it as one that enlarges perceptual consciousness into the reality gestured at by others in their talk of content or object.

Can reflective and affective consciousness, thinking and the like and desiring and the like, be understood in a way that fits in with the nature of perceptual consciousness as we have it? Might it be that the non-perceptual parts or whatever of consciousness also are best reduced or enlarged into something like what others regard as their contents? That again the best and indeed the necessary policy is to get rid of a funny relation?

Certainly it will at least be embarrassing if the shortcomings of the other views of consciousness are escaped in the case of perceptual consciousness and then have to be put up with just as they are in connection with reflective and affective consciousness. We can hardly put together what we have about perceptual consciousness with a real materialist view of thinking or wanting. We would not only be falling into a kind of inconsistency, but we would be back with the problems of real materialism.

Might it be that the non-perceptual parts or whatever of consciousness also are best reduced or enlarged into something like what others regard as their contents? That again the best and indeed the necessary policy is to get rid of a funny relation?

3   Reflective Consciousness – Possible Worlds, Concepts, and so on

You can try to bring reflective consciousness, thinking in a wide sense, into a taxonomy.

1. There are the sorts of thinking that actually enter into and are part of what we have been concerned with so far, perceptual consciousness. These reflective things implicit in perceptual consciousness include conceptualizing, mentioned already, and also attending, studied a good deal in psychology.
2. Reflective consciousness also includes memory – both the activity of remembering and the result of the activity.
3. There is curiosity and inquiry. We ask questions, try to measure, seek causes and effects, experiment, guess, reason, seek to prove, and do philosophy, science, morals and politics.
4. Whether or not as a result of curiosity and inquiry, we suppose, judge and believe things to be the case. This is

our thinking in a narrow sense – thinking that such-and-such in whatever way, thinking somehow that something has a property or relation.

5. We imagine things, make up stories, create art.

6. In sleep we dream.

This is a poor taxonomy of the genus reflective consciousness, partly because much of a species or category of it may also fall into another. But let us not try to do better. The thing aims us in the right direction.

It does remind us that reflective consciousness is not like what perceptual consciousness seems to be – a somehow bounded and filled whole, what used to be called a perceptual field, what it is very natural to call a world of perceptual consciousness. Reflective consciousness seems to consist, rather, in disparate activities, from conceptualizing in perceiving through believing a truth of arithmetic to dreaming while asleep. It also has in it the different operations of our intelligent and intellectual existence.

Still, does the earlier account of perceptual consciousness in terms of an actual world tempt you to regard reflective consciousness in a related way? Are you tempted to the idea that thinking in the wide sense consists in their being possible worlds or anyway possible things, no doubt with a special dependency on one thinker's brain? It is the idea that to think something, in whatever way, is for a thing to exist in whatever way it is that possible things do exist. My theorizing with my eyes shut, say, consists in possible objects having possible properties.

Although some of us are capable of forgetting it, partly because the usage has helped out with some formal logic, the clearest sense in our saying there are possible worlds is that our actual worlds, perceptual and physical, have a certain character or certain features. To say there is a possible world in which Jane Austen lived all her life in Bath is to say our actual worlds are such that it could have happened that she did. What that comes to, in brief, is that our actual worlds are such that our laws of nature and logic do not preclude her having lived her life in Bath. So with talk of possible things as against possible world. To talk of them is to talk of things that are not precluded by our laws of nature and logic.

So if we do not go in for the metaphysical prodigality of worlds mentioned earlier, the idea that our thinking in general is to be understood in terms of possible worlds and things is the idea that it is to be understood in terms of the natural constitution or operation of our worlds of perception and physical worlds, along with our conceptual schemes with respect to them.

Whatever is to be said of how the idea fares with our adequacy-criteria for theories of consciousness, there is an immediate objection. It is plain that reflective consciousness goes far beyond this limited subject-matter. In the relevant sense, for a start, and despite what was said of an intermingling of reflective and perceptual consciousness, I can think impossibilities. I can have thoughts that go beyond both kinds of limits on possibility. We commonly think of what physically cannot happen, and too often think contradictions.

The point that our thinking does far outstrip possible worlds and things certainly persists, by the way, if you feel that what has just been said of them in terms of our laws is too deflationary, insufficiently generous. Possible worlds can be as real as mushrooms, popping up in ever-greater numbers every metaphysical spring, watered by modal logic. They remain, as their name reminds us, different from *impossible* worlds. But our thinking in general also has to do with impossible worlds.

Something very different from possible worlds and things may come to mind at this point. This is the idea that reflective consciousness consists in *concepts and propositions*, to which can be added *images* – images of the same order of reality or unreality.[3] It can be said for this idea that it does not defeat itself by putting a mistaken limit on the reach of our thinking. So in place of a view that may be conventional, that our thinking in the general sense has concepts and propositions *in it*, that it is something that *has* this content, should we consider the idea that what thinking in general comes to, all of what it comes to itself, *is* just concepts and propositions?

In addition to the recommendation of no mistaken limits on thinking and, you may say, no superfluous addition to what others call the content of reflective consciousness, the idea may have other recommendations. Might it be carried forward in such a way as to satisfy the criteria of adequacy for accounts of consciousness having to do with reality, subjectivity, and differential phenomenology?

With respect to subjectivity, presumably you can say that my reflective consciousness will be different from yours, and different from any set of concepts and propositions that has been ordered by us in a cooperative enterprise – the defining of a common language. Also, reflective consciousness will certainly be different in its seeming and actual nature from perceptual consciousness. The idea of concepts and propositions can also seem to have another virtue.

Like its predecessor, about possible worlds and things, it allows us at least to wonder if being reflectively conscious is other than the fact of there being stuff literally in one's head.

But that is the end of the possible recommendations and virtues. The idea of concepts and propositions ordinarily understood has a large flaw unmentioned in connection with its possible-worlds predecessor but very likely shared with it. If reflective consciousness is taken to consist in concepts, propositions and images, and these are *abstract objects*, not things or events taking up space and time, then there is the immediate result that reflective consciousness is not real in our required sense. It fails the reality test – and also is not itself in causal connection with the events of input and output. Abstract objects are not events, not things in space and time. Whatever else is to be said of them, it seems they cannot be effects or causes. They have nothing to do causally with, say, locations of croquet balls.

Even if you do not share exactly my impulse about the real, you will agree, I trust, that any view of any part of consciousness that denies its causal efficacy or functionality, makes it epiphenomenal, is intolerable? Will it not take more than a brave philosopher, indeed a philosopher of bravado, to defend epiphenomenalism? Will it not take such a philosopher to defend what has recently been correctly defined or anyway expressed as the view that 'remembering our childhood plays no part in the writing of our memoirs' and 'it is never pain that makes us wince, nor anger that makes us shout'? This is more than what is granted, that it is 'an affront to common sense'.[4]

So much for the idea by itself that what there is to reflective consciousness – my remembering the look of my father or thinking a sceptical thought about something – is the stuff of concepts, propositions and equally abstract images. Can we get to a better view by marrying something to the idea?

We can add to it, for a start, that while my two pieces of thinking are not causes of my subsequent behaviour, the wholly neural processes that are associated with them are exactly such causes. They cause, for example, my subsequent speech-acts, the physical sentences that report my pieces of thinking. And further, to come to the essence of the strategy, we add in that an abstract piece of thinking can be required or necessary for an associated neural process in something other than what is impossible – a causal or other nomic sense. So since the neural process *is* causally required for the later behaviour, that will give the right role to the pieces of thinking.

Or rather, this much being familiar enough, the real essence of this third strategy must be to try to conceive of a suitable relation of necessity between the abstract thinking and the neural process. It will be a long way from a causal or otherwise nomic relation, of course, given that the thinking is abstract. What relation then? It can hardly be that the relation between a neural process and my thinking of the look of my father is *deductive*. It is not that a description of one entails a description of the other. Neuroscience is not an *a priori* discipline. Might the funny relation be a constitutive or part-whole relation? But hitherto those have been nomic or logical. Might it have the name of being a *metaphysical* relation? Easily said, but what is one of those?

Being in bad trouble, and wanting to leave it behind, do you now stick to the idea of thinking being abstract concepts and propositions, but just give up on a funny relation that gives efficacy to consciousness? Contemplate epiphenomenalism after all, contemplate that remembering our childhood plays no part in the writing of our memoirs and that it is never pain that makes us wince nor anger that makes us shout? Maybe your mind turns to consolations.

This epiphenomenalism of reflective consciousness being taken as abstract, you can say, goes perfectly well with *perceptual* consciousness having no tinge of epiphenomenalism to it. Worlds of perceptual consciousness *are* made up of things in space and time. So what you are swallowing is only a partial epiphenomenalism. Why shouldn't our conviction of the efficacy of the mental or mental causation be owed to and have to do with only part of the mental?

Maybe so, but this fourth idea – abstract thinking somehow connected to the brain – has a larger problem. It is not just that we would need a new sort of relationship between thought and neural process for the purpose of escaping epiphenomenalism. We need such a relation actually to *have* such a view of reflective consciousness to consider. We need such a relation for this fourth view that we have been gesturing at really to exist. Its very essence is a relationship between what is abstract and what is physical. The problem for it at bottom is the mind-body problem or input-output problem. What is the relation it offers? Without at least the beginning of an answer to the question, we do not actually have a view to consider.

That is not all. Making our thinking into concepts and propositions, with whatever funny relation to the brain, plainly runs up against another difficulty. It might satisfy some of our adequacy-criteria, but there is the very first one to think about. Consciousness is a reality. Thus it is something physical or, as we said at the very beginning, of the sort of the physical. We achieved this with perceptual consciousness, but on reflection we are not achieving it with the idea on hand of reflective consciousness as no more than concepts and propositions.

In these straits, let us not weaken and fall back into physicalism or materialism about reflective consciousness, even a fancy kind – say functionalism or some related doctrine that in fact leaves out the fact of consciousness as we have a grip on it and in particular its subjectivity. All of that falls victim to our conviction that consciousness isn't cells.[5] Let us rather reflect on something new, or anyway something else, for the excellent reason that nothing old works.

4   Reflective Consciousness as Existence – Outer Representations

Let us start again, as in the case of perceptual consciousness, with the so-called phenomenology. As they say, what is reflective consciousness like? What is it now *like*, as they say, for you to remember the look of your father? That is, what is the seeming nature of the fact of your remembering the look of your father? The experience is a lot different from seeing him. To take another piece of reflective consciousness, what is the seeming nature of your consciously believing something? That the squirrel is going up the other side of the sycamore tree, or that some philosophy is up the spout? What about dreaming? It also has a seeming nature that is different from the seeming nature of daily life. So does picturing this room after you leave it, or otherwise imagining something.

Is there one answer to this question of differential phenomenology as persuasive as the answer that what it seems to be *perceptually* conscious is for a world somehow to exist? Would that there were. *Something* is a reality when I remember the look of my father, or believe something, or dream, or imagine. That reality isn't cells. But how *are* we to think of it? There seems to be nothing to hand with which reflective consciousness can enlighteningly be compared, and by which it can be got into view – as perceptual consciousness could be compared with the perceived part of the physical world.

And, to revert to our earlier reflections on possible worlds, there really is no phenomenological temptation to speak of reflective consciousness heuristically as *a world*. Someone thinking with his eyes closed can be said to be in a world of thought, maybe mathematics, but that is a poor metaphor at best. Thinking with your eyes shut isn't at all like being aware of this room. The closest thing to perceptual consciousness that can be found in reflective consciousness is dreaming, and for several reasons that is a good way off.

Still, it is not as if direct reflection on our thinking produces nothing. Something can be said of the phenomenon. It is that in all of our thinking *things exist that may be true of other things or may come to be true of other things*. In the case of me and my father, there is an image or the remains of one. In the case of me and the squirrel's going up the other side of the tree, there is a sentence of English or a part of one. Without asking about the ontological standing of the image and the sentence, we can make this our start of an account of our thinking. We can take it that what we actually seem to know about reflective consciousness, as remarked above, is that it is a matter of *representations*.

These representations, it seems, even if they turn out to be like physical things rather than abstract, cannot be adequately described just as effects of the things of which they may be true. That recent hope was futile. There are many more effects of my father than such signs of him.[6]

Here is another idea. You make a better start on saying what a representation is by saying something about it itself being causal rather than the thing it represents being causal. More particularly, a representation is what shares some of the effects of what it represents. A representation can make you smile, or go into the next room, and so on. The picture of a tiger, or the image of a man or woman of a kind or doing something, or a symbol for fire, has some of the effects of what is represented. That is more or less what it comes to for a representation to stand for something else, isn't it? Anyway it's a good start.

Before we get into any philosophical deep water, say about relations between representations, and about systems of representations, remember that we have a real grip on a certain kind of them. These are such instances of written or spoken words as those you are now reading – and the equally more or less physical images, photos, drawings, icons and what-not that fill and litter our lives. There are also other things, a multitude of them, that have a representative side to them.

I admit straightaway that we are not really sure how these various things have become representations, and have not quite worked out in general the related matter of what class of effects they share with what they represent. But we do in one clear sense know what they are, and this is of great importance to our present project. These representations are things that turn up in our worlds of *perceptual* consciousness. If your actual chair is in your world, so too is something else of the sort of the physical – the actual words or whatever that represent or are true of your chair.

So as to have a proposal clear quickly, here it is baldly. Reflective consciousness is partly a matter of certain representations – instances of representations, if you want. These are actual representations or signs in our worlds of perceptual consciousness. They are items like other items in these spatio-temporal states of affairs. To go further with the proposal, what reflective consciousness more or less comes to in part *is* these actual representations. Reflective consciousness so conceived, you will note, is no more than the sort of thing, or one sort of thing, that others take to be its content.

This proposal, to remember our adequacy-criteria, makes reflective consciousness a reality – what it consists in is of the sort of the physical, part of the reality of worlds of perceptual consciousness. Reflective consciousness so conceived, further, is as subjective as perceptual consciousness. It also makes it private in the way of all contents of perceptual worlds. It is something that causes and is caused by physical things – it passes the mind-body test. And, clearly, the proposal makes reflective consciousness very different, as indeed it is, from perceptual consciousness.

What about what can be contemplated for a while as almost another criterion of an adequate analysis of consciousness – the uncertain and unsettled idea that consciousness is not in the head? Evidently we do not have to say of reflective consciousness as so far conceived that it is inside our heads. The representations in question aren't there at all.

Do you not rush into agreement with the given proposal about reflective consciousness? Are you delayed by that question of how the actual representations become representations? I myself am not much concerned with this interesting and large matter. Our problem is the nature of consciousness, an analysis of consciousness, not an explanation of how it or any part of it comes about. No doubt the story has something to do with chimps making an involuntary sound while running away, and then coming to use the sound voluntarily and purposively to give advice about running away. The story will also have to do with the causes that are natural signs, so called, such as footprints in the sand.

Are you delayed in your agreement with the given proposal about actual representations because you object, as was tempting with the existential analysis of perceptual consciousness, that the given analysis of reflective consciousness is no analysis but a case of something like circularity or *petitio principii*? That in fact we have set out to analyse thinking, and said it consists in part in some representations, but in fact ended up with the non-analysis that thinking is *thinking about* representations?

That is, you say a representation is only a representation if it is taken as such. For someone not in the know, the same item is no representation at all. So, to repeat, there is the embarrassment that we set out to say what it is to be in a way conscious, we come up with the answer that it is for certain representations to occur, but it transpires that the answer when explicit is pointless. It is such that our endeavour reduces to the circularity that to be conscious in a way is to be conscious of some representations. If this is not full circularity or *petitio principii*, it is no great advance.

It seems to me this is not the case – that the objection can be resisted. What it is for me to remember the look of my father, so to speak, is importantly for my subjective representations to exist for a while, no more that that. They represent or symbolize away, so to speak, without my helping them by doing something else conscious. The label hereby put on the view, *reflective consciousness as existence*, is in fact apposite. There is no more to this consciousness, as so far characterized, than the existing of the mentioned things.

That is not to deny a burden of what has just been asserted, however. Representations *are* representations only for those who are in some special way related to them. That is part of what it is for something to be a representation, but not necessarily something that gives rise to a circularity. What comes into view here is also a larger, more general consideration, as follows.

Our subject-matter has been and is consciousness. We all have a grip on it. Indeed in a sense we know what it is, know nothing better. You will not need much reminding that our subject-matter is not other nearby things. For example, it is not doing things without being conscious. There is a significant subject-matter there. If it can be called 'mental function', and if it is spoken of in terms of some recent piece of neuroscience, say blindsight, it is as old as the hills, or anyway our relations to the hills. Philosophers noticed a good while ago that we walk without conscious planning, do some of our driving of cars while only aware of what is on the radio, and so on.

The main nearby subject-matter that is not ours in this inquiry, though, is not doing things without being conscious. It is the non-conscious side of conscious proceedings. There is a lot to thinking, you can say, that is not part of the conscious thinking.

This subject-matter of neuroscience, cognitive science and so on, is larger and more important than that of doing things without being conscious.

A decent account of consciousness, and more particularly of consciousness as representations, does not have to transform the non-conscious side into a matter of consciousness, and will be absurd if it tries. Rather, to come to the main point, a decent account of consciousness will make use of the fact of non-conscious mental functioning where it is needed.

To revert to the objection about circularity, it was that it is futile to try to understand consciousness as *being* certain representations, since that must really be to understand it as a matter of being conscious of the representations. I don't think so. My line is that sometimes your being conscious, your thinking of your father, may *be* the fact that something is representing him in a certain way – that something in your world of perceptual consciousness is having certain effects, effects it would not have in the absence of certain facts of non-consciousness, but that is nothing to the point. That something is a representation because of a lot of other things is not the proposition that it is a representation because someone is separately conscious of it as a representation.

The point can be put more graphically. Somebody says that symbols are dead unless they are understood. Or they're not symbols unless they are understood. That is fine. The point is that what it is for symbols to be alive, to be understood, to be symbols – *is* for them to share certain effects with what they symbolize.

There is something else to be said of reflective consciousness and representations, but pause for a moment and think again of intentionality or aboutness. We found no such fact in perceptual consciousness. We now have such a fact, explained, in reflective consciousness. There is more of it to come. Were you tempted, in connection with perceptual consciousness, to say that intentionality or aboutness is a fact about some consciousness or other? That here we have another criterion of an adequate theory of consciousness? Well, the theory of consciousness as existence is now in course of satisfying it – satisfying a properly limited criterion.

5   Reflective Consciousness – Inner Representations

Will you say there are more representations than the actual ones in our worlds of perceptual consciousness? More representations than the ones on paper and in sounds and so on? And that they have to do with our thinking, reflective consciousness? Will you not give up the familiar idea that certain representations can be said in a way to be definitely *in the head*, making up a stream of reflection?

It needs to be granted. Certainly I grant it. Reflective consciousness is also a matter of a *second* class of representations, inner rather than outer. They are states and events of ourselves and other forms of life of which we know and maybe other things. These representations – things sharing some effects with what they are said to represent – stand in a certain relation to the contributing organism. It is a relation that is analogous to the dependency relation of perception, so to speak, in which the contributing organism stands to its world of perceptual consciousness.

These representations, then, items in an actual language of thought, have an existence different from but related to that of the contents of the physical world itself – the perceived part of the physical world. These inner representations, as you will anticipate, have a subjective character as clearly as do things, including the outer representations, in worlds of perceptual consciousness.

To take this line, of course, is in this sector to give up on the idea that consciousness is not in the head. To take this line accepts the truth that generality can be pursued at too great a cost, an overriding of recalcitrant facts. An analysis of consciousness may have a recommendation on account of satisfying some idea *for the most part*. While an adequate analysis of consciousness has to avoid saying that consciousness is always stuff *inside heads*, we can have a little in there. This ecumenical spirit might also be adopted with other objections.

Instead let me conclude quickly about reflective consciousness, or rather repeat, that we can take it to consist in representations in our outer worlds of perceptual consciousness and also representations in our heads, in both cases things that are acceptable to a tolerant physicalism. As a result, we still have an account of reflective consciousness that does all right in terms of the criteria of adequacy.

All the representations in question have reality, and they are subjective. How I alone contribute to my cranial ones – the question of the counterpart to my perceptual apparatus and so on in the case of my perceptual consciousness – that question is for friends in the laboratories. To say that my representations are subjective is also to say they are not exactly your representations, or of course the agreed representations of our physical and objective worlds. Further, they are private in something like the way of things in perceptual worlds and they have, so to speak, no uncontemplated existence – which facts do not subtract them from an actual world. As for the remaining adequacy-criteria, all the representations in question can enter into causal relations, and they make reflective consciousness another sort of thing from perceptual consciousness. There is also the explanation of the intentionality or aboutness of some consciousness.

6   Affective Consciousness as Existence

We come now, a little late, to affective consciousness or desiring and feeling in a general sense. It has more in it than is spoken of as *affect* in psychology. Here too we can contemplate an informal taxonomy.

1. Evidently particular desires and wants of very many kinds, and, quite as important, satisfactions and frustrations of them, are at least part of affective consciousness. The desires and wants range from inclinations and hankerings, through wants and appetites, to cravings and lusts, to irresistible compulsions, which is but one sorting-out of them. They seem to be separable in general into attractions and repulsions.

2. Affective consciousness includes a wide range of sensations, feelings, emotions, attitudes and sensations, different in their subjects or objects and also a good deal else. They include pain, pleasure, hunger, satiety, hope, fear, courage, pride, shame, happiness, anger, sadness, love, loyalty, respect, wonder, depression, calm and so on.

3. This consciousness also includes what is somehow separable from all this, which is valuing. Almost all things can have some value for us. They are good or bad for me or you from the point of view of self-interest. They are right or wrong morally.[7] They are legal or not, rational or not, beautiful, expensive, preferable, tolerable and so on. Other persons as well as things have these values.

4. We have intentions of two kinds, the forward-looking or inactive kind, such as the intention today to travel by train tomorrow, and the active kind of intentions, these being involved in the actual initiation and carrying forward of actions. Active intentions are close to what have traditionally been regarded as willings, volitions and the like, but they need to be understood, less traditionally, as being a considerable part of what can be called our consciousness of or in acting.[8]

A little reflection on this attempt at taxonomy brings out its shortcomings. Very clearly, at least many of the particular desires and wants in the first category enter into the sensations, feelings, emotions and attitudes in the second category, and vice versa. So with the sensations and so on, and the valuing. Pride cannot be taken in what is worthless, of no value, and to think one has done right is to respect oneself for a while. Also, all three sorts of affective consciousness are involved in the fourth, the intentions. To intend to do something, tomorrow or now, is to want something, feel about it, and put some value on it.

To speak differently but as truly, there is the fundamental fact that the first category's particular desires and wants and their satisfactions and frustrations are more or less pervasive in and are much of the stuff of the following three categories of affective consciousness. Some of the sensations, feelings and so on of the second category, say hunger, are close to being desires themselves. All of the sensations, feelings and so on include desires. Think of fear or hope.

So with the third and fourth categories. Think of what is good for America or right for all of us, or of intending to do this rather than that. These at least have desire or want as a component. Evidently forward-looking intentions can be regarded as complexes of a desire for what is said to be intended together with beliefs of several kinds, and active intentions as such complexes with the addition of an executive element, something that can have the name of being a command to one's body.

As in the case of reflective consciousness, then, all that can be claimed for the taxonomy is that it aims us in the right direction.

Here is one of three quick proposals about affective consciousness, and in the first instance and most clearly with the first category of particular desires and wants. The proposal is that what it is to desire a thing is for the thing to have properties that it has independently of the desirer. For reasons just remarked on, the pervasiveness of desires in affective consciousness, this is also part of what it is to have feelings about something, value something, and intend something.

The proposal goes against what philosophers have sometimes seemed to drift into or anyway towards, the attitude that someone's desiring something is just a fact about that person. To this a salutary response is that the thing has to be *desirable*. That is, it has to have some property, whatever mistakes are made about it, in virtue of which the person desires it – whatever desiring comes to. The thing has to be bigger, sweeter, more highly paid, quiet or whatever, or of course dirty, dangerous, ignorant, fatal or whatever. This is no matter of projecting value onto a world, gilding a world, and so on,[9] but of value being in part in the world.

Here we also encounter a common inclination and also some faded philosophy, to the effect that things have not only natural but also non-natural properties, and the latter are what is in question with valuing and the like. There is the non-natural property of goodness. The existence of such a thing was supposed to be proved by the proposition that it is an open question whether any natural property is the or a property of moral goodness. It would not be such if there was a definitional or conceptual connection between the two items.[10]

This is not the time for a return to all that. Let me say simply that nothing can obscure the fact that I want to meet someone because of their smile, reputation or what-not. And that I may take a policy as right because it distributes goods to those in greater need or, very differently, in favour of my already well-fed nation. We do not agree about what is desirable or right, and hence certain definitions are not written into language. But this has no tendency whatever to show that the properties in virtue of which we have feelings about things – hope for them, are shamed by them or whatever – are not ordinary properties of them.

So, a part of what it is somehow to desire something is for it to have certain actual properties. That is to say, to come to a crux, that part of what it is for you to desire something is for things in *your* world of perceptual consciousness, or as we can add, for things as represented in *your* reflective consciousness, to have certain properties. It follows that what it is for you to desire something is a fact or reality, and subjective in a clear sense, of course, and that it involves no barrier to causal connections.

That cannot be the end of the story of affective consciousness, however. We need a second proposal, since the first one has nothing in it about differential phenomenology, the different nature of affective as against perceptual and reflective consciousness, desiring in general as against seeing and thinking. To take the first species of affective consciousness, there is a difference that asserts itself between desiring and just seeing something. To turn to the second species, there is a difference between having the pain of being burned and seeing a match burning. Similar remarks are to be made about valuing and intending. All of desiring is different from seeing and thinking.

The difference has often been taken as having to do with our behaviour and our bodies. A ludicrous view here, reduced to useful parody, was the radical behaviourism that made my wanting to get a book for my son no more than my movements in ordering it from Amazon.com. Not my *actions*, note, since the ordinary idea of an action imports mental content excluded from radical behaviourism's idea of wanting something.

But if behaviourism is gone, and is now preparing a last resting place for neural functionalism, it is clear we must not put aside everything about behaviour and bodies in attempting an analysis of affective consciousness. Indeed it is impossible to do so with pain and the rest of what are rightly referred to as *bodily* sensations – some of the items in the second category of facts of affective consciousness. These, to come to a point, can presumably be treated somehow along the lines of reflective consciousness. To have a headache is for something in my body in a way to exist. As with bodily sensations, so in ways and degrees with the rest of what is in the second category of affective consciousness. We can give some place to the existence of inner bodily items with feelings, emotions and attitudes. In fact a bodily component in fear, courage, shame, even respect and wonder, has been a reasonable assumption before now.

A related account can be given of the particular desires and wants of the first category. So with the two kinds of intentions. With respect to active intentions, those involved in the actual initiation and carrying forward of actions, there is what we ordinarily call direct awareness of items of bodily movement. Something similar if weaker can be said in connection with valuing.

A third proposal about affective consciousness, separable from what has just been said, has to do with behaviour or action in another way. Again to take simple cases from the second species of affective consciousness, fear and courage involve somebody's thinking of whole actions, say fleeing and attacking. To be afraid is partly a matter of the existence of representations of actions. So affective consciousness takes into itself some reflective consciousness. Similar remarks can be made about particular desires and wants, values, and of course intentions.

The conclusion about affective consciousness, then, is that it is to be understood as consisting in (a) a side of perceptual consciousness, this having to do with actual properties of things and people, and in (b) states or events in our bodies, and in (c) reflective consciousness having to do with actions. This view of affective consciousness thus inherits the recommendations of its components with respect to the adequacy-criteria with which we started. It makes affective consciousness into kinds of existence of things. It reduces or elevates consciousness into content. It gives a place to intentionality or aboutness.

7   Uncertainties and a Certainty

Consciousness as existence, the whole theory in sum, is that what it is to be conscious perceptually, reflectively or affectively is *for certain things in a way to exist*, different things in each case. Consciousness is near to what others have called its content, with at least the implication that there is more to consciousness than content, a mistaken implication.[11]

Of what worth is the whole theory? A philosopher, even a philosopher-proprietor, should be able to stand back and ask. Well, the stuff on perceptual consciousness seems to me an enlightening reorganization of thinking on the subject, a conceptual revision that serves truth a lot better – the truth of the criteria of consciousness. Anyway it seems to have this recommendation on a clear day, in the morning. The stuff on reflective and affective consciousness is not a lot more than preliminary sketches. These sketches seem to me promising. They leave you uncertain to a degree. They need to be made into more proper theories, of course. Surely they can be?

The certainty is that although consciousness as existence may not be true, or a good reorganization of our thinking, or as persuasive with reflective and affective as with perceptual consciousness, it has another use. It has the use of illustrating how much change is needed in the plodding industry of our current philosophy of mind. A lot of it is only philosophy of mind so-called. It has or aspires to strengths other than those of philosophy, more or less scientific strengths. It is not good at logic in a large sense. While the essential science goes on, we need to get back to the philosophy and start again. Whatever the worth of consciousness as existence, that is a certainty.

As for its worth, there is more to be said of that, more argument on several fronts.

Notes

1. In my recent experience the fact has been illustrated in discussions with a couple of scientists, Susan Greenfield, author of *The Human Brain: a Guided Tour* (Basic Books, 1998) and *The Private Life of the Brain* (Penguin, 2002), and Roger Penrose, author of *The Emperor's New Mind* and *Shadows of the Mind* (Oxford University Press, 1989 and 1994).
2. David Lewis, *On the Plurality of Worlds* (Blackwell, 1986).
3. Alastair Hannay, *Mental Images: a Defence* (Allen & Unwin and Humanities Press, 1971).

4. Keith Campbell, Nicholas J. J. Smith, 'Epiphenomenalism', *Routledge Encyclopedia of Philosophy*, ed. Edward Craig (London & New York, Routledge, 1998).
5. Another word or two will be said of the conviction (p. 206). It is made good use of, by the way, in a piece only bits of which got into this books. That is 'Consciousness and Inner Tubes', a critical discussion in the *Journal of Consciousness Studies*, 2000, of David Papineau's book, *Introducing Consciousness* (Icon/Totem, 2000).
6. Representations were, of course, the subject of a lot of earlier reflection, in 'Seeing Things', Synthese, 1994. But that reflection was in another world.
7. For a view of moral propositions as owed to human desires and rationality, see my *After the Terror* (Edinburgh University Press, 2002).
8. My *A Theory of Determinism* (Oxford University Press, 1988) or *Mind and Brain* (Oxford University Press, 1990), pp. 216–31.
9. cf. Simon Blackburn, *Essays in Quasi-Realism* (Oxford University Press, 1993).
10. G. E. Moore, *Principia Ethica* (Cambridge University Press, revised edition ed. Thomas Baldwin, 1993).
11. Francois Tonneau has lately drawn to my attention the doctrine of neo-realism advanced at the turn of the last century by the Americans Holt, Marvin, Montague, Perry, Pitkin and Spaulding. See Tonneau's 'Consciousness Outside the Head', forthcoming in *Behaviour and Philosophy*. Neo-realism is said to be an account of consciousness as outside the brain and head, an account of consciousness that identifies content and object. It is clear, however, that consciousness as existence is very different from neo-realism. For the latter, consciousness is in the environment, a part or cross-section of the environment. Conscious experiences, further, veridical or otherwise, exist wholly independently of being perceived or not. Consciousness does not depend on brains. A person's conscious experience at any time is the part of the environment acting on the person, and nothing else. The doctrine is a wholly general one, about all consciousness. Neo-realism has it that dreams exist outside the head, as do hallucinations, illusion, mental images and memories. It faces up to the seeming absurdity of this, and develops a certain reply having to do not with present or momentary things outside the head but with constituents of the environment over a longer time scale. The doctrine of neo-realism gave way to critical realism – Santayana, Sellars and Lovejoy – which denied the identity of the contents and objects of experience.

Chapter Eleven

Spiritualism, Devout Physicalism, Brains in Vats, Neuroscience

A number of philosophies of mind contemplated by us are said to be physicalisms, identity theories, materialisms, reductionisms, monisms, naturalisms or neuralisms. To a great extent they do fall together, and are one option with respect to the problem of this book. There is a second option that seems in fact to be the choice of more of us. In a democratic philosophy of mind, or rather a democratic philosophy that counted timid or uncertain votes, maybe ignorant ones, this other option would prevail.

This choice-situation, the first subject of the last paper of this book, throws a further light on consciousness as existence. Light is thrown on it too by some informal characterizations of it, one being the idea that it consists in metaphysics rather than the philosophy of mind. The main business of the paper, however, is something else.

It is what may be a resolution of a problem as significant and persistent as any in philosophy, or philosophy in the English language. That is the problem of the argument from illusion, given to us by Locke in the seventeenth century and lately rechristened the problem of the brain in the vat. It can happen that a new way of looking at things can have not only the hoped for but also an unexpected upshot, a happy one. Is this the case with consciousness as existence?

Other questions have to do with the need for a theory of consciousness to be a little baffling, and finally the relation and repercussions of the existence theory with respect to neuroscience, cognitive science and also physics if you want. Certainly some philosophy motivated by science has been put aside in this book. There is another matter. Does consciousness as existence make consciousness other than or any less of a subject for science? Does it make it *more* of a subject for science?

There is also a postscript about all inquiry such as this, and the choosing of lines of it, and the effect on truth.

---

1   Only Two Other Alternatives

There is another way of looking at the arguments for the theory more or less expounded of perceptual consciousness as existence and the theories gestured at of reflective and affective consciousness as existence. The great reason for taking up or considering these theories is that very generally speaking, very broadly speaking, there are only two other sorts or families of answers to the question of the nature of consciousness, and both still terrible. Nobody believes the first sort of thing when they are not half-dreaming. Nobody believes the second family of theories when they are on automatic pilot, their realism overcome by what is admittedly a kind of good sense and science.

You can still half-dream, maybe, that what may still have the misleading name of dualism is the case – that *consciousness is a non-spatial thing and stuff, maybe somehow in the head*. The mysterious tension or contradiction about space, the temptation to non-spatial cranialism, probably helps. Consciousness *is* a mysterious fact, and so some mystery in an account of it can seem right. But forget the half-dreaming. It seems you are committed to something like the so-called dualism as a philosopher, however quiet you are and however much you keep your head down, by being unable to swallow real physicalisms but having nothing else to say.

It could be that this is the default position of most philosophers, maybe even most philosophers of mind. Certainly it is the position of a lot of other people, some of them literary and imaginative but unpractised in plain thinking about the mind. It is the position of enough people for it to be internal to our conceptual scheme. Is there a very great deal of philosophy that comes down to this sort of thing? Is it what non-materialists privately think they have to believe? Despite Wittgenstein's behaviourism, is it the implication of his piece of self-indulgent audacity that whatever thinking comes to, there is nothing happening in the brain that corresponds to it?[1] Certainly this immaterialism is in a good deal of elevated reflection by the philosophers of origination or free will.[2]

The dream shouldn't be called dualism, though, since these days most physicalisms, monisms, identity theories and even materialisms are dualistic in the sense of adding something else to physical properties or ordinary physical properties. Davidson, you will remember, says his monism is not nothing-but materialism, whatever it is that he adds to it. Searle's impulse to and inconsistency about dualism is plain. The idea that consciousness is non-spatial is better called *spiritualism*. It is only usefully called dualism in a traditional and in fact outmoded use of that term, more or less that of Descartes. His dualism was intrinsically and fundamentally a proposition about the nature of mind as against matter.

The other option from spiritualism now deserves the name of being *devout physicalism*. You can say and write, in a career that keeps an eye on some of science, maybe two, and is forgetful of reflective experience, that *being conscious or aware of something is only having certain physical properties in the head*. Usually this cranialism is a matter of only neural properties as we know them – thought of computationally or with microtubules to the fore or in any other way you like.[3]

Nobody not on the philosophical job of trying to approximate more to some of science or horse sense believes this either. We all know, to make use of a perfectly proper and enlightening parody, that consciousness isn't just *cells*, however fancily or fancifully conceived. Everybody on the job tries to give a place to or register what they *know* when they're not on the job. But they can't do it if they have it that consciousness has only neural properties, or conceivably silicon or otherwise physical properties, no matter how they are conceived additionally.

To linger a last time at this crux, real physicalism or materialism runs up against the most resilient proposition in the history of the philosophy of mind. It is a simple one you know about, that the properties of conscious events aren't neural ones, or aren't only neural ones. Consciousness isn't cells. The proposition recovered its strength and defeated the corpuscular materialism of Thomas Hobbes in the seventeenth century. It also produced the decline of early neurophysiological materialism in the nineteenth century. It eventually left behaviourism dead as a doornail in the twentieth century. It will, as it seems to me, leave neural functionalism that way early in the twenty-first.

Is it possible to prove or confirm the resilient proposition? You may not feel any need at all for a confirmation or proof. Indeed scepticism about the existence of consciousness – something other than neurons – seems to call for even less of one's philosophical attention and time than scepticism about the external world, something existing outside my head. You may say, too, that it's pointless to try to provide a proof of the existence of consciousness. A proof requires a premise – a proposition *firmer* than the one that is the conclusion. Can there be one of those with respect to the putative conclusion we know so well, that consciousness isn't cells?

Let us not delay, but let me say that the resilient proposition got its first piece of support from each of us when we first distinguished between milk and our idea of milk. Later we put our bodies in the category with the milk, and then a lot later our bodily cells, and remained as confident about distinguishing between them all and any consciousness. You could say, a little pompously, that something like the resilient proposition is a foundational or structuring fact of our thinking lives. To persist in real physicalism, in the face of this, is certainly to be devout.

There are, as you know, criteria of adequacy for a concept or conception of consciousness, widely-agreed constraints on a good concept or conception. The main ones have to do, as you know, with consciousness being of a certain seeming nature or natures and being subjective, these being fundamental to the resilient proposition, and with consciousness as a reality and the mind-body problem. There are other lesser tests.

Devout physicalism is mainly a product of a simple and pious attention to the reality criterion and the criterion about causal interaction. The laboured-on ideas of devout physicalism, despite declamation and philosophically-unproductive technicality, do indeed fail the subjectivity test dismally. Subjectivity isn't bits of protein. The physicalist ideas also fail the so-called phenomenology test. The theory of consciousness as existence, none the less, is certainly closer to devout physicalism than to spiritualism. Despite being a contemporary dualism, like so much else, it is indeed *near-physicalism*.

Like physicalism it is certainly not just a piece of conceptual or linguistic analysis – as might have been said before now. It does not purport to give what we ordinarily have in mind in talking of being aware of this room, and in talking of perceptual consciousness generally. We do not have in mind a state of affairs outside the head. Cranialism has a hold on us and our language. We no more have a state of affairs outside the head in mind than we have the state of affairs that is neural clicking or pulsing of whatever kind within the head. The enterprise in hand, rather, instead of being only conceptual or linguistic analysis, is one of conceptual *reconstruction*, of which a little more will be said in the end.

So – what it really is for you to be perceptually conscious is for things out there to have properties, be in relations, undergo the changes that are events – as a result of both things in your head and things underlying those things in your world of perceptual consciousness. Your awareness is what others call the content of your awareness, or very close to that. But have you perhaps been digging in privately? Have you been saying that this state of affairs can be redescribed more plainly just as a property or attribute *of the person*? That we ordinarily say that consciousness is a property of a person, and that we must be able to stick to this line here?

Well of course you can *say* something like that. You can *say* that somewhere's having a three-piece suite in it is the fact of an armchair's having the property of having another one next to it and also a sofa. Or that the Atlantic Ocean is in fact a large basin in the earth's surface, one having the property of being full of water. But your being conscious is no more a property of you, strictly speaking, than it is of the underpinning atoms and what-not. Your being conscious, on the present story, is ordinarily and more enlighteningly described as a state of affairs including things and depending on things.

Certainly, on this story, your being conscious is not just the particular fact of the state of affairs being in part dependent on your neural activity. *That* dependency-relationship, reportable by a true conditional proposition, does not begin to have the features required by the five criteria of consciousness. No doubt there might be profit in a lot more general philosophical reflection on things or substances, and on properties, relations, events, states of affairs, worlds and so on – in short on the categories of reality, the metaphysics implicit in all our ordinary talk and science. But we have a grip on these things in advance of the further reflection.

It seems to me that to insist that your being conscious has to be your having a property, where that is to insist on more than the possible careless use of an expression, is just to be wedded to a ghost of the sort of idea to which consciousness as existence is opposed. So maybe your proper response is to dispute what is said for the theory. If so, let us have your argument.

So much for a last look at perceptual consciousness in particular. The accounts of reflective and affective accounts in terms of existence are less neat. But they continue much of the same story. Perhaps more important, the accounts make perceptual consciousness pretty fundamental and certainly permeating with respect to reflective and affective consciousness. Perceptual consciousness newly conceived is more than the basis of consciousness as existence.

Reflective consciousness consists, first, in the existence of representations or symbols in perceptual consciousness – that is, actual things in space-time with the character of all symbols. That character, in brief, is that they have some of the causal properties of the things represented. Reflective consciousness, secondly, consists not in these external but rather in internal representations – a personal language of thought and feeling if you like.[4] What others call the *contents* of reflective consciousness are upgraded into the thing or stuff itself. In the consciousness there is no funny relationship to the representations. Whatever multitude of relations may be involved, including a causal one issuing in the activating of representations, no such relationship with a self or whatever is part of my thinking in its various forms.

Affective or desire-related consciousness is in that respect the same – no internal relationship. It consists, firstly, in things in perceptual consciousness being of certain kinds that we ordinarily desire: bigger, faster, quieter, deadlier and so on. It is, secondly, certain bodily things – say the sensations connected with fear. It is, thirdly, representations of behaviour or action.

The existence-conditions or dependence-conditions of the parts of reflective and affective consciousness that are not in perceptual consciousness will be analogous to those parts that are in it. With these internal representations, there will be a kind of double-dependency, related to both the double dependencies of things of perceptual consciousness and things of the perceived physical world. The story is as close to devout physicalism as you can get and still be true to the actual subject-matter of consciousness.

The theory of consciousness as existence is certainly different from what has been going on in the philosophy and the science of mind. It is different from what has been going on in my own philosophy of mind – left behind are ideas of a subject, inner content, and baffling relations in consciousness. Consciousness as existence turns out as a result to have a recommendation so far unmentioned, one that is remarkable. It has to do with the argument from illusion, the matter of brains in vats. Does this bring to an end the traditional dispute about the argument from illusion as well as preserve our theory from it?

2   Representative Theory, Realist Theory

Some time back (p. 154) we were thinking that consciousness as existence, in so far as it concerns perceptual consciousness, is closer to one of the two large families of theories of perception in the past of philosophy – and indeed its present. You have heard of them pretty regularly in the course of our progress.

The representative theory of perception and the related doctrine of phenomenalism are to the effect that what you are aware of and what I am aware of, when, as we say, we both see the chair, is not numerically one thing. I am aware of my sense-datum, percept, sensation or whatever, and you are aware of yours. However qualitatively alike, there are *two* of these internal things to which we are limited in our perceptual experience. Such a theory is of course identified with the empiricism of Locke, Berkeley and Hume. The best discussion of it in the twentieth century, and a tentative defence, was given by Ayer.[5]

The other theory of perception is closer to ordinary belief. It has the tremendous recommendation, as against the representative theory, of getting each of us out of solitary confinement. It is that when you and I see the chair, as we say, what we are aware of is indeed one thing, a physical object.[6] The representative theory, as Dretske usefully remarks, confines us in our seeing to mental television.[7] The realist theory saves us from this, puts us in touch with the real world. But what this relation, this being-directly-in-touch-with, comes to – this is not clear at all. Remember that the realist theory is indeed about consciousness in the widely-shared sense, not the relation of photons, retinas and the visual cortex.

The theory of perceptual consciousness as existence is indeed closer to the realist theory. The existence theory is also about something outside the head, and on the way to being physical. As against this, there is a large difference between the existence theory and the realist theory, and also between the existence theory and the representation theory of perception. This has to do with relations.

The realist theory of our seeing things necessarily involves not only the physical world but our unclear relation to it. The relation has to be in there. How it is to be conceived is certainly unclear – all that has ever been said is that it is not an inferential relation, certainly not a relation of conscious inference. More generally, it's not a relationship such that one becomes aware of something, maybe a chair, by in a prior sense being aware of something else. Don't say

the relation isn't photons and so on but is just *seeing*, by the way –
that is what we're supposed to be analysing.

An obscure relation has been as much a part of all representative
theories, I suspect. Brentano's idea of consciousness serves as an
example.[8] When I see a chair, as we ordinarily say, there is something
called activity directed onto an object, or activity with reference
to a content, which latter pair of things are of course internal to
the experience and are of the order of a sense-datum, percept or
whatever. In addition to them there is the directedness (p. 164).
Elsewhere in philosophy, there is a lot of stuff, less clear, to the effect
that all consciousness is or includes self-consciousness – here too
something is added to an internal content.

It is a further recommendation of consciousness as existence, as
you have heard before, that it is different in not loading a funny relation into its conception of consciousness itself. Needless to say, your
awareness of this room involves the dependency-relations that have
been mentioned – to your neural activity and also a world of atoms
and so on. That is not to say that what it is for you to be conscious
of this room includes in itself a relation to something. What your
consciousness consists in no more includes relations explanatory of
it than an apple includes its relation to a tree.

3   Deluded Brains in Vats

These comparisons with the representative and the realist theories
are of use in clarifying the theory of consciousness as existence but
they also lead to something else. There is that large objection to the
realist theory – to which, as remarked, consciousness as existence is
closer. The objection, which has kept on coming up, is in fact the
proposition or family of propositions that leads to the representative
theory.

The argument from illusion, better named the argument from hallucination or the argument from a brain in a vat, is not the proposition that there are variations in the experience of different persons
having to do with their different perceptual situations and equip-
ment – the look of the penny and the warm hand in water and so
on.[9] That we see a thing differently, as we say, is no reason for concluding that we do not see one and the same thing. You can add that
something that did not look different from different points of view
would not be a physical object.

The essential proposition, to rehearse it one more time, is that matters could be arranged so that there did occur some perceptual experience that stood in no relation at all to the surrounding physical world – an experience of delusion. The brain in the vat in the laboratory is stimulated by attendant neuroscientists, it is said, so that the visual cortex and so on carries on in such a way that there is experience or awareness as in ordinary experiencing of, say, Wenceslas Square. But, *ex hypothesi*, Wenceslas Square is not there in the laboratory. Since there is something indistinguishable from actual perceptual experience of Wenceslas Square, it follows that the realist theory of perception is refuted and the representative theory is vindicated.

What is also true, you may suppose, is that the account of perceptual consciousness as existence is done for. There is no Wenceslas Square in the right place to be the state of affairs that is the brain's awareness or experience. Here, as some have said, is a disaster that finishes off an unlikely idea.

There have been attempts made by holders of the realist theory to avoid their own disaster, of course. One is the retort that the brain in the vat wouldn't be seeing Wenceslas Square, but just thinking it was seeing it.[10] That is a little factitious, not quite solid enough to defeat all of Locke, Berkeley, Hume and Ayer. In fact it seems to me doubtful that the realist theory can by this or other means survive the objection. And what of my own attempt to defeat the brain-in-a-vat argument by treating it as a *reductio ad absurdum* (p. 156)? By claiming that phenomenalism is so unacceptable that the argument that issues in it must be somehow mistaken. Well, that was brave. Is it possible we can get to the desired end without bravery?

Something is implicit or explicit in the realist theory and explicit in brain-in-a-vat ruminations. It is possible to forget about it. It is that in ordinary perceptual consciousness, as in the case of the brain in a vat, there is a neural process that is causally or in some other way nomically *sufficient* for the consciousness. There is a complete causal circumstance, wholly neural, for the consciousness. That is why it is possible for the attendant neuroscientists to get the brain, as is said, to have perceptual consciousness of Wenceslas Square – have the experience without the aid of the square.

Let me forget about the realist theory now and stick to perceptual consciousness as existence. The short story is that the brain-in-a-vat rumination does not defeat *it*, for a clear and certain reason. Rather than defeat the given theory of consciousness, the brain-in-a-vat rumination is a recommendation. It offers the possibility of *testing* the existence theory.

The theory, as you will remember, is that your being aware of this room is a state of affairs in space-time outside your head, a local world, that depends *both* on underlying things – atoms, and so on – and also on your neural processes. So each of those lots of things, to speak ordinarily, is only nomically *necessary* rather than nomically *sufficient* for your perceptual consciousness. It is only together that the two lots form a causal circumstance for the awareness. We have left behind that once-redoubtable proposition, the Correlation Hypothesis (p. 23), and thus also, whether or not wistfully, the Union Theory (pp. 61, 65).

So, to come to the nub, or a first nub, consciousness as existence specifically does not have the brain-in-a-vat consequence. Rather, it excludes the proposition that a brain in a vat, anyway on current assumptions, could possibly be perceptually conscious. On this theory, there is no neural sufficient condition to be assembled.

Or, to put the matter differently, there is a way that the theory of perceptual consciousness as existence could be falsified. It can or could be falsified by producing real perceptual consciousness of a certain kind in a brain in a vat. It could be falsified if there was as much reason to believe the brain was as conscious of Wenceslas Square or this room as there is reason to believe we are when we are there. You will anticipate that I have to, and happily do, put my money on no brain in a vat ever having perceptual experience just as a result of monkeying around with the brain itself. There isn't a possible sufficient condition in the brain for a perceptual experience.

To change the whole speculation, I guess something else is conceivable, a wild theoretical possibility. It is that somebody could produce perceptual experience in the brain in the vat of the laboratory surroundings rather than Wenceslas Square if they added in a perceptual apparatus and so on to the brain. Then the situation could approximate to what I say is sufficient for perceptual consciousness. If you added in the perceptual apparatus and there still wasn't perceptual consciousness – I guess according to the brain's reports – then consciousness as existence would again be refuted.

But all that is science-fiction. The important point is that you cannot refute the idea of perceptual consciousness as existence by employing the argument from illusion, hallucination or a brain in a vat. No such thought-experiment is possible. A premise is missing.

Notice, by the way, that the theory of consciousness as existence does not make *all* of *reflective* consciousness in itself dependent on both what is outside and what is inside a head, like perceptual consciousness. In so far as reflective consciousness is a matter of only internal representations, which presumably it can be, it is not dependent on anything extra-cranial. So the theory of consciousness as existence, despite what it says about perceptual consciousness, doesn't from the start absolutely exclude *all* successful brain-in-a-vat neuroscientific monkeying. That is probably a good thing. My guess is that a lot of neuroscientists would say that there are some things their successors may be able to do and some things they won't be able to do.

4   Consciousness as Baffling

Let us go on to something related, having to do with the battered old question of whether computers could ever be conscious. That is not the question of whether they can think in the mere sense, if it is a sense, of compute, process information or anything of the sort. Rather, it is the question, in part, of whether they can consciously think – consciously think about absent things.

Could a computer consciously think about Wenceslas Square? There is doubt about that, which is to say that a lot of well-informed and good judges are uncertain about it. As it seems to me, such judges are not just in the grips of habit – the wide and deep habit of restricting consciousness to biological entities, living things. Surely there must be some other reason than a prejudice for neurons over silicon that explains why we good judges are uncertain. There must be something else about consciousness that explains this. It is reasonable to suppose that there must be something about consciousness itself that explains the doubt.

That reflection can lead to another one, more important to us. It is that a good theory of consciousness itself will have the recommendation of explaining why we are uncertain about whether machines will ever be really conscious. To use an analogy, it is rightly said that a good theory of something will include a viable explanation of why other people than the theoretician are in error about the thing. A good theory of moral judgements, maybe one that makes them a matter of desires, will include an error-theory in this sense – an account of why a lot of other people think some moral judgements are really true. Similarly, you can expect a good theory of something to explain *uncertainty* about its subject-matter.

A good theory of consciousness, to mention another analogy, will certainly have to give an answer in itself to the question of why there has been a mind-body problem. As remarked earlier, it will have to give an answer to why almost all philosophers have found it hard to see how consciousness and brains can interact causally. Devout physicalism, in making it incomprehensible that there ever was uncertainty already has a strike against it, maybe two.

To get back to the point, or nearer to it, we can contemplate theories of consciousness from the point of view of whether they explain why we are uncertain as to whether computers will ever be conscious. If you think of the two large families of theories mentioned at the start, you will not be long in coming to a thought about one of them, devout physicalism. If it really were the case that a persuasive reconstruction of consciousness was as a sequence of purely neural events, then there wouldn't be any reason in principle why computers couldn't be conscious. No reason at all. We wouldn't be uncertain at all. We could just say that no doubt it will happen some day – they'll get there.

Let us skip over the spiritualism family in this connection and come to consciousness as existence. Can *it* explain why we are puzzled about what computers might become? That question can be subsumed in a larger one. It's late in the day of this book, so let us also skip to that.

It is very clear that all of consciousness – forget about computers – is somehow baffling. To say it is the hard problem about our behaviour and its antecedents, as David Chalmers does,[11] seems to me a wonderful understatement – as wonderful, incidentally, as the idea that there is any other significant problem at all about consciousness itself. There is nothing else at all like this problem about consciousness itself.

So there is a larger challenge for a conception of consciousness: it should have something to say about why it is so hard to come to a decent conception of consciousness, about why agreement or convergence doesn't really happen, despite what is said in hopeful articles in encylopedias. Indeed, to come to the sharp end, a point that is only superficially paradoxical, a good theory of consciousness should explain why *it itself* doesn't secure wide agreement. A good theory of consciousness, in short, needs a theory of its own degree of failure.

It is a *good* theory I'm talking about, so it can't be that the theory has in it an explanation of its total failure or real hopelessness or anything well on the way to that. What we need, then, in a pretty good theory – one that does well or not badly on the other criteria we started with – is an explanation of a degree of failure. Let us say a good theory has to be baffling to a tolerable degree. You will anticipate that it seems to me that consciousness as existence does well here.

Why? A reason to consider is that this theory makes your consciousness into a plenitude. Consciousness is all of what other theories take to be the content of your consciousness, or at least akin to that. On this theory, it's not just a *relation* to what they call the content. There is a fullness and variety here over any minute, indeed a richness – in perceptual, reflective and affective terms. To think of your consciousness over longer time is to think of a plenitude to the power of what? This plenitude has in it your representations or symbols, your intentions in action and your hopes and values and other desire-related things, and the flow of perception. Your consciousness on this theory is not a relation to an abundance but the abundance itself. It is near enough a literal truth that on this theory the fact of your consciousness is the fact of your *life*.

To come to a simple conclusion quickly, this plenitude that is your life, if you set out to think about it, is defeating. To try to sum it up generally in thought, to try to come to an analytic abbreviation of it, is necessarily to be in a way baffled. This is no sophisticated, complicated or elusive point, say about the available capabilities and representations and what-not being inside the subject-matter. The point is the size and nature of the thing, *a life*. Your consciousness is not some aspect of a life, just a picture of it or whatever, let alone some odd or puzzling feature attendant on computation, but a life itself. There must be a good sense in which there is no larger subject-matter.

To look quickly at the competititon, can it be said that spiritualism is a theory of consciousness that is to a decent extent baffling? Well, as remarked earlier, some sort of spiritualism is in fact a kind of default position, and a lot of philosophers and others are in that position. But it is rare nowadays actually to *think* about consciousness and embrace spiritualism. Popper and Eccles presumably did it, but they didn't inspire confidence.[12] Spiritualism can barely have the name of a theory, since it is more question than answer. What is this gossamer stuff? How can you have a cause that is nowhere? And so on. This is not a decent theory with an explanation of our resistance to it, but a frustration in itself.

As for devout physicalism, however the pill is coated, you'll know that the situation seems to me much the same. To put it one way, this theory too is far *too* baffling. Anyone not in a way scientized finds just about ludicrous the idea that their consciousness actually consists in no more than action potentials, transmitter-substances, the useful bits of protein, magnetism, someone's favourite interpretation of quantum mechanics or the like.

5   Neuroscience, and some Attendant Philosophy

Let me turn now to the relations between the theory you have before you and ordinary neuroscience rather than neuroscience-fiction. How does the theory stand to neuroscience? The first answer is what we already have in connection with the deluded brain in a vat.

It follows from the theory that the business of ordinary neuroscience is the discovery and understanding of neural correlates of consciousness in two senses: correlates that are necessary conditions, and correlates that are sufficient or necessitating conditions. The former have to do with perceptual consciousness, the latter with reflective and affective consciousness. The distinction has to be understood in a way consistent with the intermingling of the three sides of consciousness, of which much might be said, and will need to be said in a fuller development of consciousness as existence.

That it follows from the theory that neurosience is in part concerned with neural events and processes that are only necessary conditions of consciousness is in one way uncontentious. Finding further necessary conditions, I take it, is the day-to-day business of neuroscience.[13] To put this point in one way, the day-to-day business of neuroscience is not discovering *laws*. It is not the discovery of causal circumstances or absolute nomic correlates in the brain for consciousness. Neuroscientific laws are thin on the ground.

Still, it is possible to think that this day-to-day business is carried forward on a certain background assumption. It is that for every neural necessary condition for a fact of consciousness, there is also some wholly neural sufficient condition of which the necessary condition is part, a sufficient condition that in theory could be found. Let it be confessed that in the past I myself have put a lot of effort into defending exactly that proposition about neuroscience.[14] It was, as it now seems, wasted effort.

But let us not fall into any of a number of nearby possible confusions.

For a great deal of consciousness in the reflective and affective sides of it, according to consciousness as existence, there *are* sufficient or necessitating neural correlates to be found in the head. It is only for perceptual consciousness that there are only neural necessary conditions to be found.

That does not mean that are *no* sufficient or necessitating correlates for perceptual consciousness, but simply that they are both inside and outside the head.

Hence there is no mysterious departure here from a decent assumption of lawlikeness or determinism. All of the consciousness of all the three sorts can be a perfect effect of a causal circumstance – sometimes a circumstance both internal and external to a head. To put this differently and with Davidson and Anomalous Monism in mind, all consciousness is subject to *psychophysical* laws, but some escapes *psychoneural* laws.

Finally, each of the neural events or processes with respect to any consciousness whatever *is* in a clear sense sufficient or necessitating. That is of course the sense in which, in a certain circumstance where everything else is on hand, including the dryness of the match, a striking of it is sufficient for or necessitates a lighting.

Do you say, despite all this, that current neuroscience falsifies the theory of consciousness as existence because the latter theory allows that some consciousnessness – roughly speaking, *seeing* – depends not only on brain events? Well, I don't agree, but I don't mind the possibility of falsification at all. The theory is testable – that is fine, and a lot better than other theories. Certainly, despite the independent virtues of each, science and philosophy are continuous, as Quine rightly believed.[15]

This is also the time to make some remarks on some propositions, mainly philosophical, to which neuroscience pertains.

There is the proposition of brain-mind *supervenience*: consciousness cannot change without a neural change, but a relevant neural state can be replaced by another without a change in consciousness.[16] That is, the neural-consciousness relation is many-one. This is denied, with respect to *some* consciousness, by the theory of consciousness as existence, simply because supervenience is a doctrine of neural sufficient conditions everywhere. Again, this is not upsetting. It leaves open the possibility, for example, that there can be different instantiations of a necessary condition.

Epiphenomenalism, you will remember, is the doctrine or group of doctrines that consciousness is a side-effect of neural activity, but has no effects itself – the efficacy of consciousness is denied. It is a pleasure to record that consciousness as existence, particularly in connection with perceptual consciousness, makes epiphenomenalism the mad proposition that the external world, so to speak, is causally inefficacious with respect to consciousness.

It is as much of a pleasure to record that consciousness as existence leaves no scintilla of doubt about the evolutionary role of consciousness. If worlds of perceptual consciousness aren't selective with respect to species, what is?

Finally, in passing, it is clear that consciousness as existence shares with anti-individualism or externalism the truth that much of consciousness is outside of heads. But consciousness as existence comes to its own different position without reliance on what can seem to be unlikely doctrines about meaning.[17]

To come back to neuroscience and the rest of science, let me make more explicit the rest of their relation to the theory of consciousness in hand. The short story here, of the greatest importance, is that *all* of consciousness is a subject for science. No part or aspect of consciousness – no qualia so-called, no 'insides' so-called of brain events, no curious facts that give Fregean sense rather than reference to terms or the vocabulary of consciousness – nothing with respect to consciousness is beyond scientific inquiry and understanding.[18]

Neuroscience, and also cognitive science when it is not engaged in philosophy, has the correlates of consciousness – necessary or sufficient – within its subject-matter. So too the perceptual processes that are fundamental to the dependency of perceptual consciousness on the physical world at its bottom level. The same is true of the main entities of the theory – worlds of perceptual consciousness, and the representations that are the main stuff of reflective and affective consciousness. The only qualification necessary is that these latter facts are not all *public* facts but in the defined sense subjective. But subjectivity, of course, is exactly what we expect of consciousness. And of course, there is no barrier to the *objective* understanding of what is not public, of what is subjective in a plain and unmysterious sense.

The short story of the relation of neuroscience to consciousness as existence, again, is that neuroscience is freed from any lingering worry that consciousness is outside its grasp. That worry has been owed to the idea that its subjectivity is an elusive fact not open to science. Plainly it is.

6   Postscript on Reconstruction

There remains another matter to be glanced at rather than considered. It was remarked at the start of this chapter that consciousness as existence is presented not just as a piece of conceptual analysis, but as a reconstruction of our ordinary conception of consciousness. It could have been said, too, that it is not a reporting of any scientific conception, but, perhaps, a reconstruction of some. What goes along with this is a certain diffidence about claiming truth for the theory.

There is a good deal of philosophy of science and other philosophy relevant to this diffidence. There is *conventionalism*, originally associated with Poincaré and now in a way with Quine.[19,20]. It is to the effect that scientific theories are conventions, or conventions in part, somehow a matter of choice rather than observation or truth. The same can be said of philosophical theories. *Instrumentalism*, which makes theories into useful instruments, wholly or partly, is along the same lines.[21]

Copernicus and Newton come to mind, along with Lavoisier, and of course Quantum Theory and relativity. So too competing geometries, and Carnap's alternative languages with different formation and transformation rules,[22] and Kuhn's paradigms in science,[23] and the under-determination of theory by data, and the simple fact that all theories seem to fail in the end. Simpler than all this are familiar facts about different ways of looking at a thing, turning them around, different classifications, and such psychological illusions as the duck-rabbit.

So, can we say the theory of consciousness as existence, which puts perceptual consciousness outside the head, and makes all consciousness more or less what other theories call the content of consciousness, is somehow and to some extent a matter of simplicity, ontological economy, usefulness, convenience, fruitfulness, or elegance? All of these considerations have been said to make a theory a matter of choice rather than truth in the best sense, which of course is correspondence to facts, and more particularly things.[24]

To cut this last story short, here are a few propositions.

We might well get a little freer in our thinking about consciousness, hang looser, see that there are things to be said for different conceptions. We might carry several forward together. We don't have to aspire to a Copernican revolution with consciousness, do we?

Despite the impulse to tolerance, it cannot be the case that at bottom there is some basis for any theory that is wholly detached from truth. I suspect the supposedly separate virtues of theories – simplicity, ontological economy and the rest – are really indicators or promisers of *more truth*. You can't say that inconsistent theories are both true, and you can't whistle it either.

Consciousness as existence is indeed a reconstruction, and maybe it should not clear the board. But in my view it comes closer than anything else to being what a theory of consciousness needs to be.

Notes

1. *Zettel*, trans. G. E. M. Anscombe and G. H. von Wright (Blackwell, 1967), Sects 608–10.
2. Robert Kane (ed.), *Oxford Handbook of Free Will* (Oxford University Press, 2001).
3. For an account of the mind in terms of microtubules, see Roger Penrose, *The Emperor's New Mind* (Oxford University Press, 1989) and *Shadows of the Mind* (Oxford University Press, 1994).
4. cf. Jerry Fodor, *The Language of Thought* (Harvard University Press, 1979).
5. A. J. Ayer, *The Central Questions of Philosophy* (Weidenfeld & Nicholson, 1973).
6. H. H. Price, *Perception* (Methuen, 1932).
7. Fred Dretske, 'Naive Realism', in *The Oxford Companion to Philosophy*, ed. T. Honderich (Oxford University Press, 1995).
8. Franz Brentano, *Psychology from an Empirical Standpoint*, eds Oskar Kraus, Linda L. McAlister (Routledge & Kegan Paul, 1973). For an exposition see David Bell, *Husserl* (Routledge, 1990), ch. 1.
9. A. J. Ayer, *The Problem of Knowledge* (Penguin, 1956), and *The Central Questions of Philosophy* (Weidenfeld & Nicholson, 1973).
10. Paul Snowdon, 'Experience, Vision and Causation', *Proceedings of the Aristotelian Society*, 1980–1; John McDowell, 'Criteria, Defeasibility and Knowledge', *Proceedings of the British Academy*, 1982.
11. David Chalmers, *The Conscious Mind* (Oxford University Press, 1996).
12. K. R. Popper and J. C. Eccles, *The self and Its Brain* (Springer, 1977).
13. E. R. R. Kandel, J. H. Schwartz and T. J. Jessell, *Principles of Neural Science* (Prentice-Hall, 1991).
14. *A Theory of Determinism* or *Mind and Brain*, ch. 2.
15. Christopher Hookway, *Quine* (Polity, 1988).
16. Donald Davidson, 'Mental Events,' in his *Essays on Actions and Events* (Clarendon Press, 1980); Jaegwon Kim, *Philosophy of Mind* (Westview, 1998).
17. Hilary Putnam, *Philosophical Papers*, vol. 2 (Cambridge University Press, 1975); Tyler Burge, 'Individualism and the Mental', *Midwest Studies in Philosophy*, 1979.
18. Edgar Wilson, *The Mental as Physical* (Routledge & Kegan Paul, 1980).
19. Henri Poincaré, *Science and Hypothesis* (University Press of America, 1913).

20. W. V. Quine, 'Two Dogmas of Empiricism', in *From a Logical Point of View* (Harvard University Press, 1953).
21. B. Bas van Fraassen, *The Scientific Image* (Oxford University Press, 1980).
22. Rudolph Carnap, *The Logical Syntax of Language* (Kegan Paul, Trench, Trubner, 1931).
23. Thomas Kuhn, *The Structure of Scientific Revolutions* (Chicago University Press, 1962).
24. I look forward in particular to one book in this area, Harold Brown's *Conceptual Systems*.

Acknowledgements

The whole book was the idea of Jackie Jones, exemplary editor.

Chap. 1, 'Anomalous Monism and the Champion of Mauve' derives from the dispute mentioned in the introduction to it between Prof. Peter Smith and me in the journal *Analysis*. It consisted in the following papers: (1) Honderich, 'The Argument for Anomalous Monism', *Analysis*, 1982, (2) Smith, 'Bad News for Anomalous Monism?', *Analysis*, 1982, (3) Honderich, 'Anomalous Monism: Reply to Smith', *Analysis*, 1983, (4) Smith, 'Anomalous Monism and Epiphenomenalism: a Reply to Honderich', *Analysis*, 1984, (5) Honderich, 'Smith and the Champion of Mauve', *Analysis*, 1984. The present paper, 'Anomalous Monism and the Champion of Mauve' is a slightly revised version of (1) and part of (5). As remarked earlier, the book *Mental Causation and the Metaphysics of Mind*, ed. Neil Campbell (Broadview Press, 2003), reprints (1), (2), (3) and (5). I am grateful to Don Davidson for comments on an earlier draft of (1), which led me to enlarge it. My thanks too to Colin McGinn.

Chap. 2, 'The Thinking of Some Neuroscientific Friends', now revised, like all the papers in this book, was originally 'Psychophysical Lawlike Connections and Their Problem', published in the journal *Inquiry* in 1981. Commenting on it in the same issue of *Inquiry* were the following pieces: J. L. Mackie, 'The Efficacy of Consciousness: Comments on Honderich's Paper', T. L. S. Sprigge, 'Honderich, Davidson, and the question of Mental Holism', Stephen P. Stich, 'On the Relation between Occurrents and Contentful Mental States', and Edgar Wilson, 'Psychophysical Relations'. *Inquiry* in 1989 carried Jaegwon Kim, 'Honderich on Mental Events and Psychoneural Laws'. I learned from all of these pieces and also from comments on the original paper by Myles Burnyeat, D. C. Dennett, W. G. Lycan, Colin McGinn, John Watling, Kathie Wilkes and critics who heard

it read at Oxford, University College London, Cambridge and elsewhere.

Chap. 3, 'Cognitive Science's Philosophy and the Union Theory' was
first 'Functionalism, Identity Theories and the Union Theory', in *The
Mind-Body Problem: a Guide to the Current Debate*, eds R. Warner and
T. Szubka (Blackwell, 1994). For comments on the original paper,
I am grateful to Jonathan Blamey, Tim Crane, John Heil, Jennifer
Hornsby, O. R. Jones, E. J. Lowe, Paul Noordhof, Jane O'Grady, and
Mike Targett.

Chap. 4, 'Anti-Individualism v. the Union Theory' is a revision
of 'The Union Theory and Anti-Individualism' from the collection
Mental Causation, eds John Heil and Alfred Mele (Oxford University
Press, 1993). I am grateful for comments on this paper to Heil and
Mele and to Tim Crane, Marcus Giaquinto, Paul Noordhof, Ingmar
Persson, Jane O'Grady, Gabriel Segal, Barry Smith, Jerry Valberg,
and Arnold Zuboff.

Chap. 5, 'Consciousness and Humble Truths', now a little changed,
was originally 'Consciousness, Neural Functional, Real Subjectivity' in the *American Philosophical Quarterly*, 1995. My thanks for
comments on the original draft to Finn Collin, Tim Crane, Owen
Flanagan, John Heil, O. R. Jones, E. J. Lowe, Simon Matthew, Gregory
McCulloch, Alfred Mele, Paul Noordhof, Jane O'Grady, Ingmar
Persson, Gabriel Segal, and Michael Targett.

Chap. 6, 'Seeing Things', now revised, was first a paper under that
title given to an Oslo conference in honour of Alastair Hannay and
Dagfinn Follesdal. It was published in *Synthese* in 1994. For com-
ments on it, I am grateful to Tim Crane, Darren Denby, Alastair
Hannay, Dagfinn Follesdal, Paul Noordhof, Jane O'Grady, Van
Quine, and Nikolaus Waldenmaier.

Chap. 7, 'Consciousness as the Existence of a World' was first the
lecture 'Consciousness as Existence' to the Royal Institute of Philosophy. It was published in *Current Issues in the Philosophy of Mind*,
Royal Institute of Philosophy Lectures 1996–7, ed. Anthony O'Hear
(Cambridge University Press, 1998). A mistake or two in the original piece have now been put right. My thanks for comments on it
to Bill Brewer, John Campbell, Geert Engels, Alastair Hannay, John
Heil, Jennifer Hornsby, Bob Kirk, Jonathan Lowe, Paul Noordhof,
Ingmar Persson, Ingrid Honderich, and Barry Smith.

Chap. 8, 'The Theory Embarked On', is a shortened and revised
version of 'Consciousness as Existence Again', given to the World

Congress of Philosophy in Boston and published in the journal *Theoria* in 2000 and in *Proceedings of the Twentieth World Congress in Philosophy*, vol. 9, *Philosophy of Mind*, ed. B. Elevitch (Bowling Green Philosophy Documentation Center, 2000). My thanks to Ron Chrisley, Alasdair MacIntyre, Kevin Magill, Murali Ramachandran, and Tom Stoneham.

Chap. 9, 'The End of Intentionality in Perceptual Consciousness', now improved, was given as the lecture 'Consciousness as Existence and the End of Intentionality' to the *Towards a Science of Consciousness Conference 2001* at Skovde and also to the Royal Institute of Philosophy. It was published in *Philosophy in the New Millennium*, Royal Institute of Philosophy Lectures 1999–2000, ed. Anthony O'Hear (Cambridge University Press, 2000). My thanks to Ron Chrisley, Anthony Freeman, James Garvey, Scott Hagan, Basil Hiley, Ingrid Honderich, Paavo Pylkkanen and Rudy Vaas.

Chap. 10, 'Reflective and Affective Consciousness' was given as a lecture to the Royal Institute of Philosophy and published as 'Perceptual, Reflective and Affective Consciousness as Existence' in *Minds and Persons*, Royal Institute of Philosophy Lectures 2001–2, ed. Anthony O'Hear (Cambridge University Press, 2003). Thanks to Ken Adams, James Garvey, Ingrid Honderich, Derek Matravers, Stephen Priest, Andrew Ross, and Barry Smith.

Chap. 11, 'Spiritualism, Devout Physicalism, Vats, Neuroscience' was first 'Consciousness as Existence, Devout Physicalism, Spiritualism'. It was given to the *Towards a Science of Consciousness 2003* conference in Prague. It has not been published before. My thanks are due to Ken Adams, Harold Brown, Ron Chrisley, William Fish, James Garvey, Basil Hiley, Ingrid Honderich, Derek Matravers, Hugh Mellor, Stephen Priest, Richard Rawles, Andrew Ross, Tim Schroeder, Barry Smith, Tom Stoneham, and Rudy Vaas.

Index

aboutness, 11, 159, 201; *see also* intentionality
adequacy criteria *see* consciousness
affective consciousness *see* Consciousness as Existence
African lad objection *see* Correlation Hypothesis
Anomalous Monism, 5–16, 19, 42, 69
anti-individualism, 67–84, 79, 148–9, 219
arthritis in the thigh, 76–84
awareness, standard, 110–11, 116, 121
    belief within, 118
awareness, unmediated, 117, 121–2
Ayer, 66, 124, 160, 212

behaviourism, 48, 54, 200, 201, 205
belief in perception, 118
Block, 3
brain in a vat, 154–6, 204, 211–14; *see also* argument from illusion, phenomenalism
brain-mind problem *see* mind-brain problem
Brentano, 11, 13, 106, 164, 178, 186, 211
Brewer, 3
Burge, 68, 76–84

Campbell, 16
Carnap, 70, 220
causal circumstance and cause, 28, 33–4, 218
causality, 4, 16, 63, 102–3, 153; *see also* lawlike connection
causally relevant properties, 8, 9, 10
causal sequence, 26
Chalmers, 3, 65, 215
Chinese Room argument, 88, 101, 102
Chisholm, 162
cognitive science, 2, 5, 47, 104, 129, 204, 219
communication, 67
communitarianism, 67
conceptual analysis, 207
conceptual reconstruction, 208, 219–21
conditional connections, 9–10; *see also* causation

consciousness, 5, 17, 127, 148, 195; *see also* Consciousness as Existence, mental events, subjectivity
and science, 47, 50, 204–5, 219
as physical, 22, 63, 89, 100; *see also* identity theories
consciousness-brain problem *see* mind-brain problem
conscious stuff, 52, 101, 130
criteria of adequacy for theories of, 128–30, 132–3, 151, 152, 159–60, 182–5, 189–90, 191, 196, 207
hardest problem, 49, 104
in space, 5, 63, 138–9, 144, 151, 153, 161
most resilient proposition about, 54, 206; *see also* functionalism, unswallowable
ordinary idea or conception of, 20, 49, 51, 57, 59, 86–7, 105
phenomenology of, 127, 183; *see also* Consciousness as Existence, what it is like
reality of, 128, 132–3, 183, 194
spiritualism, 3, 52, 147
trinitarianism, 3, 149
Consciousness as Existence, 126–222, 127, 130–1, 148–9, 177–8, 202, 208, 210–11, 220
affective consciousness, 182, 184, 187, 198–202, 201, 208
and science, 47, 204–5, 219
as baffling, 204, 214–17
circularity objection, 131, 133–4, 135–45, 160
dependencies, 135–8, 140–1, 144, 156–7, 208, 209
intentionality, 159–60, 159–81, 177–80
perceptual consciousness, 105, 126–47, 148–58, 159–81, 185–7, 194, 196–7, 200, 212–14
phenomenology, 130–3, 147, 149, 156, 192–4
reflective consciousness, 182, 184, 187–98, 209, 214